26 MILES TO BOSTON

A Guide to the World's Most Famous Marathon

Revised Edition

MICHAEL CONNELLY

LYONS
PRESS

Guilford, Connecticut

An imprint of The Rowman & Littlefield Publishing Group, Inc.
4501 Forbes Blvd., Ste. 200
Lanham, MD 20706
www.rowman.com

Distributed by NATIONAL BOOK NETWORK

British Library Cataloguing in Publication Information available

Library of Congress Cataloging-in-Publication Data

Names: Connelly, Michael (Michael P.) author.
Title: 26 miles to Boston : a guide to the world's most famous marathon / Michael Connelly.
Other titles: Twenty-six miles to Boston
Description: Revised edition. | Guilford, Connecticut : Lyons Press, [2020]
Includes bibliographical references. | Summary: "Features mile-by-mile sights and sounds experienced by the runners. Interwoven throughout is the colorful history of the men and women of manifold skills who have competed in this preeminent event over the span of more than a century"— Provided by publisher.
Identifiers: LCCN 2019046363 (print) | LCCN 2019046364 (ebook) | ISBN 9781493046393 (paperback) | ISBN 9781493054817 (epub)
Subjects: LCSH: Boston Marathon. | Marathon running—Massachusetts—Boston.
Classification: LCC GV1065.22.B67 C66 2020 (print) | LCC GV1065.22.B67 (ebook) | DDC 796.42/5209744/61—dc23
LC record available at https://lccn.loc.gov/2019046363
LC ebook record available at https://lccn.loc.gov/2019046364

My son, Ryan—I'll take the half moon
My wife, Noreen—Thanks for our eternal dance
Mom and Dad, for your selfless love and guidance
My siblings, who aren't just my brothers and sisters, but also my friends
And to Jack's beloved wife, Mary Radley

Contents

ACKNOWLEDGMENTS

In my attempt to provide the reader with the quintessential look at the Boston Marathon experience, my labors would be for naught if it weren't for a number of friends and associates who helped to make it all possible. I would like to acknowledge their efforts with an insufficient mention of their name: my wife, Noreen Connelly, who was stuck driving the route, listening to me whine, and providing encouragement for her spouse, no matter how slowly he ran, or wrote; my son, Ryan, who inspires me every day; my mother, Marilyn Connelly, who has spent her life reading my term papers, book reports, and now, my manuscripts; and my father, John Connelly Jr., who provides the ideal devil's advocate.

My passion for writing is equaled by my passion for research. It is within the pages of history that I can transport myself through time and start to connect the puzzle pieces of the Boston Marathon, linking common threads in order to share a story. The Boston Marathon comes to life in the archives of local newspapers, like the *Boston Globe*, *Boston Herald*, *Boston Journal*, and *Boston Traveler*, which served as amazing resources. I thank the authors of those thousands of articles—mostly Lawrence Sweeney and Jerry Nason, who were the custodians of the race for over seventy years—as well as their contemporaries Tom Fitzgerald, Joe Concannon, John Powers, Shira Springer, Bob Dunbar, John Vellente, John Gilhooley, Jack Thomas, Ray Fitzgerald, Victor Jones, Leigh Montville, Mike Madden, Marvin Pave, and countless others (my sincere apologies for any omissions). Others who are referenced in the book include Wellesley historian Beth Hinchliffe and Bob Brown.

I would also like to thank Tom McCarthy and Meredith Dias, who ran the extra mile for this project; Jack Fleming and Gloria Ratti of the Boston Athletic Association, to whom I owe more than just thanks; and champions that represent over fifty laurel wreaths, especially John "The Elder" Kelley, Uta Pippig, Bill Rodgers, Geoff Smith, Jean Driscoll, and Jim Knaub, along with other runners, such as soccer great Kristine Lilly, Olympic gold medalist Summer Sanders, runner John Treacy, musical personality and son of Boston Joey McIntyre, Rick and Dick Hoyt, mayor Ray Flynn, NBA executive Pat Williams, and Henry Staines, for sharing their stories.

I also thank Maria Mello, Mariellen Gipson, Charlie Gaffney, Martin Duffy, Bruce Shaw, Maureen Connelly, Angela Heffernan, Tom McLaughlin, Richard Twombly, Mike Radley, Jack Radley, Pat Williams, Tom Ratcliffe,

Acknowledgments

John Cronin at the *Boston Herald*, Roy Clark, Al Larkin, Chris Young, Dan Shaughnessy, Dorothy Dolongschamps of the Natick Historical Society, Dick Fannon of the Ashland Historical Society, Carolyn McGuire of the Framingham Historical Society, Susan Abele of the Newton Historical Society, Laura Nelson of the Wellesley Historical Society, Bob Sullivan of the Brookline Library, Becky Saletan, Aaron Schmidt and Charles Longley of the Boston Public Library, Tracey and Jeff McEvoy, Dr. Diane English (orthopedic surgeon), Dr. Caroline Foote (cardiologist), Jennifer Worden, Sandra Southworth, the Boston BullPen Project team—Steve Alperin, Ben Levin, and Al Stern—and last but not least, my partners in crime, Bob Tracey, John Wilson, Jody Goodwin, Lianne Thibeault, and Rebecca Gardner.

FOREWORD

by Bill Rodgers

When Michael Connelly contacted me to write a bit about his book *26 Miles to Boston*, I wasn't overly enthusiastic. It seemed to me that the race had received enough attention as it was. Was I wrong! Connelly writes about the race from many new and interesting angles. You can't help but be seduced by this book. The stories flow one after another, like a marathon runner's footsteps. Each story adds to the razzle-dazzle of the race's long and colorful history.

Of course, that's exactly what the Boston Marathon has to offer—lots of colorful history over the 123 years of the race. But no one has told the stories of the race beyond those of the top runners. Connelly gives other perspectives and thoughts, and I salute him for doing so, as it is only in recent days (as you'll see from reading the book) that the top runners have received respect as world-class athletes. As recently as my win in 1975, a well-known Boston sports commentator indicated that the runners at the Boston Marathon weren't athletes at all.

Because of my own background as a competitive runner, I've always been interested in reading about the top runners at the Boston Marathon, and enjoyed the accounts of the race. People like Clarence DeMar, Johnny Kelley, and Joan Benoit Samuelson have told of their exploits as champions at Boston. Today's top racers have been of interest, too, but what I truly enjoyed reading in *26 Miles to Boston* were the stories that are never told—accounts of volunteers, police officers, medical personnel, merchants in stores along the route, spectators, officials, and, of course, the so-called "average runner." The athlete's challenge is what the Boston Marathon is all about. The athlete's heart beats inside all of us.

Having run the race thirteen times, won four, and dropped out of the race twice, I know what it feels like to take on the challenge of running the Boston Marathon. Michael Connelly does, too, but he goes on to explore why a simple foot race has the impact it has on runners and non-runners alike. An overly intellectual, sedentary fellow once observed that runners never seem to smile as they run; surely he was never at the Boston Marathon.

Had he been, he would have seen the real smiles, the ones with really deep satisfaction behind them.

To run the Boston Marathon is not an easy thing. To write well about it and explain its charisma is even harder. Michael Connelly's *26 Miles to Boston* succeeds in this regard. Not many sports books have the capacity to make you feel as though the event was happening only ten feet away. This one does that. Connelly has exposed the special qualities of the Boston Marathon foot race and why it is more than an ordinary sporting event.

The Boston Marathon endures; it continues on, just as its athletes have done, despite the violent attack in 2013. Maybe the Boston Marathon's ultimate strength is that it is a great equalizer of humanity—that it brings people together in peace and friendship. Anyone who has been to Boston knows that.

Maybe it's too narrow to say that the Boston Marathon is a road race. Maybe it's more accurate to say that it's a celebration of life itself.

Bill Rodgers is a four-time Boston Marathon winner, including three straight wins in 1978, 1979, and 1980, and a four-time New York City Marathon winner, between 1976 and 1980.

PREFACE

26 Miles to Boston is a look back at both the Boston Marathon and my run on that April day in 1996, over two decades ago. Almost a quarter of century after standing on the starting line in Hopkinton, I still consider my participation in the Patriots' Day event as life-changing. It was on the streets between the start and finish of the race that I found layers of potential that I did not know existed.

This book, which is in its fourth rendition since 1998, is written in two voices. One voice is a reflective first-person account of my humbling—but totally fulfilling—run. The other voice is that of the race's history. For over a century, the April run has graced the streets of our community. The book will travel from start to finish and every mile in between. Within each mile, history, topography, and strategy are represented.

The perspective that I draw upon for this story is threefold. First, I have compiled and incorporated more than 120 years' worth of research into the narrative. Second, the Boston Marathon is in my blood. Five generations of Connellys have lined the sidewalks of the race over its history, and I have personally attended the race for more than fifty years: as a son on my father's shoulders, as a college student with a red cup in my hand, and as a father, with my own son on my shoulders. Lastly, I experienced the race as a competitor in the one hundredth running of the longest continuous running event in the world.

The Boston Marathon is one of the jewels of Boston's crown. A gem that helps to make the Athens of America so special. A thread that has been woven through our quilt of history that connects years and generations. An event that is so much more than a road race. The Boston Marathon represents everything that is good about the human condition. It's on the roads from Hopkinton into Boston that dreams come to life every April, allowing fan and runner alike to experience the magic of the world's greatest race.

INTRODUCTION

My Nana Kenny used to talk about life being a journey—a never-ending odyssey that compels one to traverse from birth to death seeking purpose and, ultimately, fulfillment. She always said that when we got to her stage in life (her mid-90s), we would start to look backwards and be amazed at the course we had traveled. It was never easy—never direct. It was up and down, around and over, and sometimes under. But it was those detours and deviations that allowed one to live life.

And with that, we start the beginning of a story full of metaphors that will connect life and the world's greatest race. Start to finish—trials and tribulations. It's on the streets (and sometimes the sidewalks) of the Boston Marathon that the hearty have chosen to challenge their essence by living out a 26.2-mile embodiment of who they are, or hope to be.

People don't come to Boston to run its race. They come to Boston to live their life. To justify their existence. In Hopkinton runners are fueled by adrenaline. On the flats of Framingham and Natick, the synapses fire commands to legs. In Wellesley, runners wage a debate in their own mind between doubt and certainty. In Newton, when you are laboring up the hills, it's heart and not legs that allows you to ascend the four hills. And then, from the 20-mile mark to the finish line, it's the kitchen sink. A bunch of runners pushing forward in some warped, involuntary, preprogrammed march to their destiny.

I'm still not exactly sure why I was drawn to Hopkinton on that third Monday in April of 1996. Maybe I was following Paulo Coelho's philosophy from *The Alchemist*: "It's the possibility of having a dream come true that makes life interesting."

For three decades, I had cheered from the sidewalks of Newton, content to watch, eat, and, in later years, drink, and go home. Although I must admit, I had always been curious. As runner after runner would pass before my eyes, I found myself wondering why these athletes moved forward in such contradictory states of discomfort and joy. I guess this annual wonderment evolved into a twisted quest to discover the answer. As I entered my fourth decade, I felt obligated to act upon my curiosity. It took thirty-two years for my heart to veto my brain's impulse to remain stationary and safe.

Why did I do it? It was not simply because the race "was there," like Mount Everest. There must have been some deeper motive that prompted me to attempt this madness. It is closer to the truth to say that, by the age of thirty-two, I was starting a process of review. I had entered a stage in which life and its offerings were no longer taken for granted; I was beginning to grapple with mortality. Now the lessons that had bored me in philosophy class years ago started to have relevance. Now Socrates' famous warning that "the unexamined life is not worth living" took on meaning.

I must admit, however, that the decision to run wouldn't have been made without peer pressure. Peer pressure brought on by friends at our weekly pickup basketball game, which we played to fight our expanding waistlines and stay connected with old friends. It was during one of those Thursday nights, between an occasional seventeen-foot jump shot and an ill-advised turnover, that buddies Richie Twombly and Michael "Rad" Radley and I were grabbing some water and talking about post-game beers when somehow the conversation shifted to a shared aspiration: to someday run the Boston Marathon.

Soon an idea filled with irrationality was roaring down the mountain, out of control. Three guys who had never run anything more than a 10K road race and were having a tough time getting up and down a basketball court were now committed to participating in an event that was deemed hazardous to your health. So much so that teacher and 1957 Boston Marathon winner John "Younger" Kelley once said that the parents of his students described a marathon runner this way: "[A] fellow has to be slightly unbalanced to run a marathon . . . all it requires is stamina and stupidity."

Some might say that the "stupidity" part applied to the three of us. We were just hoping that the "stamina" came with it. Either way, we were committed and excited. We had eight months to prepare for the race. But not just a race—a life-changing experience. A chance to change our destinies. A new item to write in our obituaries.

I was all in, giving Richie and Rad my word that I'd do it. And just in case I got an inclination to forgo the jaunt for a more dormant Patriots' Day, I made a point of telling every friend and family member I could that I was running the 100th in April. There was no turning back now; I was stuck.

To commit to such an undertaking, you have to have both feet in. In my heart, there was no doubt that I would see this adventure to its conclusion. I was determined, as were my running partners, to reach the summit of Boston, with or without Sherpas.

In the ultimate book about seeking one's destiny, *The Alchemist*, author Paulo Coelho explains that committing to a cause is the first step in any possible life-changing experience. "He still had some doubts about the decision hc had made. But he was able to understand one thing: making a decision was only the beginning of things. When someone makes a decision, he is really diving into a strong current that will carry him to places he had never dreamed of when he first made that decision."

To participate in an undertaking of such scale is like a current carrying you, but this one felt more like a Class V whitewater rapid. It was a decision that would sweep me along, forcing me to challenge myself on so many levels. It meant the beginning of countless personal conversations with myself about probability, where I was in my life, and how this race could serve as bridge from the lost days of youth to a world of serious, purposeful decisions.

It is within these conversations that dialogue has to be honest. The website Inc.com once published a list of "Ten ways you can tell if someone's lying to you," suggesting that it could be a change in voice levels, or filling the story with irrelevant details, or maybe eyeballs sliding to the right, along with other tells. The story also said that the average person is lied to as many as two hundred times a day.

When you run the Boston Marathon, you don't have to worry about people lying to you. The question becomes more "How will I know when I'm lying to myself?" I knew that participating in an event of this magnitude would challenge the core of who I am. This meant that at some point my brain and heart would look to sabotage my intention by conspiring against me to concoct excuses that would serve as an escape hatch, allowing me to flee the scene and return back to my previous world of safe living. That's why in *The Alchemist*, the boy vacillated over taking his journey, saying, "I prefer to just dream about it."

The one defense I had against this counterproductive instinct was knowing that running Boston was a longtime dream of mine. This, combined with the fact that it was no longer an individual quest, but a solemn pact by friends to support, encourage, ridicule if necessary, and push each other forward when everyone else (including myself) was telling me that my ambition was silly and non-sensible.

Just to make sure there was no turning back, at the end of that night of basketball, the three of us put our hands together, like some sort of over-the-hill Three Musketeers, and made a pledge to each other that in the spring of 1996, we would celebrate the 100th running of the Boston Marathon by making good on a lifetime dream.

The first time I went out for a run, I jumped off my porch with zest. One mile later, I returned, panting, wondering what I had gotten myself into. But soon one mile became a 5K race, and then a 10K, and I starting to do things that I never believed possible.

While I trained, my family failed to recognize my resolve. When the subject of "running Boston" was forced into a conversation (as it often was), they would respond with halfhearted words of encouragement like, "That's good, Michael. Have fun." It was like a toddler telling his parents that he was going to be an astronaut or a professional baseball player—when a goal is that unrealistic, the best response is tainted with a tone of vague, loving indulgence. They assumed that I would go out and train for a couple of weeks and then be shocked into submission. My wife and parents guessed that running was so alien to my being that it would be impossible for me to evolve in eight short months from trotting a mile with cramps to running twenty-six of the most challenging racing miles in the world.

But I believed, and that's all I needed. Since I can remember, I had always had a belief in myself—even if it was misplaced. I was that undersized guy with the wise mouth and a chip on his shoulder. I thrived off proving people wrong. I was actually glad people were doubting me. It only served as motivation.

I knew that getting to the starting line would mean hard work. And not just running miles, but immersing myself fully in the cause. An immersion that would include my family, my job, my total being. The sacrifice would have to be mighty. Seven-time winner of the race Clarence DeMar trained each year by refraining from alcohol and smoking, and spent his free time reading the Bible. But I preferred 1931 winner Jim Henigan's approach to training and diet, as reported in the *Boston Herald*: "Good ale, he says, hurts no man. It is a tonic. It promotes appetite."

So, the mission was to stand on the starting line in Hopkinton. To stand where Rodgers and DeMar and Kelley and Switzer stood. To stand where men and women—both "abled" and willing—stared down the beast known as the Boston Marathon course. To stand where the warriors of running have stood for over a century and pledge to commit one's soul to the 26.2 miles that awaited. To be part of the 1 percent, a special fraternity of individuals who are possessed by a pioneer spirit to extend themselves beyond the boundaries of their perceived limitations. To blaze a trail that will take them to the Promised Land, a destination where those who enter will be granted enlightenment. A state of nirvana that says they are now capable of running any race, scaling any mountain, overcoming any obstacle.

That is the magic I sought when I said yes to running the Boston Marathon. It wasn't going to be a race, but rather an affirmation of life and the great blessings bestowed upon me.

When I agreed to run Boston, I didn't realize that my life could change. I didn't realize that, beyond eating up miles, part of the process would be taking an inventory of my life. During my first three decades, I had lived a life devoid of discovery. Now, something was telling me to endeavor outside of my element and test my limitations, because if I didn't now, I would always wonder. I would always ask the questions, but I would never have the answers.

So, I went to Hopkinton that year to explore while I could still climb. I ran to write a new chapter in my life. I ran from Hopkinton to Boston both to run a race and to prove myself worthy of my gift of life.

———

A poem by Harry Blythe that appeared in the *Boston Journal* before the 1909 Boston Marathon reads:

> *They will run their thumping hearts out*
> *through the winding, chocking miles—*
> *while the people crowd to see them*
> *casting comment, pity, smiles—*
> *they will crucify their bodies*
> *like the fearless Greeks of old—*
> *but their crown is not of laurel,*
> *'tis a bit of fame and gold.*

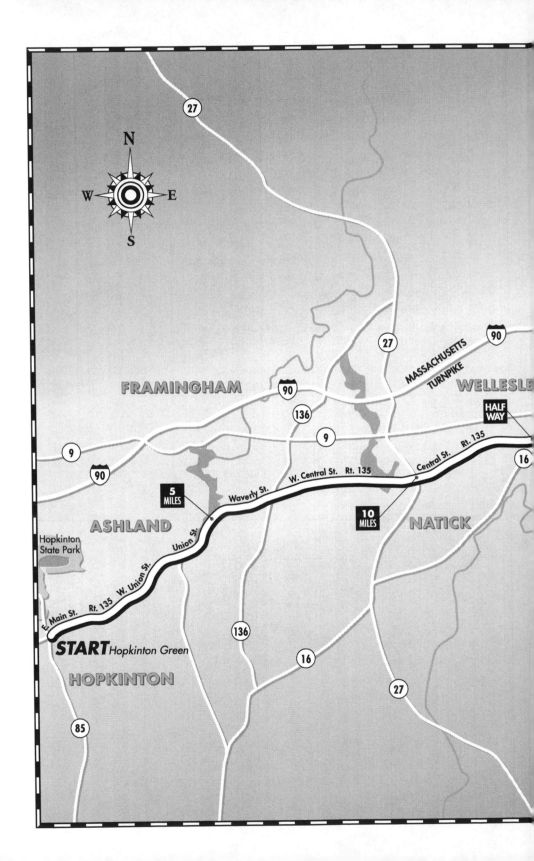

95
128

16

93

1

26 MILES, 385 YARDS

25 MILES

NEWTON

90

BOSTON

Commonwealth Ave.

Beacon St.

FINISH

Rt. 16

ngton St.

20 MILES

9

93

9

BROOKLINE

28

15 MILES

95

1

128

Detail of Downtown Finish Line

CAMBRIDGE

Boston Common

Charles River

Dartmouth Street

Beacon Street

Hereford Street

Boylston Street

Commonwealth Avenue

Copley Square

Newbury Street

FINISH

Beacon Street

Commonwealth Avenue

Boylston Street

DOWNTOWN BOSTON

93

1

95

28

Fairy Tale

In the spring of 1996, I was thirty-two years old. I had a big person's job, a wife, and a four-year-old son who was starting to assert his will upon our house. After work, there were games of catch and walks around the block. At night, my wife, Noreen, and I watched *Seinfeld* and *Friends* and ate ice-cream sundaes. That was a lot better than suffering through carrot sticks and watching the nightly news, where the bearded Unabomber was found in some cabin and Bill Clinton was trying to convince me that he "did not have sexual relations with that woman . . . Miss Lewinsky."

It was during that year that *Jerry Maguire* would give us "Show me the money," and wives and girlfriends would drag reluctant dates to *The English Patient*. In Oklahoma City, domestic terrorism took lives, while in Boston the worst winter in over a century had blanketed the region with more than 110 inches of snow, causing schools and work to be interrupted throughout the winter. For Rad, his brother Jack (who had joined the Three Musketeers), Rich, and I, the snow was problematic. We were trying to prepare for the 100th running of the Boston Marathon. Snow and snowplows made miles much more challenging than just having to tie our sneakers and get out on the road.

Unfortunately that year, April showers were bullied by a winter that simply refused to quit. It was during Marathon week that winter showed us who was in charge by punishing Boston once again. In the days leading up to the race, seven inches of snow fell, bringing with it fifty-mile-per-hour winds. Hopeful daffodils and overly optimistic purple crocus were victims of the whims of bipolar New England weather. Over 100,000 homes had their power knocked out, and runners hoping to cram for the Marathon test by sneaking in more miles were now faced with risking injury on icy sidewalks, thus destroying their months of training.

Elements beyond the racecourse have impacted the race for over a hundred years and add to the degree of difficulty of the run. It's not just about running Hopkinton to Boston. In some ways, just training for Boston can be as challenging—and as fulfilling, in some ways—as running the actual race. Finding babysitters, early-morning jogs when the moon and sun are out at the same time, long Sunday runs on the course—all earn you the right to stand in Hopkinton.

During the week leading up to the race, runners come into Boston from every corner of the world. The four of us already lived here, so that was one challenge we didn't have to confront. But for others, traveling across the country—or even the world—could be problematic.

In 2010, flights from Europe carrying runners were delayed because of the blinding ash that blanketed skies from an Iceland volcano. Almost a century before, it wasn't airline flights runners were waiting on, but trains. Like back in 1917, when runner Chuck Mellor was trying to find his way from Albany to Boston. Hoping to avoid having to pay for his passage, he decided to let the train leave the station, after which he would access the moving train by jumping down onto the tracks and then leaping onto the train. This he did, holding on to the railing for dear life. He tried to climb the stairwell into the last Pullman car, but physics worked against him. As the train rolled down the tracks, he hung on for dear life. The train rocked forward and gained momentum, causing his legs to swing outside of the doorway. With his body almost horizontal, the train came upon a bridge, where his legs slammed into a girder. The impact with the iron post badly bruised his leg. Mellor managed to climb aboard the train and make it to Boston, where, despite the painful injury, he would finish in sixth place. Eight years later, he would win Boston.

Because Boston is the mecca of all races, runners do whatever it takes to participate in the race. Three-time winner Uta Pippig would call her annual visit to run Boston a "fairy tale." It's not just a journey to run a road race, it's a trip to experience an epiphany, one that is shared with hundreds of thousands of other people who cherish the Marathon experience as a spiritual, physical, and emotional journey. It is so relished that in 1955, Argentinian runner Ezequiel Bustamante sold furniture to pay for the trip to run Boston, where he would finish ninth.

In 1988, Irish runner John Treacy didn't have to sell furniture, but he did have to hurry up. On the Thursday before the Marathon, he rolled over in his bed in Ireland and told his wife that he had decided to run Boston. Three days later he was leading the race in Mile 21, only to finish third, with a sub-2:10 time of 2:09:15. "I was convinced I could win the Boston Marathon," he recalled. "I had a great week of running, and felt I was as prepared as I could be. I knew I'd run well; sometimes that's enough."

In 1941, the Boston Athletic Association (BAA) made the following recommendation: "[It is] inadvisable for anybody to attempt the race without proper preparation." Although this warning is seemingly self-evident, the process of running twenty-six miles is so foreign to the ordinary mortal that the governing body of the world's greatest race felt compelled to remind people that the journey they had agreed to undertake was so awesome that the BAA would be *irresponsible* not to provide forewarning. The BAA was operating under the premise that the decision to run Boston in the first place proved someone's reckless nature.

Running Boston is a passion reserved for the possessed. For the honor of traversing the eight towns of Boston, one must prepare accordingly. To make sure that runners understood the honor and magnitude of such an enterprise, in 1905, the governor of Massachusetts, Curtis Guild, felt obligated to caution runners prior to the race that they must be willing to sacrifice. "[The runner] has first to deprive himself of the luxuries of life and learn what real hardship is. And by this, I mean he should dispense with all tempting viands. No matter how nice the good things appear that Mother makes, if they come under the head of pastry, they must be put on the 'excluded' list."

One must make serious sacrifices to even get to the starting line in Hopkinton: Show restraint at the dining-room table, show obedience to that alarm clock, choose sneakers over couch and television after work, and show the discipline to do cardio work on the weekend when friends and taverns are beckoning.

From frontal lobe to temporal lobe, the challenge of Boston will dominate every waking thought. Like *Nightmare on Elm Street*, the race shadow chases and haunts runners from the moment they say "yes." It is the thesis paper to write, the leaves to remove from the gutters, the report at work, the teenager to pick up—all wrapped into one. The restrictions placed upon a runner's conscience are immense. "I sacrificed many opportunities to be here," Men's wheelchair champion Jim Knaub said after one of his five conquests.

The runner needs to know that the Boston Marathon isn't run in April, but instead, in the winter months prior, when there are no cheering fans, cameras, or medals—only self-discipline. Champions understand this, and endeavor year after year to develop a system that best prepares them for the coming April.

John "The Younger" Kelley finished second at Boston five times—despite having the lead—and was determined never to be caught from behind again. He amended his training to wear a twenty-pound pack to help build stamina.

It must have worked, as he would go on to win the 1957 Boston Marathon, setting a course record. Marathon winner Uta Pippig left Germany to run in the high altitude of Colorado. Clarence DeMar, who never missed a day of work, even the night shift just hours after the Marathon, ran the eight miles back and forth to work every day. Finnish runner Heikki Olavi Suomalainen ran in two feet of snow to strengthen his hips, while four-time winner Gérard Côté from Canada did his speed work in off-season snowshoe competitions.

For most, their mission is not to win, but to run. Because running is winning. They know that they can use this experience to run all of life's races. That a successful run at Boston can serve as a catalyst to venture farther, higher, and faster. A virtual crowbar to pry open all of life's possibilities. Because isn't that why they come to Hopkinton—to live, and learn how to live? It is an exercise of self-discovery. To test themselves when the sun seems hottest, the hill seems highest, the next water table farthest away. It's on the road to Boston that runners are willing to bare their very being, not knowing if their heart can push forward when every other muscle pleads with them to stop. From Hopkinton to Boylston Street, all runners confront their perceived limitations. Ultimately, their success is a function of a single thing: will.

For me, I felt like I had plenty of will. But there was still doubt. In the nights leading up to the Marathon, I had several dreams about the race. In some of these visions, I ran the last yards of the race jubilantly, while in others I missed the start for various reasons. Apparently my subconscious was quite aware of the magnitude of this event and the significance that it played in my life. After a number of these dreams, I became concerned that my quest to run Boston had evolved into an obsession.

In the months leading up to the Marathon, many runners find that even in their sleep they can't hide from the coming race. Two-time champion Joan Benoit Samuelson admitted that she dreamt of missing the start because she was window-shopping in Hopkinton boutiques. Clarence DeMar claimed that he was visited seven times in his dreams by an apparition who assured him of victory—and he went on to win all seven of those races. Meb Keflezighi dreamt of running down Boylston stride for stride with another runner. He would wake up before he found out who won. Days later, in 2014, he would live the end of the dream and answer who won when he broke the tape.

There is no lying to one's subconscious. It knows when we are nervous, tentative, and insecure. The subconscious seems to revel in its ability to produce visions of failure, knowing that the runner is trapped in the theater of REM sleep.

In 1971, Irish runner Pat McMahon found himself overwhelmed by a recurring dream in which he was winning the Boston Marathon, the finish line in sight. Sadly, his vision would always end with him being caught from behind, victory eluding him. He'd sit straight up in bed in a cold sweat. On the actual race day, McMahon was running in the lead with 150 yards to the finish line when Alvaro Mejia of Colombia ran up next to him, elbowed him out of the way, and ran on to victory. McMahon was left to watch him from the side of the road—the best seat in the house—as the Colombian runner broke the tape. His nightmare had literally come to life.

＊＊＊

On the night before the race, the four of us knew we were either ready or we weren't. With the race just hours away, my three friends joined me at my house in West Roxbury. My wife cooked us the marathoners' dinner of pasta. Like warriors going off to war, we were strangely quiet. Dinner was filled with nervous chatter. We were less than twenty-four hours away from partaking in an event that could change our lives. We had gone from huffing and puffing on a basketball court to getting carried away with a discussion about running Boston to now being on the verge of toeing the line. It was a chance to blindly leap into the abyss, hoping to change ourselves from "I think I can" to "I did it."

I sat at the table with my friends, a virus of doubt pulsating through my being. I was trapped in a state of denial. Running nonstop for over twenty-six miles is unhealthy, if not asinine. Sure, I'd always had wild and exciting ideas, but acting on them was a different matter altogether. As the months of the calendar had flipped toward spring, I'd buried the fear of failure deep in my subconscious. In reality, I had no right to be standing on the starting line. But I was determined to stare down the course and those who told me I couldn't. I had no parachute, yet I was prepared to jump.

With just hours to go, all avenues of escape were closed, and now the fear of failure was starting to flow from the subconscious to the conscious. I was starting to realize that I had swum out too far and was now caught in a Nantucket riptide. Who was I kidding? Maybe I should stay home. Perhaps dreams and reality occupy different states of consciousness for a reason. Maybe, just maybe, I had bitten off more than I could chew. But the tide was taking me, and I let it.

Race Day

Prior to the 1933 race, the *Boston Herald* wrote on the morning of the event about the uniqueness of the average participant. "Marathon runners are a bit eccentric in their ways, some of them picturesquely so. They have been known to arrive in Boston wearing their running suits as underwear and carrying their shoes in their pockets. Others have been recorded as [having] deserted their jobs, homes and families in order to take part in one of the classic road grindings. Most of them would rather run than eat."

Running Boston isn't physics, but rather metaphysics. It is one of those rare experiments in which one volunteers to test his or her will for the purpose of transcending human boundaries. It's an opportunity to defeat one's perceived limitations, to overcome the hindrances of the innate, to turn back the ticking of time, to be an instrument of a Superior Being. All on a stage in which your adversary is malicious and unforgiving.

You came to Boston to run on the road that stretches 26.2 miles from suburban Hopkinton to downtown Boston. But it will not be until you take that first step that you will come to understand that the course is so much more than hot top and pavement. Instead, it's seemingly the creation of a mad scientist, born in test tubes to defeat any runner who risks crossing the "bridge" that separates failure and success. A concoction of hot top and potholes and manhole covers, surrounded by teeth-baring dogs and overzealous fans ready to lash out at anyone so bold as to dare to pass. If you stayed home, or never took the first step, then you would never be confronted by the breathing and vengeful leviathan that is the Boston Marathon racecourse.

But that's not who you are.

Prior to the 1912 race, the *Boston Journal* printed an ode to the world's greatest race. "Today, of all the days in the year, Boston can, with beaming pride, display her title of the modern Athens, for this is the day when our athletic no less than intellectual city presents the classic contest appropriately known as the marathon race."

On the morning of the Marathon, the four of us tied our sneakers and hydrated, and hydrated and hydrated. I took in at least six liters of a brew of three parts water, one part green Gatorade. In 1907 they said about hydrating, "[W]ater is almost fatal to a runner's chances, and only the *in*experienced ask for it during the run."

Ready or not, we made our way over to Hopkinton Center to find the starting line. Over 40,000 runners joined us that morning in a town of only 14,000 people. Back in 1911, one of the pre-race favorites, Clifton Horne, missed the train out to the starting line and had to run a mile from the hotel. With the gun ready to be raised, he had no time to claim his number for the race, so his handlers drew the number 18 on his shirt as he raced to beat the gun.

———

Hopkinton is a middle- to upper-class rural town that for 364 days of the year would be described as bucolic. But not on the 365th day. While this sleepy colonial town typically rises to welcome each new morning in a leisurely fashion, on Marathon Day, no matter if Hopkinton tries to hide her head under the pillow, she cannot escape. On that morning, the sound of chirping birds perched on the budding maple trees around the town common are drowned out by a parade of shuttle buses; the smell of fresh coffee is overpowered by the aroma of muscle-soothing liniment; the sound of a thrown newspaper hitting the front door is replaced by the knock of a total stranger with a bursting bladder, requesting the use of a bathroom.

On this day it is the center of the running world. It is NASA. It is where people come to embark on the greatest journey of their life. Since 1924 the race has started in the small New England postcard town. The starting point was across the street from the Phipps farm, which had been in the family since the 1700s. In the papers that year it was said of the race's new host town, "The new start is on the state highway at the top of [a] slight incline."

The town of Hopkinton was founded in 1715, when money donated to the town from John Hopkins was used to buy land from the Natick Indians. The town has a long history of devotion to its country. In the American Revolutionary War, 115 of its men fought for freedom, including warrior Danny Shays, who was recognized by General Gilbert du Motier, Marquis de Lafayette, because of his valor at the Battles of Lexington and Bunker Hill. Both battles are recognized each year on the day of the Marathon, run on the Massachusetts holiday of Patriots' Day.

When Shays returned to Hopkinton after fighting for the new country, he was penniless. In 1786, Shays would lead a rebellion against unfair tax collection from veterans, and was called in front of Governor John Hancock and ruled to be insolvent. (Ironically, Hancock's image would be the face of the insurance company that would later save the Boston Marathon as the race's main sponsor.)

Two generations later, the Union Army would call upon Hopkinton's young and bold residents. Reportedly the town committed more men to the war than any other town in the nation. In all, 330 men answered the call, many never to return home. No family suffered greater loss than the Bixbys. When President Lincoln was informed that Lydia Bixby had lost all five of her boys in battle, he penned the following note to the bereaved mother:

Executive Mansion
Washington, Nov. 21, 1864.

Dear Madam—
I have been shown in the files of the War Department a statement of the Adjutant General of Massachusetts that you are the mother of five sons who have died gloriously on the field of battle.

I feel how weak and fruitless must be any word of mine which should attempt to beguile you from the grief of a loss so overwhelming. But I cannot refrain from tendering you the consolation that may be found in the thanks of the Republic they died to save.

I pray that our Heavenly Father may assuage the anguish of your bereavement and leave you only the cherished memory of the loved and lost, and the solemn pride that must be yours to have laid so costly a sacrifice upon the altar of freedom.

Yours, very sincerely and respectfully,
A. Lincoln

It turned out that three, not five, of Lydia's sons had perished. The two that were mistaken for Lydia's children were actually her nephews. Nonetheless, her sacrifice was still enormous.

The history of Hopkinton's patriotic commitment was further evident during World War I, when a hundred members of the town fought in the "war to end all wars," including George V. Brown. Brown would return home from the war to continue a tradition that started in 1905, where a member of the Brown family would fire the gun at the start of the Boston Marathon. Brown would go on to fulfill this role for more than three decades. (A member of the Brown family has started the race every year, except in 1990.)

George Brown, an 1898 graduate from Hopkinton High School, later became the manager of the race, overseeing everything from measuring the course to approving applications to setting the race's rules. His name is inscribed on the doughboy statue that stands guard at the starting line. (The statue depicts a World War I infantryman with a rifle on his shoulder. It should be noted that the soldier is walking in the opposite direction of the runners, as if he knows something the athletes will discover during the next twenty-six-plus miles.)

Along with its commitment to the nation, Hopkinton is also known for being home to the family of Brigham Young; as the place that George Washington and General Lafayette would stay when traveling from the south up to Boston; and for the fact that the mills and factories that comprised the Davenport Block in the mid- to late 1800s were some of the top producers of shoes in the country.

As the clock ticks toward noon (or whatever time your designated starting corral is sent off to Boston), the spirit at the starting line is one of community. Runners from every corner of the world are joined together for one shared quest. Back where we were standing in 1996, about a half-mile from the starting line, there was no animus or jealousy or pettiness. We were all excited for each other. Any stresses we had in our lives, whether at work or home, were put on hold. It was just about running and making it to Boston.

On the loudspeakers set around the starting line, a disc jockey was playing music, causing adrenaline to spike. At one point, the song echoing off the bandstand and church steeple was the Steve Miller song, "Fly Like an Eagle." Around us you could hear people rocking back and forth with nervous energy, humming the song that would build into a 40,000-person chorus. It was awesome.

After the goose bump–raising singing, the Hopkinton High School band played the National Anthem. Americans sang with pride. Foreigners stood in respect. Up above, F-14 fighter planes zoomed over us in a ceremonial flyover. It would take them just one minute to travel the length of the Marathon course.

Seconds later, Walter Brown, a Vietnam veteran, took to the starter's perch situated on the sidewalk, continuing the long-standing family tradition. With the starter's gun loaded, the runners make peace with the Lord (or Yahweh or Muhammad or the Golden Sneaker god). Minutes slowly tick by on the digital watches of the runners just as surely as they ticked by on the timepieces of derby-clad gentlemen in years gone by. The last-minute stretching, the faraway stares, the nervous babble—all of these final rituals seem to speed the clock forward.

In 2013, Summer Sanders stood in her corral, debating when to start her watch. It was essential that she run at the proper pace in order to achieve her desired time. But then she looked around and suddenly realized something: She didn't have to run a particular time. In past marathons she'd been obsessed with time because *she had to qualify for Boston*. But now, she was here, *at* Boston, the starting line of which she had dreamt. She turned from her watch and decided to run with just pure joy in her heart. She would appreciate every aspect of Boston: high-five every kid, smile at every well-wisher, share with every running neighbor. She ran to pay homage, because it was Boston, and that's what you do there. She smiled. She let the sun shine on her face and the breeze wash over her. She took her place as a member of the running community. As a temporary resident of this community, she discovered what other runners had known before and will know after: The world is good. People are good. It takes a day like the Boston Marathon to reaffirm these truths.

The racers fall into place as they await the sound of the gun; with stern faces and elbows extended, they strike the same pose that runners have struck for the past century. Whether mill workers with scally caps on their heads and leather shoes on their feet or Kenyans with speed pulsating through every muscle of their being, in the moments before the crucible, they are all one, linked from era to era, country to country. They are all now brothers and sisters of the Boston Marathon, sharing a collective gasp, frozen in time, while the starter cocks the gun.

Mile 1

No Regrets

One of the saddest obituaries I've ever read included the following line: "He ran daily and dreamed of doing the Boston Marathon." To still have dreams on the table when your last day comes is sometimes as sad as death itself. This actually personifies a quote that I find profound, uttered by professional football player Aeneas Williams: "Cemeteries—some of the wealthiest places on earth are the cemeteries. There are unwritten books there. There are songs that were never written. There are so many people that have gone to the grave with unrealized potential."

Standing on the starting line of the Boston Marathon is all about not having regrets. It's about living your life to the fullest, which happens by acting on your dreams. Part of running Boston is having an understanding of who you are and what you are capable of. It's not about running—it's about self-exploration. The run from Hopkinton to Boston is not a race but an exercise in discovery in the sincerest sense.

Regrets are those moments in life that pass by but are never forgotten. A memory painted in disappointment, surrounded by the question of "what could have been." By answering the gun at Boston, you will never have to ask the question, "I wonder what running Boston would be like?"

Anne Frank said in her short life, "Dead people receive more flowers than living ones because regret is stronger than gratitude."

Bang!

"[S]harp at 12, when the sun is highest in the heavens, the report of manager George V. Brown's pistol will start the big pack." On race day, the average marathoner will take over fifty thousand steps—with none more important than that very first one. The simple act of raising one's foot for the first time at Boston means you are giving permission for the soul to take control over the body; the irrational to rampage over the rational, for the mind to challenge matter.

When 1919 champion Carl Linder was asked what elements were necessary to conquer the living, breathing specter known as the Boston Marathon, he replied:

- First—You must have a well-muscled body, developed by sports other than running.
- Second—You've got to stick to the job.
- Third—You must be ambitious and determined.

When it came to Richie, Rad, Jack, and myself, we were determined. We only hoped that we were up to the challenge. The sounding of the gun was played over the loudspeakers. We weren't in sight of the starting line where we were standing. We were stuck down a side street over a half-mile from the starting line. It would take us more than thirty minutes to make it to the bandstand. When we finally arrived, I jumped over the starting line. Up on the podium overseeing the race was Teresa Heinz, one of the heirs to the Heinz ketchup dynasty, and wife of former Massachusetts senator John Kerry. She was waving at runners as we passed under. As I looked up, I contemplated yelling, "Teresa—bet you a million dollars I finish." I decided against it. I had never run even eighteen miles before, and I didn't have a million dollars to pay up if things didn't go as I hoped.

Bet or not, I paused in my mind to enjoy the moment. I had bet on myself, and now I was running in the world's greatest race. I, Michael Connelly, was running where Clarence DeMar had run. Where Bill Rodgers, who was twice on the cover of *Sports Illustrated*, had embarked on his historical runs. Where Roberta Gibb Bingay in 1966 had jumped out of the shrubs to run where women weren't supposed to run.

Now don't get me wrong; my goal was to finish this thing. But it's also an accomplishment to get to the starting line. To do those miles, to be true to your word to get there, and to take your best swing at the course. And I was ready to swing. I was scratching that itch I'd felt for years, to someday run Boston, and it was so satisfying. I would never live with the regret of wondering what it was like to run in the Boston Marathon.

I was stretching myself and who I was. Like motivational speaker Tony Robbins suggested about the boundless capacity of the individual spirit: "I believe life is constantly testing us for our level of commitment, and life's greatest rewards are reserved for those who demonstrate a never-ending commitment to act until they achieve. This level of resolve can move mountains, but it must be constant and consistent. As simplistic as this may sound, it is still a common denominator separating those who live their dreams from those who live with regret."

Like warriors going off to battle, the runners are sent off to the ballad of drums and cheers. Staring down the first mile, it is apparent that the limitations of the road's width is challenged by the chain gang of runners who now stretch from curb to curb, slowly navigating the narrow, winding roadways of Hopkinton bordered by bare-branched maple trees and evergreens.

Newspapers described the 1905 race as "one of the grandest aggregations of amateur long-distance runners the world has ever seen." The *Boston Herald* described the 1911 start as a "perfect avalanche of humanity swept down the road"—and that race was run by less than two hundred athletes. In 1996, there were over forty thousand of us, shuffling forward like rows of ducklings in the Boston Public Garden, twenty-six miles away.

Almost all competitors proceed with caution through this early stretch. The course takes them east, dangerously down Route 135 in the direction of Boston. You won't see any skyscrapers but rather a sharp decline and a blind turn at the bottom of the first hill. With adrenaline pumping, the runners must hold back and make an effort here to move smartly and safely. The start is very narrow: just under fifty feet, fitting only twenty-one bodies across. A disorderly start could result in injury, or even death.

Greg Meyer, winner of the 1983 race, feared the start with a passion: "With the course starting on a narrow street and moving downhill, all of your training could be for naught with one trip over someone's feet. I wish I could fall asleep and wake up somewhere in Natick."

The downhill combined with the excitement of the race is tempting to the runner. John "The Younger" Kelley called the early miles "seducing." Runners can be lulled into a false sense of security, thinking their early fast pace is a function of some newly acquired superpowers. This belief would be foolhardy, and for many it's sadly dispelled up ahead on the hills of Newton.

While most experts beseech runners to control their early pace, in 2017 Yuki Kawauchi, from Japan, ran the first mile in 4:37, an insane breakneck speed. Kawauchi, who is known as the "Citizen Runner," averaged a marathon a month leading up to the race. His reckless first mile was an approach that defied Boston Marathon dogma. Twenty-five miles later when he broke the tape in Boston, people weren't questioning his sanity.

Down the hill, the road winds and falls like a Robert Frost poem. For runners who had been hydrating throughout the morning, the calming trees on their right not only help quiet their nerves but also may provide a spot for an impromptu bladder release. Marathoner and Orlando Magic executive Pat Williams calls this stretch of the course "the best fertilized."

For wheelchair competitors, their start is paced by an official's car to control speeds. In 1987, the lack of restraint allowed able-bodied competitors to reach speeds in excess of forty miles per hour in the first mile. Inevitably, as in any sport with committed competitors, the risk of success led to a heart-stopping accident in which chariots were flipped, athletes injured, and onlookers aghast. In New York, race director Fred Lebow took a shot at Boston's "tolerance" of wheelchair runners, saying the BAA "is flirting with disaster."

The attractive opening descent can be treacherous to any of the runners. With thousands of lemmings all going in the same direction—at the same time, with the same purpose, and all hoping to be first—there are endless risky possibilities. Runners must watch their step, keep their elbows down, and stay patient. Some are forced to adjust their game plans and pace because traffic is mimicking Boston's average morning commute—slow!

At the halfway point of Mile 1, the course teases your muscles with a preview of the monster that lies ahead by making the runner shift from downhill braking to uphill grinding. In the last quarter of the first mile, the runners move by a nursery. Just beyond the nursery sits a barn from old Tebeau's Farm. From the 1920s to the 1940s, runners used to gather at this spot to change clothes and receive their pre-race physicals.

Mary Tebeau, an Ashland schoolteacher, eventually sold the land to the Mezitt family. The Mezitts—the largest landowners in Hopkinton, with over nine hundred acres—still work the land under the name of Weston Nurseries. Here they grow everything from Christmas trees to a special rhododendron that blooms for the race. Brothers Wayne and Roger Mezitt remember when the race started on their farm at a ledge called "Lucky Rock," so dubbed because of a streak of quartz that ran through the middle. Although they have fond memories of this day, their business suffers badly throughout the holiday because of the tight traffic control maintained around the race.

At the end of the first mile, the competitors can look over Mahar's Meadow to their left. The first chapter of their journey is complete; 25 miles and 385 yards to go. Hopefully the harriers at the back are approaching the starting line. In all, the runners have descended 130 feet in the first mile, the greatest drop of any mile on the course. The starting line is at the highest point on the route, approximately 490 feet above sea level. In the first four miles, the course falls over 300 feet.

As I fell down the first mile on my way to Boston, I was honored to be running in a race that had been so important to me and five generations of Connellys. I was the first one in the family to ever dare to jump off the sidewalk and answer the question, *Why do they run?*

It was Viktor Frankl who warned in his book *Man's Search for Meaning,* "Woe to him who saw no more sense in his life, no aim, no purpose, and therefore no point in carrying on." It's in the first mile that you understand you've embarked on a journey that will give you aim and purpose.

MILE 2

"Never Mind the Bullshit"

For the last two decades, I have worked with a man by the name of Bill Olsen. Bill comes from the blue-collar town of Everett that sits on the northern border of Boston. Everett is proud of its high school football team and doesn't suffer fools. Bill's grandfather was a roll-up-your-sleeves, no-nonsense type of guy who worked down on the fishing piers. He wasn't one to listen to why you didn't get a better grade, or a job promotion or a base hit. You either did or you didn't. He lived by a motto that we adopted at our place of work for its raw frankness, the essence of which speaks to the difference between winning and losing—"Never mind the bullshit."

In 1996, the four of us were prepared to succeed under any circumstances. We would either finish or not. There was no excuse that would justify failure. We had to "never mind the bullshit" and put one foot in front of the other all the way into Boston. We would run with only one purpose, in which no excuse was acceptable. We would fight any instinct to rationalize walking off the course. We had to be honest with ourselves and do what was necessary to cross the finish line in Boston. We were here to run. To stop, to fail to seek reasons for "why not," was not on our agenda.

At minimum, we had made it into the race, and our intentions to complete the task were sincere. But we didn't want to just be the man in the arena for whom Teddy Roosevelt spoke so eloquently back in 1910, about at least trying. For us on this day, that would be nothing more than a loser's lament. "Only trying" wouldn't carry the day for any of us. We hadn't trained for eight months to just pull up on a sidewalk in some town far from the finish and feel fulfilled, or like we'd achieved some sort of a moral victory even though we'd failed to realize our goal. For us, only a finish in Boston would fill our hearts and souls with that sense of nirvana we yearned for.

Throughout the history of the race, other runners sought more than the mere satisfaction of participating, and this included Stylianos Kyriakides, who ran in the 1946 race.

Kyriakides came to Boston from Greece, leaving behind his starving family—and nation—who were still suffering from the effects of the rampaging Nazi war machine. During Germany's occupation of his country, Kyriakides sold every one of his possessions to feed his wife and two children. His country was destroyed; there were no roads or trains or harbors left. "There is nothing—nothing except the soil of Greece and a people determined to survive and be great again." When asked if he had the stamina to run the race, because of his hunger and the effects of war, he humbly answered, "I think I have the strength for it. If not in my legs, then maybe here in my heart."

In the days leading up to race, the *Boston Traveler* printed a headline that spoke to the emaciated runner's desperation: "Greek Food Relief Rides on Marathon." The runner was hoping that a win would bring attention to his plight and inspire others to help.

On race day, Kyriakides wrote two notes to himself. At the starting line he opened the first one, which read, "Do or Die." The message spoke to his desperation and the no-excuses approach he would adopt on this day. Twenty-six-plus miles later, he broke the tape and opened his other note, which proclaimed, "We are Victorious!" Kyriakides would return to Greece with a boatload of supplies. He would send a letter of thanks to the citizens of Boston, which was printed in the Boston papers: "The people of Greece are everlastingly grateful to the people of your magnanimous country."

At the first mile marker, a statue of the 1946 winner Stylianos Kyriakides graces the Marathon course, reminding all runners that just being in the arena is not enough. So, we ran, channeling the courage of the great Greek runner and attacking the course with a genuine spirit that would pass muster with Bill Olsen's grandfather. No excuses would be offered.

On Marathon Day, everyone has something wrong with them. Sore knees, sore feet, lack of sleep, chafing, new sneakers that are too tight or too loose, or a shirt with material that is abrasive. But you are here to run. People don't want to hear why you didn't make it to the starting—or the finish—line.

In 1919, runner Frank Gillespie from Chicago was running with brand-new footwear that were too tight, causing the skin on his feet to rip and blood to pool. With five miles to go, he stopped on the side of the road and procured some scissors which he used to cut off the front of each sneaker. He ran the last five miles, all the way to Boston, with his toes dangling on the ground, finishing fourth.

Running Boston isn't supposed to be easy. That's why those who run it are so unique and special. That's why only 1 percent of the entire world has a marathon "conquest" on their résumé. Everyone who toes the line in Hopkinton understands that the challenge is mighty. They know that they can only conquer if they suffer. It was this very motivation that compelled Guy Gertsch to finish Boston in 1982 despite breaking his thighbone at Mile 7. He would collapse over the finish line and be brought to a local hospital where he underwent a five-hour surgery to mend his shattered femur.

In 1951, Guillermo Rojas from Guatemala finished twenty-seventh, despite a ruptured appendix that would require emergency surgery after he finished. In 1953, Kiyoshi Shinozaki was told not to run because of a leg issue. He went on to finish twenty-second, and was brought right to the hospital to have a cast placed on his decimated leg. Thirty-two years later, Welsh runner Bryan Price ran Boston sixteen months after receiving a heart transplant.

This is what running Boston is all about. The great Greek runner Kyriakides exemplified the power of the Boston Marathon. It is an event that transcends the arena. From start to finish, the effort must be Herculean. It was this mind-set that drove champion Clarence DeMar, who possessed a no-excuses spirit. When asked once about the challenges of running in extreme conditions, he said, "A champ can run in any weather."

In Mile 2, the course continues to slide downward toward Boston in a moderate descent, allowing runners to test Sir Isaac Newton's law of universal gravitation. The runners serve as the apple in a maniacal experiment, falling 165 feet from Hopkinton's town common to the border of the next town of Ashland.

In the early steps of the race, the athletes move as a solid mass. Spectators waiting for the runners to come around the corner, or down the street, can hear and feel the oncoming stampede. The herd moves east in what appears to spectators as a mosaic of hats and bounding hair. This collection runs without distinction—one monstrous regiment of buoys bouncing up and down on a rough sea.

Up until now, most runners have been unable to open up to a comfortable pace. Each step must be carefully placed to avoid another runner's foot. On the sidewalk, the contingent of spectators mostly comprises locals, as the streets of Hopkinton are closed to normal traffic early in the morning. The second mile continues with a series of quick-hitting ups and downs, and an occasional house among the woods and fields that line the road. Halfway through the mile, the runners pass Clinton Street and its admiring residents.

Later in Mile 2, as runners begin to extend their strides, they also start to assess their pre-race strategy, deciding to either respect or ignore it. In planning how to best attack the race, the runner must decide whether to run with consideration, or with a lack of restrictions. While the race can't be won in Mile 2, it can be lost. For the elite, it's critical to get to the early flats of Mile 2 before others do.

This is especially true for the wheelchair athletes. If a runner can't move in a shared cocoon with others, then he or she faces the same fate as the slowest antelope in the Serengeti, with the course playing the role of the lion. Tardy wheelchair competitors left behind are forced to run Boston on their own as the lead group of wheelchair racers work together to share the burden of fending off the resistance of wind, thus moving faster. An elite wheelchair competitor who loses contact with the lead pack on the first incline is unable to draft off the front group, and thus faces the daunting task of running on his or her own. It has been estimated that separation from the pack here can add as much as ten minutes to a competitive racer's overall time. If you don't crest the first big hill back in Mile 1 with the lead pack, your day is probably over, so it is essential to push the envelope here.

Five-time wheelchair champion Jim Knaub puts it this way: "If you make it to the top side of the first hill before everyone else, you have a great chance of winning. It's like God picked you up and dropped you in the lead, and said, 'It's your day.'"

The decision to run fast, or deliberately—to run with the lead pack, or to let them go—is a determination that runners have mulled over and discussed for more than a century. The decision is as simple as the riddle posed in Aesop's fable, "The Tortoise and the Hare":

> *Hare ran down the road for a while and then paused to rest. He looked back at Slow and Steady and cried out, "How do you expect to win this race when you are walking along at your slow, slow pace?"*

The methodical plodder sees the tortoise as wise and calculating. In 1941, the *Globe* wrote about a champion who ran at a pragmatic pace, similar to the tortoise, in the previous year's race. "Leslie Pawson showed everybody how to run this course last year. He started away from that crazy fast early pace. He hung back until the leaders tired. Then he ran away from them." The radical runners, however—well, they are all hares. To them, the hare is the *essence* of running. It's putting one foot in front of the other without regard for winds or sun or competitors; if it's their day, it's their day.

While Pawson used pace to run to victory, others find that running with restraint is counterintuitive to the very act of running. Bill Olsen's grandfather would say you came to Boston to run—so put your head down and go. That's what the hare does. The emboldened runner is like the Italian speedster Franco, played by Raul Julia in the 1976 road race movie, *The Gumball Rally*. As Franco prepares for the start of the race, he rips off his rearview mirror and declares, "What's behind me—it's not important."

The runner who wants to run without restraint is a piston-firing Corvette, not a peace sign–stickered Prius. Runners of haste don't spend their days worrying about global warming—they create their own energy. These runners run hard because that's what they do. In their minds, all fables are open to interpretation. Morals of stories are subjective, hinging on the perception of the reader. The runner knows that the hare's only problem in Aesop's fable is that he *stops running*.

The greatest competitor in Boston Marathon history was a hare. Seventime champion Clarence DeMar ran not to run but to win. He was wired to let his legs—not his brain—decide where to go, how to go, when to go. "I always annoyed marathon coaches by telling them that the main thing was to get there as quickly as possible and to let the styles chips fall where they would."

Like DeMar, in 1978, Gayle Barron also ran like a hare. She showed up at the starting line of the Marathon with training sneakers instead of her running sneakers, assuming her run that day would be respectable but not winnable. As she ran, she felt light and relaxed, despite the fact that she was running in the lead. When she came upon friends who were there to support her, they implored her to slow down, as she was running beyond her means on that day. But *slow* wasn't in her nature. She would say later, upon reflection, "I said to myself that I'd run that pace as I could for as long as I could." After running through the tape as the Women's champion, she said, "Can you believe it? I've never run that way in my life. I never, never would have picked me to win."

To run a marathon means that the enormity of the undertaking should be matched by the effort. To cross the finish line with more left to give, with more run in your legs, more fuel in the tank, is considered by some to be disrespectful to the course and those who have run before. Some view it as a sin.

In 1978, Jeff Wells ran with great speed, but in the end, he had more to give. When he sat after the race with beef stew in hand, he felt guilty for finishing two seconds behind winner Bill Rodgers, and begged God for forgiveness. "I had too much left in me. I hadn't given out 100 percent as I had promised Him. And I didn't. I had too much left."

Jeff Wells never ran with the lead that day, but for those who have run the final yards of a marathon with no one in front of them, and the gleaming, unbroken tape in front, they claim something beyond victory. With that victory comes the knowledge that is bestowed upon someone with a marathon championship on his or her résumé and a laurel wreath in the trophy case. From that point on, the runner runs with a level of confidence and chutzpah that other runners are simply not wired for.

It's the "been there before" attitude that allows the veteran to run the race without getting swept up in the challenge of the course or the threat of competitors. Boston Marathon champion Rob de Castella explains the core of his strategy: "I have a pretty simple theory, really. If you run as fast as you can, you should finish up there with a pretty good time. If you're fitter than others that day, you may win. If someone's with you the last couple of miles, then you've got to start racing. But I worry about that when it happens."

Past winners Geoff Smith and Jim Knaub concur with the "run for the tape" mentality. They will tell you that there is no such thing as a game plan. Both runners have a common strategy: Attack every inch of the course the same. Knaub says: "Go for broke from the beginning to the end. If it's not your day, then it's not your day." Smith agrees, and adds, "Line up and let's see who's best—whoever wins was the best that day."

World-class runners have to run Boston with two game plans. The first is logical, composed of the best running strategies ever incorporated in road races. The second plan must be a spontaneous fire drill that compels you to react to weather, course conditions, and, mostly, the will of your competitors.

For the most part, you must run Boston at least once before you can win here. Very few runners have showed up at Boston and won the first time. Johnny Miles in 1926 and Geoff Smith in 1984 were both exceptions to this rule, while marathon greats Frank Shorter and Greta Waitz came to Boston for the first time and "withered" away, never to come back.

Somewhere in Mile 2, your breathing begins to regulate and your pulse becomes more controlled. Adrenaline is still pumping, but at a more reasonable rate. In the first two miles, you work your way through the crowds of slower competitors. Richie and I spent the first two miles navigating runners, which only added extra steps to our journey. Some runners are still peeling off layers of clothes and throwing them on front lawns, while others are answering nature's call.

Between the downhill running and the meandering around others, the early miles seem more like a slalom event than the world's greatest race. The farther you run, the farther you separate from the masses.

Richie and I hugged the left side of the road along the sidewalk, Richie showing his appreciation to young well-wishers by high-fiving them. This was no different from the competitors in the first race in 1897 who thanked supportive bystanders who were waving handkerchiefs by bowing. I, on the other hand, knew that I couldn't afford to waste a single ounce of energy, and reminded Richie that we still had twenty-five miles to run. He smiled as only Richie can smile.

At the end of the second mile, you cross into the town of Ashland, Massachusetts, where the race started all those years before.

MILE 3

It Started Here—Ashland

As a Bostonian, I am a traditionalist. History fascinates me. It's one of the reasons I love the Boston Marathon. But for me it's not just the connection with history; I also have a personal relationship with the race. Throughout the 1970s and '80s, I used to watch the race at my uncle Paul's house in Newton, located just feet from the course.

In our later years, my older brother, John, ran track at Providence College on one of the top track and field teams in NCAA history. Three of my brother's teammates were All Americans and future members of the Providence College Hall of Fame, as well as being authors of finishes at Boston that placed them in the top three, including Irishmen John Treacy and Andy Ronan, as well as Englishman Geoff Smith, who would win Boston twice. In Smith's second win of back-to-back championships, in 1985, the Connellys would cause a controversy that would provoke the race's biggest change in its history. This was when my brother introduced Geoff Smith to my uncle Paul's company, Prime Computers, which would sponsor him that year. This came at a time when the race was mulling over whether to remain amateur or introduce prize money, in order to help entice world-class runners.

Geoff Smith wore a singlet with Prime Computer emblazoned on it, winning his second straight Boston Marathon in 1985. When Geoff passed us in Newton, you could hardly see Uncle Paul's company logo, as Geoff was on pace to pulverize the world record that day. He ran the first half of the race in an unheard-of time of 1:02:51. On his hand he had written the splits he would need to run to break the record, and he was blowing the times away.

But that's when the course reared its ugly head. For a hundred years, the Marathon has had a way of humbling even the greatest runners, and this year was no different. With hamstrings pushed to the limits, Geoff was forced to shift down and turn from hare to turtle, running slowly and cautiously to the finish line. Nonetheless, Smith has two Boston Marathon wins on his résumé, as well as being one of the few people in the world to ever run a sub-4:00 mile, a sub-1:02 half marathon, and a sub-2:10 marathon.

While five generations of Connellys have attended and supported the race over the years, none of us had ever participated in the event until I crossed the starting line in 1996. Now, more than a decade after Geoff had won his two, back to back, I was running in his footsteps, along with those of Ronan, Treacy, DeMar, Kelley, and Gibb. It was heady stuff to think I was running in the same arena as the greatest that had ever laced up sneakers.

It is this link to history that makes the race so special to me, and to those who come to Boston to run or give witness. The race, like ivy, has wound itself through both the towns and time. It has provided the community with a constant. This is what is so special about running Boston. It's not just being part of a road race; it's being part of history.

When the first race was run, there were over a million veterans of the Civil War still alive. It is likely a former Union Soldier watched the first Boston Marathon. On the morning of that first-ever race, a Vermont newspaper called the *United Opinion* reported that "Sixteen runners entered for the Boston Athletic Association Marathon race." Right below was a note that read, "Survivors of the first volunteer company sent to the front of the Civil War were banqueted in Cambridge."

When Boston woke up to their April 19, 1897, *Boston Journal*, a new sporting event was being introduced to the city. It was on those pages that the route of the new road race was presented to the readers:

> *Will cover just about 25 miles, across the steam railroad track to the trolley tracks and then follow electric line straight, through South Framingham, Natick, Wellesley and Newton Lower Falls to the large signboard. At this point two roads begin. Through the Newtons leaving Chestnut Hill reservoir on the right, thence by Beacon Street, Massachusetts Ave., Boylston and Exeter Streets and Huntington Avenue to the (Irvington) Oval, one lap of which is the final burst of the race.*

The Boston Marathon was inspired by an athletic event first introduced at the original Olympics, hosted in Greece in 1896. The race was a twenty-five-mile endurance event in which runners honored the historic trek of a heroic Greek soldier named Pheidippides. The soldier had run from Marathon to Athens in 490 BC to declare Greek victory over the Persians by proclaiming, "Rejoice, we conquer!"

Bostonians Herbert Holton and John Graham were present at those Olympics and were captivated by the distance event. When they returned home, they vowed to bring a similar event to the city. After receiving support from the local sporting club, the Boston Athletic Association, the men set off to map out a course. The two men rode their bikes west from the Boston Athletic Association building in Boston, using the train tracks as their guide. With cyclometer in their hands, they pedaled all the way into Ashland, where their instruments read 25 miles. They then climbed down from their seats, grabbed two rocks, and proclaimed the bridge next to Metcalf's Mill as the starting line for the American Marathon.

Reports would say of the newly designed course in the following day's paper, "There are seven hills, the hardest one being just past the Chestnut Hill Reservoir in Newton. There, not so bad, as John Graham rode up all of them on his wheel."

From 1897 to 1923, the Boston Marathon started in this small, thirteen-square-mile town. For years runners took steam trains, electric trolleys, and barges out to Ashland to participate on a racecourse that was dusty and, in the eyes of one reporter, not the cultural equal of the course and starting line at the Olympics. "The road from Ashland to Boston is hardly as rich in classic memories as the road from Marathon to Athens, but it appears to have been honored with as swift runners."

It wouldn't be until 1924 that the Boston Marathon would begin in Hopkinton. The amended course was necessitated when the universally accepted marathon distance was increased to 26.2 miles in 1908, at the Olympics in London. (This was to allow the race to start at Windsor Castle and finish in front of the Royal Box.)

It was in Mile 3 that Richie and I pushed forward and were starting to hit our stride. The course continued to fall toward sea level. The mile was more of the same: wooded areas with houses mixed in, congenial families cheering us on to the next mile.

In the old days, the village of Ashland used to hose down the early miles of the course, into the next town of Framingham. It was said that the "roadway for the first 12 miles is soft and heavy, but after they strike the Newton boulevards it is almost as good as a track." In 1907, the sand was said to be "ankle high."

Mile 3 moves up only to fall for the rest of the mile, dumping the runners into Ashland center. Throughout the mile the route moves left and then comes back right, almost as if it were a driver overcompensating in the snow, causing rear wheels to slide back and forth like Vin Diesel cruising around corners in *The Fast and the Furious*. Halfway through the mile, the runners pass the local Knights of Columbus and Ashland State Park. From there, the course moves downhill precipitously for the last half of the mile.

At approximately the 2.7-mile mark, the runners go by Steven's Corner. It is here where the race was started from 1899 to 1924. It was on the bridge at Metcalf's Mill where the men pushed and carved out space at a starting line literally drawn with the heel of a race official's shoe. Surrounded by officials and gamblers alike, the runners would crouch, awaiting the gun as thousands of fans cheered them on, just as they did for the first Boston Marathon in 1897. As the *Globe* reported, "The crowd at the Ashland station was good-natured, and as it formed a line for the athletes to pass, the sleepy old town rang with the cheers of her lusty sons."

Like every Boston Marathon runner who has stood on the starting line, all those in Ashland—that day, and for the following two-plus decades—hoped to realize glory hours later on the streets of Boston.

Richie and I weren't running sub-five-minute miles like Geoff Smith did in 1985, and we didn't have attendants to wipe our brows or hand us sponges soaked in brandy. We put one foot in front of the other and kept running east. At the end of this mile we would find more of a commercial zone than a residential one for the first time in the race.

In Mile 4 we would be in our comfort zone.

MILE 4

Pedigree

Part of that journey Nana Kenny talked about was finding yourself. Finding out what you are capable of—who you are—what you believe in—what you stand for. It wasn't just about existing. This is why the four of us were running the Boston Marathon.

In the book *Tuesdays with Morrie*, Morrie Schwartz talks about how it's a shame to not take this journey of discovery. "The biggest defect we human beings have is our shortsightedness. We don't see what we could be. We should be looking at our potential and stretching ourselves into everything we can become."

At the end of my high school career in baseball, my coach sat down with me and the other seniors and indicated the players he considered talented enough to try out for their respective colleges in the coming fall. He pointed to the teammate on my left and then my right, electing not to judge me worthy.

From that moment forward I realized that I actually thrive when people doubt me. I sat there in the locker room that day, considered not good enough by a coach who was unaware of the power of words. But that's all right, I thought. Fuck him. Don't ever tell me I can't do something. I knew better than anyone what I was capable of. He saw a second baseman who was vertically challenged and harnessed by a limited arm strength. What I saw when I looked in the mirror was a person capable of pushing past perceptions. Where my coach saw a slap-hitting second baseman with average arm strength, I saw myself as someone who would never quit, never say no, never surrender.

Television writer David Hudgins once spoke of such a scenario. "You can do anything. Don't let anybody tell you that you can't, and don't tell yourself that. If you don't believe in yourself, nobody else is going to."

That following autumn, I made the baseball team at Bentley College and turned myself into a three-year starter. And despite being the smallest player on the roster my senior season, I led the team in extra base hits and runs batted in while hitting over .350 with men in scoring position. At the end of the year, I was presented the Most Improved Award and the Wayne McCrae Award, for my "dedication, hustle, and love for the game."

——◆——

Each mile on the course has its own characteristics, presenting its own unique challenge for the runners. In the first steps of Mile 4, the runner moves downhill and to the right. It is here that the runners are introduced to ankle-high cement traffic islands that rise from the ground, often tripping unsuspecting competitors. The islands stretch for a tenth of a mile as the road curves to the right. These are known as "Three Mile Islands" (even though they occur in Mile 4)—a nuclear metaphor that implies danger if they're not properly navigated. These obstacles enhance the degree of difficulty of this mile, making this segment of the course a virtual steeplechase, and proving that the intricacies of the course itself are just as much a part of the competition as the distance.

Wheelchair competitors need to be especially careful rolling around the bend, as they may be traveling in excess of twenty-five miles per hour coming down the long hill approaching the first of the islands. Although the island early in the mile is well marked with cones and police tape, it can jump up on the runner in hurry—especially if you're drafting or following another competitor too closely. This is one of the spots in the race where being unfamiliar with the course can be a real disadvantage.

For Richie and me, the fourth mile of our training was always a fun and entertaining distance, whether it was in training or on Marathon Day. We talked, joked, and laughed. Our muscles were firing and our breathing had settled.

After Richie and Rad and I put our hands in and pledged to run the Boston Marathon, I'd left the gym that night ready to tell everyone I knew I was going to run Boston. It was my way of locking in the commitment. I couldn't go back on my word. Whenever I told someone, I studied their face and voice inflection to determine whether they believed I could run twenty-six-plus miles. Sure, up to this point in my life the farthest I had ever run was a 5K, and that had been challenging, to say the least. But I was determined, and committed to achieving this goal. To me, the Boston Marathon wasn't a road race; it was an opportunity to live outside of the lanes in which people had always told me I should stay. The race was literally one of a few crossroads in my life that would allow me to challenge my perceived boundaries. Why not? Living isn't sitting on the couch. Living is for exploring who you are and what you are capable of.

So, from that day on the basketball court to running the race, I was all in. And what better way to embark on a road of discovery than with friends. Rad and Richie and I had been buddies for years, sharing laughs and many a beer together. We jumped into fights for one another and stood up at each other's weddings. We weren't just buddies; we were the type of friends you hope you will have in your life.

In the months leading up to the race, we had advanced far enough in our training that we were ready to take part in some extended Sunday runs along the course. Jackie would join us. We would get a ride out to the beginning stages of the route after leaving a car just after Heartbreak Hill. Before we started our first long run, we agreed that it was important to always run at a pace that was comfortable. I was the slowest of the four and didn't want to extend myself too far; I also didn't want them to train at a pace slower than their natural ability.

During these Sunday training runs, the four of us would settle into our pace. We would run in single file on the side of the road, teasing and encouraging each other. We laughed and enjoyed each other's company. Our runs together were the personification of our friendship: four individuals sharing a dream and wishing the best for each other. For this odyssey to be successful, all four of us would have to realize success. If one of us were to fail, then our mission would be incomplete.

In the fourth mile Rad and his brother Jack would usually push ahead while Richie and I stayed behind, catching up on each other's lives—families, jobs, local sports teams. Strangely, the conversation always morphed from immature to serious the farther we got down the road. Within this dialogue we challenged each other. We wondered if we were pushing ourselves to be the best versions of ourselves. Training for the Boston Marathon has a way of making you take inventory of your life.

Both of us had come from middle-class families of Irish descent. Our families weren't prominent like the Forbeses, Endicotts, or the Lodges. Our great-grandparents had been pushed out of the Beacon Hill–like neighborhoods to the peninsulas of South Boston and Dorchester, forced to build their own way in a harsh world of the haves and the have-nots. Other than the Kennedys and Fitzgeralds, for the most part Irish families politely fit into the low or middle classes and worked in subordinate jobs around the city.

Richie and I both had good and decent parents who provided for us. We didn't have extra, but we needed nothing. This is all we knew. We knew comfortable. The Connellys had six kids, two parents, one bathroom, one station wagon. It worked. But our parents wanted more for their kids than they had. We both wanted more. So, we asked the question: How do you achieve more? How do push yourself to break through the unspoken caste system that keeps one from leaping into a world above where your families existed?

In the book *Epiphany*, Esther Perel shares an approach to surviving that her parents had applied in order to survive the Holocaust: "You better do big things—only if you are really big, really daring, really cunning, really determined and lucky would you survive."

To climb society's economic and social ladder, you must be bold. It's only by being audacious that you can change a family's trajectory. Running the Boston Marathon is bold. If we could make it to Boston, we would have a living, breathing touchstone we would be able to draw upon. We would know that we were capable of great things. We would have validation that by being bold in life, you can truly live.

To run Boston we would have to channel the audacious and even brash state of mind that Boston runner Arthur Roth competed with in 1916, when he won the championship, "When did I start thinking I could win?" He mulled over an answer and then brashly stated, in part, "I just piled confidence into myself. I don't like to sound fat-headed, but I might say that when I started this morning I didn't think for a minute I was going to lose."

For us, our grandest ambition was to run the Boston Marathon. We weren't runners by trade. We didn't run qualifying times. We didn't know about glycogen stores or VO2 max. We were all about putting one foot in front of the other. About being one step closer to Boston. Sure, it was our first marathon, but no one had ever run this race with more sincerity than the four of us on this day. We ran because—why not? Why couldn't we do great things? In *The Alchemist*, the narrator speaks to the challenges faced by people who aren't used to confidently reaching for great things—the things that seemed to be meant only for those deemed worthy. "People are afraid to pursue their most important dreams, because they feel they don't deserve them, or that they'll be unable to achieve them."

So, why *not* us? Why couldn't we run in the footsteps of DeMar, Kelly, and Benoit? We loved this race just as much as anyone else. Why couldn't we advance our families even further than our parents or their parents had gone? Why should we accept less—expect less? Running Boston would be our first steps on a road toward grabbing more going forward. So, in 1996, we ran the fourth mile with love and hope in our hearts.

Overall, the course plummets three hundred feet—almost thirty stories—in the first four miles. Mile 4 turns flat and straight as the course moves briefly through a residential neighborhood before creeping past an old burial ground, and then a school on the left. At the next set of lights, marking the Main Street intersection, the runners pass the spot where the old Central House and the Columbia House were located. In the early 1900s, these places of lodging offered runners their physical exam and pre-race meal of steak and eggs. Most didn't finish their plates because of nervous stomachs.

In 1928 seven-time winner Clarence DeMar didn't suffer from that problem. Prior to the race—in which he won his sixth championship—he devoured two prunes, two hard-boiled eggs, oatmeal, two pieces of toast, and a glass of milk. In current days the pre-race meal, compliments of the BAA, is held the night before on the grounds of Boston City Hall, and the fare is pasta, and more pasta. (The 2019 menu included, among other dishes, penne marinara with fresh Italian herbs and three-cheese macaroni and cheese.)

Back in the days when DeMar was winning races, Ashland was known for manufacturing clocks and watches per the designs of a local inventor named Henry Warren. Warren created the first self-winding clock during the Great Depression. People moved to Ashland to find work in the prospering clock factory. In later years, the town's—and Mr. Warren's—wallets expanded when General Electric joined Warren as a 49 percent partner. Time and clocks remain integral to the town of Ashland today. The high school sports teams go by the nickname of the Clockers, and a clock tower stands in Ashland's epicenter, down the road in Mile 4.

Toward the end of the mile, the runners pass the Ashland clock tower on their left. This large timepiece is mounted on a commercial building called the Ashland Technology Building. During the days when there were no clocks along the racecourse, DeMar used this clock to check his pace early in the race. As the runners pass the clock nowadays, they hardly glance up at the old dinosaur; they all have digital watches and numerous clocks along the route to remind them that they should have trained harder.

At the end of Mile 4, runners need to remain focused and stay to the right. In the middle of the course there is yet another traffic island rising from the ground, forming the second half of the Three Mile Island sandwich. Runners are relieved to survive this mile and look forward to the comparatively boring setting of Mile 5.

At this point runners start to gain their stride and stretch it out, glad to be checking Ashland off their list and moving on to Framingham. Any thoughts of stepping off the course and calling it a day at this juncture would raise the ire of the demanding spectators, who won't accept this decision. This sentiment was shared by local marathoner Mark Coogan, who said in 1994, "Boston is the only marathon where you can't walk off the course. The fans are going to push you right back out there."

At the end of the mile, I was slowing my pace and preparing to release the tether connecting me with my friend Richie. As we crossed over the mile mark, I felt like Jack in *Titanic*, slipping into the water, while Richie (Rose—sorry, Rich) floated away on his raft. I was now by myself. Living in the moment, step by step, same goal—keep pushing forward, but now alone.

MILE 5

Sisters

In Jane Austen's book *Pride and Prejudice*, Elizabeth Bennett says about the spirit of women's independence, "There is a stubbornness about me that can never bear to be frightened at the will of others. My courage always rises at every attempt to intimidate me." In the town of Ashland back in 1967, such a streak of feminine willfulness was on full display when Kathrine Switzer ran through its streets in what was seemingly an innocuous run. In the end, Switzer's run would be historic.

The story actually started one year before. Women weren't allowed to run Boston until 1972. But in 1966 a young lady from the Massachusetts town of Winchester known as Roberta Gibb Bingay was the first woman to ever run the Boston Marathon. She ran the race from Hopkinton to Boston. In the papers the following day it was written, "Roberta Bingay didn't do badly at all. She finished well ahead of lots of men." Another paper called her a "blond 23-year-old beauty." When race officials were asked about Roberta's run, they ignored the individual runner and spoke about the gender instead. "They don't have the 'physigammy,' or whatever you call it." Another official suggested that he would consider allowing women to run under the following condition: "If someone would guarantee that all future lady runners would be as pretty as she."

In the following year, Kathrine Switzer and Roberta Gibb both proved they had the proper "physigammy." Gibb jumped out of some nondescript shrubs in Hopkinton and ran quietly toward Boston. But Switzer's run wasn't as inconspicuous. Switzer ran with number 261 pinned on her gray sweatshirt, which race officials interpreted as sacrilege when they discovered that she was a woman. They were so outraged that they jumped on the press bus and chased her down into the town of Ashland.

When they pulled up beside her, Jock Semple and Will Cloney leapt from the bus. Jock Semple was first onto the pavement and hit the ground running. Little did these defenders of the gender know that they would have to get by Switzer's muscle-bound boyfriend, Tom Miller, a collegiate hammer thrower at Syracuse University who was running side by side with his girlfriend. Semple got to her first—"Cloney tried to catch her first—he was too bloody slow," Jock later recalled—and yelled for the woman to "get out of my race!" Unaware of Miller's presence, he reached for Switzer and began to pull off the number 261 bib. Instinctively, the runner's boyfriend knocked Semple to the ground, allowing Switzer to escape to Boston. (Semple later claimed "that he never hit the ground," and that, "If Cloney wasn't so fat and slow he would have been to the girl before I got there and did what I did, and then women wouldn't hate me.")

With Semple flying through the air, Switzer and her Syracuse posse continued down the course. An enraged Semple would later call the group a "close-knit bunch of scoundrels," stating that the "Syracuse bunch would never run in this race again."

After the bizarre confrontation, the "Syracuse bunch" would keep running east. The next miles were sad and eerie, Switzer recalled. "Everyone was silent. The only sounds you heard were the quarter-sized snowflakes hitting the leaves of the trees above and the runners' feet pounding the pavement." Switzer did what any focused marathoner would do: She kept putting one foot in front of the other—but in her head, she was confused. "I was embarrassed and mortified. I was treated like a common criminal when I was only hoping to run a race," she said. Switzer would finish the marathon that day, and in the process, she would change the race—and women's sports—forever.

At the post-race press conference, Cloney and Semple were rabid. "I am surprised that an American girl would do something like this, and go someplace where she wasn't invited."

⊸〜

John "Jock" Semple was a hot-tempered Scot with a shrill brogue who was determined to protect the race under all circumstances. Semple had sacrificed all for the race—his marriage, his legs, his health. He was loyal, committed, and inflexible. Over the years, he did more to give color and identity to the Boston Marathon than any other individual in the hundred-plus-year history of the race. Born in Glasgow, Scotland, the raging Scot traveled across the sea to Philadelphia at age eighteen. In 1929, Semple hitchhiked to Boston to run in the world-famous marathon. He ran that year, and eighteen more times, finishing in the top ten six times (his personal record was 2:44:29).

Eventually Semple traded Philadelphia for Boston and joined the BAA. The marriage between Semple, who would become known as the "Cardinal of the Race," and the Boston Marathon was a special union. Semple treated the race as a classroom and the runners as its students. He demanded that the pupils be attentive and respectful, but when he spoke, his cantankerous demeanor was more scolding than educational. Whenever a potential runner requested an application to run in the race, Semple was known to loudly demand: "Are you *sure* you can run twenty-six miles?" Runner Ken Parker of Canada looked forward to being yelled at as almost part of the experience. "It was an honor to be yelled at by Mr. Semple," Parker said.

Jock passionately administered the race from 1947 to 1982. And though he will be most remembered for his failed extrication of Kathy Switzer, the race wouldn't be the premier event it is today without his contributions. Jock died in 1988 at the age of eighty-four, but many swear that they can still hear the echoes of his abrasive brogue back in Hopkinton, commanding that the runners adhere to protocol, run with honor, and conduct themselves with dignity.

After Switzer's and Gibb's rebellious runs, local sports columnist Bud Collins would write in support of women runners. "The Marathon is Boston's finest sporting event because of its wide-open nature. Its embracing of everyman, demented and the daring, the heroes and the hopeless. It's everybody's race. It isn't the Olympics, remember. It's the unique, marvelously mad Boston Marathon."

As far back as 1915 women were interested in running the city's famous race. It was that year women were seen training on Blue Hill Avenue in Boston in bloomers, blouses, and leather gymnasium shoes. It was five years before women could vote when a woman wrote to the race's governing body, the Boston Athletic Association, asking, "Wanted to know if ladies are permitted to run in the marathon, and if not, why not? For women now have the same rights as men. If ladies are permitted to run, please set aside a dressing room for them. We are going to run anyway." After female applicants were denied entrance, the *Herald* would write: "[A]s yet no arrangement for a 25-mile marathon race by the girls, who were barred out of the big race Monday."

The women's missive to the BAA would prove prophetic, because women *would* run, and with a competitor's spirit. Following the trailblazing runs of Switzer and Gibb, the BAA would vote to welcome women to the race starting in 1972. That year, seven women stood on the starting line as official runners. At the 100th running in 1996, more than ten thousand women ran Boston, and in the overall history of the race, more than two hundred thousand women have competed. This is not because they are Susan B. Anthonys, but because their hearts tell them to run. In 1996, Uta Pippig would win her third race while fending off the course, challengers, and female biology. The following day, *Boston Globe* writer Eileen McNamara would write, "Uta conquered her own body as well as the competition."

In the first steps of Mile 5 the runners continue right, as the traffic islands extend from the previous mile into the next one. Beyond the islands, runners can look to the left and see the refreshing sight of Bracket Reservoir, which stretches over the next mile, flowing into the Framingham Reservoir. After the runners slide past the cement protrusion in the middle of the road, the course moves up a hill and to the left.

At 4.2 miles, the road continues to hook left like a Tiger Woods drive. The course leaves Union Street and forks left up a slight incline onto Waverly Street, past Ashland Landscape Supply on the left. In the past, the shopkeepers posted the names of friends and associates running the race on a display board outside. It is here that runners must shift muscles to work the uphill. The increased exertion begins to warm them as the rising sun causes many to peel off layers and toss their sweatshirts, hats, and gloves into the parking lot.

In Mile 5, I ran by myself for the first time. On some level it was almost sad to be partaking in something so monumental in my life all by myself. But fortunately for me, I had family positioned throughout the course, ready to cheer me on and support me through this endeavor.

American poet and novelist Eleanore Marie Sarton (known as May Sarton) once said, "Loneliness is the poverty of self. Solitude is the richness of self." This speaks to the core difference between marathoning and running. While training, the runner enjoys the time to run and separate from the world, while a struggling marathoner feels the pain of detachment. It is a lonely pain. The struggle of a marathon is personal, as if the course holds some type of grudge against the runner.

Up ahead my sisters—Maureen, Cathy, and Susan—were waiting for me with a sign and guarded optimism. (I had warned my family before the race that no matter how bad I looked, they must lie and tell me that I was doing great. I knew that my margin for error was slim, and there was no room for doubt.) As I came upon them, they waved and yelled their good wishes. I was surprised at how excited I was to see them.

Every step I took on this day was a product of who I was and where I'd come from. As a member of a big family, my motivation and purpose was a collective state and not an individual sentiment. This was the great thing about growing up in a big family. I drew energy from all my brothers and sisters and parents on this day.

I grew up in a typical Irish Catholic house. There were a lot of mouths to feed and a busy mom and dad. In the driveway there was a wood-paneled station wagon where the kids were piled with no regard for seat belts, only where you got to sit in the car. We were a close family. My father was stern but loving; my mother, skilled in the art of managing a house, kids, and husband, all at the same time. At the dining-room table, there was no singing or silliness. Conversation focused on current events, the day's lessons in school, and outcomes in sporting events.

After dinner we were assigned chores—clear the table; wash, dry, and put away dishes. After chores were complete and homework finished, we squeezed into the TV room around the color Zenith where we watched *The Brady Bunch* and Disney while eating Jiffy Pop popcorn and drinking Kool-Aid.

Our neighborhood was middle-class. We risked life and limb sledding down Sherbrook Street, and played street hockey and touch football in front of the house, using hydrants and telephone poles as goal-line markers. Next door was an old lady who would knock on the windows when a ball rolled on her lawn. On the other side were the Kirbys, who revved jalopies, while up the street was our most famous neighbor, detective Phil DiNatale, who caught notorious serial killer, the Boston Strangler, allowing women to sleep safely.

Holidays were always fun with a big family. At Christmas we lined up, shortest to tallest, at the top of the stairs and practiced our downhill running after my father confirmed that Santa had come. At Halloween, the Connellys would circle the neighborhood yelling "Trick or treat," with the smell of burning leaves in the air.

But now we were adults, with children of our own and real jobs and real responsibilities. That didn't mean we didn't still lean on each other. And that's what I was doing in Mile 5—leaning on my sisters. They were a sight for sore eyes. It's a blessing to have people in your life who provide support and have your best interests at heart. Morrie Schwartz echoed this sentiment in *Tuesdays with Morrie*: "That your family will be there watching out for you—nothing else will give you that—not money, not fame."

I was disappointed to leave them behind. From this point on, I started to appreciate that there is a significant emotional dimension to running a marathon. I was only five miles into the race, and I was already emotionally vulnerable. I knew that going forward, each time I came upon a family member or a friend, I would remember that I was loved, and that I was not alone on the course. I ran with their hope and love for me in my heart.

A marathon invokes the crests and troughs of pathos. When the gun goes off in Hopkinton, the runner alone is responsible for the day's outcome. No amount of support or motivation from loved ones can help a competitor once he or she is on the course. Their presence may provide a momentary and critical reprieve from the arduous endeavor, but when the runner parts ways with his or her loved ones, it's just runner against the racecourse, in a battle of wills.

One thing was for sure: I wasn't going to fail on this day because of lack of love.

❧

Halfway into Mile 5, up until its end, the course snakes back and forth, left and right, testing the runner's rack-and-pinion steering. In the final steps, there is a mixture of residential, commercial, and undeveloped land. It's too easy to feel indifferent during this stretch, and runners must bear down in order to stay focused.

Back in 1907, reports stated that the runners ran into Framingham with dirt up to their ankles. For the first three decades of the race, witnesses would say that the dirt of Ashland would create a human dust bowl, kicking up a cloud that absorbed the runners into its haze. Runners were said to enter Framingham with soiled faces and tired legs.

In the final tenths of the mile, the runners have a chance to genuflect when they pass the Sri Lakshmi Temple at the Framingham–Ashland border. The temple draws Hindus from all over the Northeast. With a mailing list of over eight thousand, worshippers come from as far away as New Jersey to shed their shoes and pay homage. On the temple's magnificent tower, which rises fifty feet into the sky, is a statue of Lakshmi, the goddess of wealth. At her sides are the *dwarapalaka*—the female gatekeepers. It is only fitting that they continue to keep watch at the end of Mile 5, the site of the battle for female equality at Boston.

I ran through the end of the mile, up a slight hill, into the third town of Framingham. My encounter with my sisters had reenergized me. Six months earlier, I had never run five miles at a stretch. Now I was comfortably putting one foot in front of the other, looking forward to whatever the next mile would present to me.

———

Two decades later, my sister Maureen, a doctor, would run Boston. A mother of four—including triplets—she found time to run while working her bigwig job with Harvard Medical School. When three-time champion Uta Pippig was asked about runners she admires, she spoke of parents who care for their children, go to work, and still find time to train for a marathon. Maureen is the type of person Uta and I both admire!

Self-Actualization

After the five-mile mark, the runners' brains are busy with calculations as they divide five into their time and then multiply by twenty-six and round up to account for the last 385 yards. The route has been fairly easy up to this point, with adrenaline helping runners maintain their pace for the first thirty to forty-five minutes.

By Mile 6, many runners are ahead of their intended splits, both because of the downhills and the early excitement. Runners who are new to the Boston Marathon can easily fool themselves into thinking they can keep up this pace for twenty-one more miles, but veterans know all too well that this optimism is off the mark. In fact, more runners than not will see splits trend up as the Newton Hills give way to the Citgo sign down the road.

The early steps of Framingham offer runners the first of many tugs-of-war that will happen between mind and body on race day. While they rejoice that they have passed the first real benchmark of the race, at the same time they realize they haven't even completed one-fifth (a mere 20 percent) of the course. The devil on the runner's left shoulder starts to debate with the angel on the right. With more than twenty-one miles to go, and the easiest part of the course behind them, it takes a calm mind and a well-trained body to take the next step and pretend that the ten-mile mark is just around the corner.

During the 1898 race, the *Globe* reported that "Framingham greeted runners with gongs and ringing of bells." Luckily, the crowds start to increase in size and passion here. Five miles into it, runners are starting to crave the much-needed encouragement of the "Looking good!" and "You can do it!" comments, provided by sidewalk supporters.

At the beginning of the sixth mile, the course moves uphill and to the right before leveling off through a wooded, residential neighborhood. The route then makes its way from residential to commercial. On the left, marathoners may notice diners stepping out of the landmark Italian restaurant LaCantina's (founded the same year Shigeki Tanaka won Boston, in 1951) with meatballs on their forks and *amore* in their heart for the runners.

After bending right, the runners get a brief respite with a short descent past another commercial area, before another right-hand bend and a slight uphill. Through this section, trees provide some temporary protection from either sun or rain, offering the runners a moment to gather themselves. Up ahead, the increasing noise signals a tumultuous welcome waiting around the corner.

In the last half of the mile, the runners pass over the intersection of Route 135 and Winthrop Street. This area proves to be an ideal viewing area, where fans stand five or six deep to get a look at the competitors, drawing the runners to them like magnets. This is one of the areas on the course where the athletes are greeted like prodigal sons (and daughters), returning home. It's an amazing feeling for both elite runners and ten-minute milers to be celebrated like Tom Brady or Lionel Messi by an adoring crowd.

This crowded intersection tends to put smiles on the runners' faces and reinvigorate their spirits as they continue down the route. As they return the crowd's salutations, they must pay attention, because the big right turn from a half-mile back is reversed here with a huge left bend that stretches for a tenth of a mile through the intersection.

At the 5.6-mile mark, the first raucous crowd of the day has gathered to remind you that you are not alone. This is the Boston Marathon, where people come together to help one another, to push runners down the road. It was the first time in my life that so many people had assembled to wish me well. It was a special feeling—like I was the only runner on the course. It was one of those times on the course when you say to yourself, "This is why I decided to run Boston." This is why I'd run through those blizzards and puddles, past those snapping dogs. This is why I got up before the newspaper was on the front stoop.

This curve in the road appears to have been molded for the sole purpose of straightening out the marathon course. For the next four miles, the route remains straight and relatively level.

It's here—in the third town of the race—that many begin to bid farewell to the runners they befriended back in their corral, at the starting line. After five miles of running and the traffic of competitors starting to spread, runners naturally begin to fall in line with those of similar talents and abilities. It's possible that runners in lockstep in Framingham could still be side by side as they enter the gates of Boston, twenty-plus miles down the road.

It's during these miles of Framingham (and later, Natick) that runners began to group together into cliques that match their comfort level. This includes runners who have aspirations of victory. At the beginning of the sixth mile, I was torn. My spirit was boosted by my encounter with my sisters, but now I was on my own. Jack, Rad, and Richie were somewhere down the road, as they were running at their own pace ahead, and the support I felt from seeing my family was fleeting. It was great, but it was over. With more than twenty miles to run, I was lonely.

I was compelled to run alone despite there being forty thousand runners around me. The solitary confinement would allow doubt to creep in, occupying a place in my psyche that would include questions similar to the ones American hero Vice Admiral James Stockdale once asked in a vice presidential debate: "Who am I, and why am I here?"

In 1985, when Geoff Smith was winning his second straight Boston Marathon, he was on pace to annihilate the race, and world, record. But, as often happens, the course exerted its will on Geoff, and he was afflicted with an agonizing hamstring pull. Although he was the one to break the tape, in the following day's paper, the article empathetically described the "lonely agony Geoff Smith was enduring out there on the course." In team sports, you can rely on your mates to pick you up when you are down, or injured, or having a bad day. When running a marathon, there is no help or escape: You either run or you quit. This is the loneliness of participating in a life-changing event all by yourself.

Race official Jock Semple had run Boston many times before he became an organizer. He once spoke eloquently on the challenge of the sport. "I never had so many funny—or awful—feelings as I did that day. It was torture! Pains racked my stomach after four miles; my legs felt like lumps of lead; I was dizzy. Worst of all, it was lonely."

To run a marathon means that you are okay with running alone with your thoughts, constantly debating different subjects. Whether it's work or marriage or parenting or finances—it will all be rattling around in your mind during training runs, and even on race day. With the drop of each foot, the merry-go-round of ideas and suggestions and recommendations whirl around inside your head.

Frank Shorter, the great American marathoner, called long-distance running both a "compulsion" and a "lonely, solitary sport." By Mile 6, I had become acquainted with this loneliness. During training I had accepted the cold nights, rainy mornings, and boring treadmill sessions because I knew it was all a means to an end. But now I was trying to accomplish that end, and found I was having a completely different conversation with myself—including the nagging question of just exactly what I was trying to accomplish on the road from Hopkinton to Boston. What was my motivation?

I guess I wanted to achieve something great. Something that was beyond what I perceived as what I was capable of.

In 1943, psychologist Abraham Maslow coined his famous hierarchy of needs, which helped to explain the order of people's motivations based around personal requirements. The tiers of the pyramid begin at the bottom with what is essential for survival, and culminate at the apex of personal fulfillment and realization. The list that follows is adapted from an illustration on Wikimedia Commons:

- **Self-actualization:** morality, creativity, spontaneity, acceptance
- **Self-esteem needs:** confidence, achievements, respect of others, connections, need for individuality
- **Love and belongingness needs:** friendship, family, intimacy, connections
- **Safety and security needs:** health, employment, property, family, stability
- **Physiological needs:** air, food, water, shelter, clothing, sleep

In reviewing the categories, I realized that my motivation for running Boston on this day touched three rungs of the ladder. I ran to further my bond with my friends and connect on a more profound level by sharing something special in our lives, thus satisfying some level of the "Love and Belongingness Need." I also sought to further heighten my self-esteem through achievement. And it would be through achieving my goal of running Boston that I would enhance my confidence. But in the end, my ultimate motivation was self-actualization.

In 1996, I was in the fourth decade of my life, and starting to assess who I was and what life really meant. Unknowingly, I was taking inventory.

How would my obituary read? What had I accomplished thus far? How was I honoring my life—my good fortune—my health. My life's mission had to be more than simply getting up each morning, shaving, showering, tying a tie, fighting traffic, and going to work, only to get up the next morning to repeat the same thing over again. The last thing I wanted to be doing was starring in my own version of *Groundhog Day*. I needed to accomplish things.

There's a line in the movie *Wild*, with Reese Witherspoon, that has stuck with me: "Are you in the passenger seat of your own life?" Now, don't get me wrong. When I toed the line in Hopkinton, I was already blessed. I had a loving wife and a happy and healthy son. My parents were still alive and still a supportive force in my life. I had friends and siblings who were a profound part of my life.

But there had to be more—mountains to climb, oceans to travel, ancient cities to visit. That's why I was running Boston. My true blessing on this day was that my primary motivation was self-actualization. I wasn't running to earn food or secure a home and safety for my family. I was running to boost an already-inflated self-opinion.

While I ran for contentment, others came to Boston desperate to break the tape and change the fortunes of their family.

Following the 1905 race, winner Fred Lorz told the press, "I am a brick-layer by trade, work all day, finding time in the evenings to do my training. I intend to go back to New York this morning and to work laying brick tomorrow."

In the 1930s several winners of the Boston Marathon ran during the days of the Great Depression, unemployed and hungry. One of these was Walter Young, of Quebec, Canada, in 1937. Young was motivated to win the Boston Marathon so that he could showcase himself as a viable candidate for a job. Following his win, a reporter asked his wife if the family would celebrate her husband's run. Demonstrating how basic the family's needs were, she retorted, "I'll say there won't be a party—have a heart, mister; it's hard enough to get enough food to live on without throwing a party."

In 1946, champion Stylianos Kyriakides ran the Boston Marathon to feed his family and his people.

In 1997, German Silva of Mexico hoped to win the Boston Marathon and use the subsequent notoriety to bring running water to his village in

Tecomate, Mexico. (When he'd won the New York City Marathon in 1994 and 1995, he was able to bring electricity to his community.)

This hunger to win under any circumstances explains why foreign runners have come to Boston and outrun Americans time and time again. Americans for the most part run for self-actualization, while some less fortunate athletes run to live. Kyriakides was prepared to die on the streets of Boston if it meant the difference between feeding his family and not; similarly, 2001 winner Lee Bong-Ju of South Korea said after the race, "I put [down] every step of the marathon thinking that I would die on the track if I had to."

When race director William Cloney was asked back in 1962 why Finnish, Japanese, and Korean runners were dominating the race, he responded like an older person shaking his head at the younger generation. "How many youngsters will even consider running 26 miles . . . most kids want the family car to go to the corner store."

Following the 1954 race, reporters asked winner Veikko Karvonen why Americans weren't winning the world's greatest race. "You Americans have too many automobiles and much too much to eat. You'll never develop men of stamina and endurance that way."

To win Boston you have to be obsessed with winning Boston. When three-time champion Ibrahim Hussein was asked why the Kenyans are dominating the race, he said, "Kenyans are winning because they train hard and leave aside everything else, like going to discos or seeing friends at night. They only concentrate on training."

Longtime race official Walter Brown said of the international dominance, "Runners in other countries deny themselves a lot of things to become great." Reporter Austen Lake further stated in 1953, just before the race, "These winners come from have-not nations which exist below poverty's belt and where ample edibles [are] scarce. We are largely a country for sports spectators . . . they are about to give us another warning that we Americans are becoming too fat, lazy, prosperous, and apathetic for our own national good."

From 1946 to 1957, runners from seven different foreign countries won Boston. The lack of American victors in a race once called the "American Marathon" was devastating to those who held the race in high esteem. So much so that in 1953, two-time winner John "The Elder" Kelley would suggest, "Maybe we should have separate sets of prizes for the semi-professional foreigners and for the Americans."

Kelley was raising the white flag. Motivated international runners were taking over the race that used to be the property of hungry American runners who laid bricks, delivered milk, and ran printing presses, among other blue-collar jobs.

In the early years of the race, the very thought of a non-American winning the race was unpatriotic. After Canadian runners won the race in 1900 and 1901, *Boston Globe* writer Lawrence Sweeney would write, diplomatically, "Canadians acquitted themselves nobly, and their performance only served to make American runners that more determined."

From the race's inception in 1897 to the end of World War II, in 1945, American men won thirty-four (of the forty-nine) Boston Marathon championships. But from 1946 to 2019, men runners from the United States have won it just eleven times (four by Bill Rodgers).

America went through a transformation after US soldiers returned from World War II. The superior athletes were no longer drawn to running and track-and-field events. Instead, they found glory running for touchdowns, earning headlines and cheerleaders' smiles. American athletes—and sports fans—no longer emulated the DeMars and Kelleys of the world, but instead the Jim Browns and Bob Cousys. Running may have brought satisfaction to some athletes, but rarely recognition. This paradigm shift allowed athletes from countries that couldn't afford cleats and shoulder pads to run right past Americans and through the tape. Some went on to hero status, while others headed right for the bank.

In the fascinating book *Born to Run: A Hidden Tribe, Superathletes, and the Greatest Race the World Has Never Seen,* author Christopher McDougall describes the attributes that comprise a passionate runner. "Virtues of strength, patience, cooperation, dedication and persistence," he writes. "Most of all, you had to love to run." This is the schism that separates other great running countries from America. Like soccer players in South America, to be great, to exceed what others think is possible, the sport has to run through your blood. If you are going to win Boston, or play for the Brazilian soccer team, the endeavor has to consume you.

It was apparent in the years following John "The Elder" Kelley's win in 1945 that there had been a shift in power in the sport. Race administrator Jock Semple was one of the people who recognized the widening abyss, saying in 1956, "[Foreign runners are] better than our guys for some simple reasons. From the country that they come from, people still use their feet and legs. They don't hop into a car to buy a loaf of bread or go to church. Walking isn't strange to them, and running is only exaggerated walking."

The shift in the long-distance running world was abhorrent to running great and World War I veteran Clarence DeMar. When DeMar won his first Boston in 1911, it roused such a spirit of patriotism that the *Boston Globe* wrote the following day: "Let the American eagle scream! Unloose the fetters that imprison the sacred codfish and let that denizen of the sea flap his tail in glee!"

DeMar saw the shift in running dominance not as a function of talent but instead as a shift in *priority*. DeMar claimed that he ran because he loved to run, and because it gave him the opportunity to prove he was better than someone else; he earned pride and self-worth at the finish line. What he saw later was runners seeking only the tangible. Athletes in other sports were driving fancy cars and wearing nice clothes. Runners wanted the same. This provoked DeMar to admonish the modern-day American runner. "All they care about here is money, money, money," he said.

John "The Elder" Kelley held out hope. He still believed in the American runner. "We are just as good as they are; if we dedicate ourselves to it, we can do it," he said. In the 1970s, Kelley would prove to be prophetic, as American marathoning made a comeback. The sport was resurrected despite spectators' obsessions with home runs, jump shots, and touchdowns. The pride of American long-distance running returned, led by Frank Shorter's gold medal at the 1972 Munich Olympics and dominance at Boston by Americans Bill Rodgers, Jack Fultz, Jon Anderson, Alberto Salazar, and Greg Meyer, who won eleven Boston Marathons between them from 1973 to 1983.

In *Born to Run*, Christopher McDougall details the resurgence of the American runner, and how the net benefit was a country rediscovering its love for the sport. "They were a tribe of isolated outcasts, running for love and relying on raw instinct and crude equipment," McDougall writes. "[T]he guys in the '70s didn't know enough to worry about pronation or supination. . . . [B]y the early '80s the Greater Boston Track Club had a half-dozen guys who could run a 2:12 marathon. That's six guys in one amateur club, in one city."

Bill Rodgers graced the cover of *Sports Illustrated*—twice. Average Americans were jogging in local parks and on neighborhood streets. Fitness was "in." But then, as quickly as it came back, it disappeared again.

Clarence DeMar was right when he mourned the "demise" of running back in 1953. He knew that American marathoners were doomed; they were running for a purpose other than the love of the sport. Long-distance running was once again dying.

The plague that had infected the sport in the late 1940s had by now metastasized. John "The Elder" Kelley had run for a laurel wreath and a pat on the back. Americans in the 1980s ran as part of the capitalist system, as Christopher McDougall, who traveled to the far reaches of Mexico in order to find pure running for his book, *Born to Run*, writes: "This isn't about why other people got faster; it's about why we got slower . . . American distance running went into a death spiral precisely when cash entered the equation."

No longer were runners doing it because they wanted to be faster than the guy next to them. They were running because they had sat down with their agents and carefully picked races that would allow them to maximize their exposure, protect their legs, and, ultimately, earn the most money possible. This focus and strategy was not built around winning, but instead, by netting endorsements, being audacious in the press's eyes, being articulate or glib, or by looking good on the cover of *Runner's World*. Professional American runners were running with an eye on their hamstrings, as though they were pork bellies being traded on the commodities exchange.

The world, meanwhile, was becoming more connected, borders more accessible, and athletes from smaller countries saw an opportunity. The door was open for athletes from countries with fewer resources but who had more drive and purpose. When five-time Japanese wheelchair champion Wakako Tsuchida was once asked whether she thought of pulling off to the side of the road when the physical toll of rolling got to be too much, she firmly retorted, "I [didn't] care if I cut my fingers or anything, I knew I wanted to finish." This is the hell-bent approach that is required to run Boston. Anything less is disrespectful to the thousands of other runners who work all year to get there, and to DeMar and the Kelleys and others who helped to make the race the worldwide event that it is today.

This pride came from the desire to run as a performative act, of declaration and defiance and, in the process, represent something greater than just oneself. When United Kingdom runner Ron Hill saw Canadian runner Jerome Drayton sitting on a curb during the 1970 Boston Marathon, he took it as an insult to the Queen's sovereignty, compelling him to shout,

"Get up and walk if you have to. But finish the damn race!" (Drayton would later famously say: "To describe the agony of a marathon to someone who's never run it is like trying to explain color to someone who was born blind.")

Most people who run the Boston Marathon have achieved the most basic levels of Maslow's tiers, and thus run to fulfill a dream or to realize their potential. Those who have run to obtain the most basic of human needs for themselves and/or their family run with an urgency that propels them forward. Over the history of the race, there have been some heart-wrenching examples of runners who ran the Boston Marathon in desperation, motivated by the more basic levels of Maslow's pyramid.

In 1914 a *Boston Globe* writer compared the desire of the marathon runner to the great Athenian runners who ran to save their country, those who run from a "confidence born of desperation."

Globe writer Jerry Nason would also call Stylianos Kyriakides "a modern Pheidippides" after his inspiring run for family and country. At the post-race press conference, the champion didn't speak of his accomplishments but instead pleaded for America to help feed his country. While speaking he broke into tears and said, "Once I think of my wife and two kids. You don't believe it, but many times they have only peas—just a few peas to eat!" Every runner and reporter in the room was moved by the runner and his country's plight. Overcome by emotion, second place finisher John "The Elder" Kelley approached Kyriakides with tears in his own eyes, put his arm around the runner, and said, "It was great that you won. It was great for your country."

This is the essence of marathoning. The piston that drives the champion marathoner forward isn't the legs but the heart. To an extent, American runners have gotten away from the soul of running. How-to tips in running magazines, innovative workout routines, and smoothies can't make a champion. Any talent the runner has must be enhanced by a primal need to get to the unbroken tape.

When sports agent Mark Wetmore talked about the key to African runners' dominance of long-distance events, he spoke not of technical advantage but instead, of the sport in its rawest form. "It's a much simpler sport for Kenyans and Ethiopians," he said. "They don't know their VO2 max [which determines aerobic capacity], they don't do treadmill tests. The sport itself is just simpler. It's just running. If you train harder, you run faster. It's not more complicated than that."

In 1963 the Boston Marathon community was treated to a glimpse of the greatness that lay ahead for African runners when Ethiopian heroes Abebe Bikila and Mamo Wolde came to Boston and almost grabbed the laurel wreath before falling off their record pace at Mile 20. Since 1988, African men have won twenty-eight of thirty-two Boston Marathons, with Kenyans Robert Kipkoech Cheruiyot winning four times, and Cosmas Ndeti and Ibrahim Hussein each claiming three championships. Since 1997, African women have won twenty-one of twenty-four Bostons, including Kenyan Catherine Ndereba's four championships and Ethiopian Fatuma Roba's three titles.

The level of dominance was so overwhelming that *Globe* writer Bob Ryan in 2002 was prompted to ask, in a piece jokingly datelined "Nairobi-on-the-Charles," "When will this Kenyan tyranny end? Whatever happened to the Finns, the Japanese, the Mexicans, and the Ethiopians? And don't even ask about the Americans." Ryan continued, "By our sadly reduced standards,

Foreign Countries Represented on the Podium of Champions

Men

Kenya	22
Canada	16
Japan	9
Finland	7
Ethiopia	6
South Korea	3
Great Britain	3
Belgium	2
Greece	2
Germany	1
Sweden	1
Guatemala	1
Colombia	1
Yugoslavia	1
New Zealand	1
Australia	1
Italy	1
Ireland	1

Women

Kenya	13
Ethiopia	8
Germany	5
Russia	4
Portugal	3
Norway	2
New Zealand	2
Canada	1
Poland	1

we actually had a good day. But the Bill Rodgers heyday seems as if it took place sometime back near the Civil War. It's hard to get excited when the first American—Keith Dowling—finishes 15th."

The quest for running dominance has shifted throughout the history of the race—not from town to town or running club to running club, but from continent to continent. From the first marathon in 1897 to the end of World War II in 1945, only one Boston Marathon was won by a runner from outside North America (1932—Paul de Bruyn of Germany). From 1946 to 1974, Europe and Asia accounted for twenty-two of the twenty-eight championships. The United States enjoyed a resurgence from 1973 to 1983, coinciding with Bill Rodgers's *Sports Illustrated* covers and a revival of running in America. From 1988 to the present day, Africa (exclusively Kenya and Ethiopia, two of the world's poorest countries, with life expectancies under sixty) has dominated the race.

We can't know where the winners of the coming decades will hail from, but they'll likely contain the proper mix of talent, drive, desperation, and purpose. Hopefully the wins by American man Meb Keflezighi in 2014 and woman Desiree Linden in 2017 will begin to reverse the trend and bring American runners back to the forefront of the sport.

———

Wherever I fell on Maslow's hierarchy, my motivation in 1996 was awash with sincerity. At that moment on the course, finishing Boston was the most important thing in my life. I had sacrificed much to get to the starting line. I was starting to become conscious of the true challenge in front of me. The first five miles had been nothing more than adrenaline. Emotion had carried me to this point. Now the primary force in my run would start the fragile transition from emotion to mind.

Life is short. Profound moments like this are sadly far too infrequent. It was time to live in the present, to soak it all in. To cherish what was cherishable. I ran that bend in the road like a swimmer hitting the wall for a flip turn, actually gaining momentum, strength, and confidence.

Following the 1917 Marathon, *Boston Journal* writer Bob Dunbar wondered if it was the crowd that motivated runners to run twenty-six miles. "The applause of the hundreds of thousands who line the course is as exhilarant as a stimulating drug."

I was now saying to myself, "All right—I can do this." As I pushed toward the next mile, there was a band on the rooftop of a nearby business playing Buster Poindexter's "Hot, Hot, Hot." Suddenly I was reminded that I wasn't the lone runner on the course as hundreds of runners at my pace and thousands of fans lining the street started to join in song. "Ole, ole—ole, ole!"

Usually reserved, I was having a visceral response to this sing-along. I realized now that I was part of a special community—not just as a New Englander, but as a participant in the Boston Marathon. For years, I had stood on the sidewalks and envied those who dared to run this race.

Now I was one of them.

Able

Before a baseball game in my junior year at Bentley College, I loosened up and came into the dugout only to discover that I'd been left out of the lineup. An inferior teammate had been chosen to play instead of me. After the game, I confronted my coach in the parking lot. For fifteen minutes we stood nose to nose, passionately stating our respective positions. Eventually, I told him that I didn't think it was fair I hadn't gotten to play. Coach looked me in the eye and flashed a wry smile that indicated he was about to impart a life lesson that would end this conversation: "Life isn't fucking fair," he said. "And the sooner you figure that out, the better off you will be."

I hate to say it, but he was right. If I'd stood around waiting for life to balance out after being wronged, then I would have been waiting a long time while life passed me by.

In his book *When Bad Things Happen to Good People*, Rabbi Harold Kushner speaks of the need to understand that pain is an inevitable part of life. To carry on, you must reconcile yourself to suffering and find purpose in your life going forward:

> *Is there an answer to the question of why bad things happen to good people? . . . The response would be . . . to forgive the world for not being perfect, to forgive God for not making a better world, to reach out to the people around us, and to go on living despite it all . . . no longer asking why something happened, but asking how we will respond, what we intend to do now that it has happened.*

In the earliest steps of the seventh mile, the course delivers runners to the ten-kilometer mark on the course. Many runners take this opportunity to review times on their watches or on course clocks to assess their pace. At this juncture, the route runs straight ahead and flat, allowing the runners to pound the pavement and continue the process of self-examination. If the runner has any ailment or malady at this point in the race, then he or she is subject to the third town's axiom: "If you're hurting in Framingham, you're dead."

When I ran through this passage, my time was just over fifty-three minutes (adjusting for the slow start). For me, this was more than acceptable. The last time I had run ten kilometers in a race was in the autumn edition of the Falmouth Road Race, five months before. In that race, I went out too fast and then struggled through the first three miles. As I waited for a second wind, I couldn't help but be disheartened by the number of runners passing me. Even so, I had run farther than I had ever run in my life.

This is one of the amazing parts of running Boston. It's a process that builds upon itself, with goals and accomplishments within your quest to get to the starting line. It's these accomplishments that feed your soul and build confidence for the April day. When you are constantly reaching heights that you've never reached before, you start believing—maybe this thing could actually happen.

Running the Falmouth 10K was concerning for my family. When I started to train for Boston, my wife and parents had assumed that it was nothing more than a whimsical lark in which I would see the silliness in partaking in something so foreign to me. But soon, one mile became a 5K, which evolved into a 10K, and suddenly they realized that my premature venture into the world of midlife crisis was more than idle talk.

After the Cape Cod race, they knew I intended to challenge my thirty-two-year-old body in April. This included my thirty-two-year-old heart, which wasn't just any heart. In my teens, I was diagnosed with a congenital heart disease called Wolff-Parkinson-White syndrome. This meant that I was afflicted by a cardiac arrhythmia that brought with it an extra passageway between my heart's upper and lower chambers, sometimes causing my heartbeat to go rogue and race more than two hundred beats a minute.

During a college baseball game, I suffered what was thought to be a related episode, falling unconscious. I was raced to the hospital. My coach came to the emergency room after the game, and once he'd been assured that I was okay, said, "Thank God you didn't die. I don't know where we would get the black armbands for tomorrow's games."

Over the next decade or so, I suffered a number of episodes, most of which turned out to be your basic rapid-heartbeat spells. I coped by slowing my breathing and relaxing my body, and eventually my pulse would revert to normal.

The years went by. I got older, hair receded, and I gained a wife and child. In the medical field they were busy developing a procedure called radiofrequency catheter ablation, which promised to rid me of my disease permanently. In the procedure, a catheter is guided into the heart and used to destroy the tissue that is interfering with the heart's normal electrical function.

Prior to this innovation, I'd spent the last fourteen years reporting to my cardiologist for a quarterly EKG exam: I took off my shirt, they connected me to some wires to confirm that my rhythm hadn't changed, and I went on my way. It was an inconvenience, but in my mind, a better alternative to having a laser traveling around my body like some video game for a doctor who used to be good at Frogger.

Now realizing that I was determined to see this running thing through to the end, my parents and my wife, Noreen, conspired to give me an ultimatum: If I was going to continue this tomfoolery, I would have to concede to surgery.

So, in October of 1995, I was wheeled into an operating room where I underwent the oblation. One hour later, my wife joined me in the recovery room. As the sedatives wore off, she stroked my hair and we joked about the wasted worry, which seemed like it had all been for naught. That is, until my heart went blank and forgot to beat. The steady beep on my heart monitor alerted the medical staff that I had just flat-lined.

Quickly, they hustled Noreen out to the hallway, sat her down, and left her to her thoughts. Around her, hospital staff ran to my bed while she pondered life as a widow and a single mother. She wondered if this was really happening. Then, down the hall came my father. Anxious to hear the results of the surgery, he was horrified to see the look in Noreen's eyes. Together they sat in the hall, hoping for the best and fearing the worst.

On the table, I survived. I don't remember much. My life didn't pass before my eyes, and I didn't hover over my bed in some sort of out-of-body experience. There was no light calling me (I hope that's not a bad sign). I sat on the precipice of life, sliding toward death. I don't know quite what went on during that period, or how long it lasted. Nurses and doctors had run to my bedside, one doctor leaping up on the gurney and preparing a defibrillator to restart my heart while an intubation tube was pushed toward my trachea.

Eventually I regained consciousness and was safe. Heated paddles were extinguished, and the tube retracted. My wife and father were allowed to join me in the recovery room. Not knowing whether to laugh or cry or kiss me, they did all three.

From that moment on, I was ready to rejoin my training. A day later I was walking around my block. Two weeks later, I ran for the first time, and was back on my way to Hopkinton. Now I would run Boston to celebrate life and to prove to all—including myself—that my repaired heart was actually my greatest strength. There was no more ambivalence. Boston would be my opportunity to put all fears and concerns to rest. I would train, and succeed, proving to my parents, my wife, and mostly myself that I could do this.

—————

On some level, no matter what, every participant in the race is impaired. While some people have afflictions that are apparent, others run in other states of relative discomfort. Some are dealing with mental issues, depression, or addictions. Other run with sadness brought on by life's tribulations.

But no matter what conditions confine the runner, the race is so much more than a physical endeavor. It is a physical and emotional challenge in which the individual is compelled to draw from all the resources at his or her disposal to overcome.

When I ran over the train tracks in Framingham, I was just six months removed from surgery. I ran in celebration. I ran because I could. Because my heart told me to.

At the first of three train tracks, runners must be careful to set their footfall carefully so as not to trip or slip on the raised rails. For those running in wheelchairs, the tracks present an even greater challenge. If a wheelchair competitor was to hit the protruding obstacle the wrong way, he or she could suffer a flat tire and be sidelined for the rest of the race.

Men's five-time wheelchair champion Jim Knaub has two suggestions for those who pass over the train tracks: First, "Go to church the day before." And second, "Attack every foot of the course with abandon, including over the train tracks. It's either your day or it's not."

The Boston course presents unique challenges for wheelchair competitors. Besides the exhausting distance all runners face, there are significant impediments between the start and finish that wheelchair competitors must be conscious of; in addition to train tracks, they also face potholes, manhole covers, and uneven pavement. The course is always ready to show its teeth to the runners, warning them to *never* lose focus. In addition to the many obstacles on the course, wheelchair athletes face risk that is magnified due to the fact they can reach speeds of up to forty miles per hour. Technology has advanced, making their equipment spin at an even more aggressive pace, meaning that the chance of injuries and accidents is enhanced.

But like every athlete on the course, wheelchair competitors accept the inherent risk associated with an event that demands so much from its participants. Since 1970, when Vietnam veteran Eugene Roberts crossed the finish line in a hospital-issued wheelchair, the Boston Marathon community has welcomed (albeit, sometimes rather slowly) all who arrive at the starting line with a will to compete.

Five years after Roberts's historic run, wheelchair-bound Bob Hall asked race director Will Cloney if he would accept him as an official competitor in the race. Cloney promised that if he ran in less than three hours, he would earn a medal. Hall rolled over the finish line in 2:58. This would eventually prompt Cloney to "reluctantly" open the doors to runners in wheelchairs in a statement in which he included the vernacular of the 1970s: "Twelve crippled contestants will join the race. They will start 15 minutes early. I'm trying an experiment," he continued. "I figure this is a community event, [and] I'm softhearted. Covering a course in a wheelchair isn't running a marathon, but they're so ambitious. So dedicated."

Back in 1978, a fan was so taken by the effort and sincerity of the wheelchair competitors that the person wrote a letter to the editor of the *Boston Globe*: "I watched the wheelers running in the marathon today—their great determination quite took my breath away."

In the same paper, in 1930, a writer marveled at the challenges all competitors overcome during the race: "The old course could tell stories of shattered hopes, of triumphs lost when the goal seemed at hand, and of men who fought off seemingly insurmountable handicaps and managed to reach the finish line."

Back in 1916, the *Boston Journal* documented the appearance at the starting line of two physically challenged competitors at that year's race: "Deaf-mutes line up in marathon side by side—Albert Parker of Natick and Sam Pavitt of Malden." When Parker signed up to run the race, he was asked by officials if he could finish, to which he responded, "I will do it if I have sunshine heat over my face, cold water, lemon." He would further add, when asked why he wanted to run, "Because I shall win!"

In 1971 two visually impaired runners, Harry Cordello and Joseph Prado, ran the race—one with a cane and one with a runner serving as a guide. Cordello would say after finishing, "Thank goodness there's no hang-ups about blind people running in [a] marathon."

For over a century the Boston Marathon has provided those willing to overcome obstacles with the opportunity to demonstrate that it's on the roads between Hopkinton and Boston where runners can push beyond their perceived *dis*abilities or afflictions. To run Boston, one doesn't need legs or vision or hearing or white blood cells of a particular level. Instead, the only requirement needed to conquer the twenty-six miles of Boston is *the will to do so.*

In 2018, the essence of such will was personified when Mary Shertenlieb wrote her own heroic chapter in the race's history. Mary was a leukemia survivor who was running to honor her gift of life and to raise money for related causes. On the starting line, a freezing wind chill and icy rain had prompted her doctor to warn against pushing herself too far with such a weakened immune system. Running the first fifteen miles with the same strength and courage she'd shown while fighting her illness, her lips began to turn blue, and her body convulsed with involuntary shivers. Devastated, she walked off the course into a Dunkin' Donuts, soaked and exhausted. She broke down, her dream seemingly shattered.

But with the support of her husband, Rich, a local radio personality, later that night at 8:30 p.m., the couple who had already been through so much walked into that same Dunkin' Donuts, where she would continue her journey. Together they ran, walked, skipped, and slid across the remaining miles of the Boston Marathon. After months of treatment, prayers, hugs, and tears, the two celebrated life by crossing the finish line just after midnight, in a run that will rival that of any runner who has ever toed the line in Hopkinton.

When John Graham and Herbert Holton presented the prospect of a road race to test the spirit of willing athletes, little did they know they would be providing runners like Mary Shertenlieb, Bob Hall, Harry Cordello and Joseph Prado, and Albert Parker and Sam Pavitt a canvas on which to etch a story that would rival Homer and Shakespeare. Love, tears, courage, fulfillment, joy—all from a race.

Mary's story will live forever in Boston folklore, along with that of tandem runners, Rick and Dick Hoyt. In all the history of the race, no runners have captured the hearts of those who love the Boston Marathon more than this father-and-son team.

The story of Team Hoyt is one of the most inspiring in the history of the Boston Marathon. Rick Hoyt, the son, was stricken with cerebral palsy as a child. An avid Boston Bruins fan and a Boston University graduate (class of 1993), Rick loved athletics, but his disabling disease and his confinement to a wheelchair restricted his participation. That is, until his father Dick, at the age of thirty-six, was prompted by his fifteen-year-old son Rick to push him in a road race back in 1977. Running with his dad opened up a whole new world for the younger Hoyt. As Rick said, "When I'm running, I feel like I've never been handicapped."

Dick started out running around the block while pushing Rick in an old wheelchair; eventually they graduated to road races, marathons, triathlons, and Iron Man competitions. (During the swimming segment of triathlons, Dick incredibly pulls his son in a small rowboat with a rope held in his mouth.) Going through these endeavors as a team, Dick and Rick formed an extremely tight bond. They now share their pain and triumphs together as a team. As Dick pushed his son through the streets of Hopkinton and all the way into Boston, another bond formed—between Team Hoyt and Boston Marathon fans. After each race they ran together, Rick would always remind his father that he beat him by one second.

After crossing over the first set of tracks, the route takes you past the Framingham train station on the left. Since Civil War times, passenger and freight trains have stopped in Framingham to deliver both passengers and supplies. In 1885, H. H. Richardson built the Framingham station, which is now registered on the National Registry of Historic Places. The station was constructed for $62,718. Considered one of the great architects in American history, Richardson also built Trinity Church in Boston, next to the finish line.

The train station not only serves as an emotional landmark, but it was also designated as one of the race's checkpoints despite its unconventional location in the race. Checkpoint locations were originally selected to provide officials with easy access by train, or to be near watering holes for the attendants' and spectators' horses. Officials would take the train from Boston out to Framingham to oversee the race and place checkmarks next to the names and numbers of runners. After the last competitor passed, officials could jump back on the train and arrive in Boston fifty-five minutes later for the finish, and the first bowls of beef stew.

Runners came to despise the odd placement of checkpoints because it made it difficult for them to calculate split times and keep track of their pace, but the BAA and race traditionalists defended them for their historical significance. It wasn't until 1983 that runners won the battle of common sense over tradition, and the checkpoints were moved to mile marks and at kilometer intervals.

As for me, I skipped over another set of train tracks at the 6.5-mile mark and pushed forward the rest of the mile. The rails now run parallel to the course on the left side. In the old days, train companies used to advertise for fans to follow the race by buying a train ticket in Framingham and riding the trolley or Boston & Albany train along the route, east, toward Boston, while watching the race.

Beyond the train tracks sit the old carcasses of factories that used to employ thousands in the old days. They made boxes and hats in these factories, until they didn't.

The course remains flat and straight, a welcome respite for wheelchair competitors, who can breathe a sigh of relief that they've survived the train tracks. They can enjoy some flat rolling for a while, knowing that down the road, the course will once again challenge them, just as it will anyone with an affliction, seen or unseen.

—◦—

I am conscious of a soul-sense that lifts me above the narrow, cramping circumstances of my life. My physical limitations are forgotten—my world lies upward, the length and the breadth and the sweep of the heavens are mine!

—HELEN KELLER

MILE 8

Talent Is Overrated

When I was in my teens, my mother called me a "dreamer." She wasn't being malicious. It was a sincere reaction to one of my many ideas or theories. I didn't really think much of it until I was enrolled in a banking program at Wharton Business School many years later.

Prior to the first day, each student was required to complete a test called the Herrmann Brain Dominance Instrument. It's a question-and-answer assessment that asks seemingly obscure questions, but when taken in its totality, will be able to ascertain how your brain processes life.

On the first day of the three-year program, I walked into the auditorium (late as usual). There were no seats on the edges, so I had to bump and excuse my way, with luggage on my shoulder, into the middle of the row. As soon as I sat down, a Wharton professor came onto the stage and asked for two students to get up and leave the auditorium. One was a woman from Kentucky, and the other was me.

Mortified, and not knowing what I had done, I now had to slide past everyone in my row and make my way out into the hallway. While out there, an official from the program explained that the professor was setting a scene with the three hundred other students and that someone would be coming to get us and bring us up on the stage in a short while to answer a question.

Minutes later the doors opened, and the Kentucky woman and I were escorted down the aisle and up to center stage, where we were asked to stand on either side of the professor. He then repeated the scenario that he had already shared with the rest of the audience.

Your Little League team just won the state tournament and you have been invited to the national championship. The problem is that you can only bring twelve of your fifteen players.

He then looked at the two of us and asked us to provide a solution. Being chivalrous, I deferred to the woman from Kentucky. Microphone in hand, she went off on a stream of consciousness about how she would retain an attorney and have them contact the national tournament. Then they would spearhead legislation to change the rule, which she would finance through fund-raising activities, including a cake sale.

After some polite applause, the professor turned to me and asked me what I would do. I leaned over into the microphone and said, "That's easy— we would cut the Kentucky kids from our team." The crowd laughed, and we were allowed to return to our seats.

Later that night, I was at a social event to meet fellow students. As I shook hands with people, one of my peers, who had already overindulged, came up to me and said, "Dude, that was fucking crazy! Before you got up on the stage, the professor told us exactly what you two were going to say." Pausing for another sip of his drink, he continued. "He said you would say something fresh and out there, beyond what anyone in this audience could imagine in their own mind. You had no control over your thoughts—the whole thing was predetermined."

Later that week, I was told that my Herrmann Brain Dominance Instrument had shown that I was different from the rest of the three hundred students in the class. The answers to my test indicated that my way of thinking placed me in the top right quadrant of the model. This meant that I was "curious, [broke] rules, impulsive, and prone to speculate." It wasn't that I was unique or necessarily smarter than others. It was just that a creative mind was unique to the usual norm in the industry of banking.

I knew my brain worked differently; I had ideas and visions. When people talked or I sat in meetings, I heard the words and immediately starting processing how to improve on the subject matter, leading to unsolicited suggestions. My brain heard a scenario and started to percolate immediately, trying to consider alternatives. This is who I was—a "know-it-all." I knew best.

But this type of brain function also meant I had limitations that would often leave me stymied. I stunk when it came to foreign languages (thanks, Mr. Hurley, for letting me "sneak" through Latin class). I wasn't someone who could read directions and then process the information efficiently, in order to, say, put together a gas grill. But I could see the instruction booklet and think of a better way to deliver that information. I couldn't read music and put fingers to keys, but I could see music and suggest to the instructor a different way to teach the application of sound and its language.

My mother had been right when she called me a dreamer. It was all about the blueprint with me, and never about the building. I think what my mom was trying to say was, "Michael, great idea—now do something about it." It was her polite way of saying "Never mind the bullshit." My mother wanted me to be a person of action, to go out there and let it fly. To not be afraid to fail. To see things through.

I was a dreamer. I know that now. My mother is the smartest woman I know. She got her master's degree while raising six children. It behooved me to listen to a person who knew so much—someone who knew me better than anyone.

When Richie, Rad, and I put our hands in together months before on the basketball court, that was my speculative side. That was the dreamer side of me. But out on the course, it was different. I wasn't just chirping about running Boston—I actually got out there and ran the miles. I put on layers and ran in the cold. I set my alarm clock and got up before work to bang out a run. I took a cortisone needle in my knee. Yeah, I was dreaming of running Boston, but I was also acting on it, and not on a superficial level, but with depth and sincerity. My parents had instilled in me a strong work ethic. I had grit. I was mentally tough. Now it was my mission to fuse my creative side with my capacity to work hard. I was channeling the spirit of Amelia Earhart, who once said, "The most difficult thing is the decision to act. The rest is merely tenacity."

When I committed to running Boston six months before the race, I could only run a mile. But I knew in my heart that I could find it within me to make up the twenty-five-mile gap by working harder than anyone has ever worked—by committing my total being to the dream.

In Malcolm Gladwell's book *Outliers*, he introduces the concept of the 10,000-hour rule to the reader. It means that to be great at anything, you need to commit 10,000 hours to the task. Included in that commitment of time was an understanding that many of those hours had to be because you wanted to do the work. That you didn't need a coach, or teacher, or parent standing over your shoulder, pushing you. If you needed outside forces to motivate you, then you weren't personally invested enough to be great at it.

I didn't have 10,000 hours to give to my training, but I did have an earnest heart, willing to do whatever it took to find a way to run twenty-five miles farther than I could on the day I first expressed my desire to run the race.

In the book *Talent Is Overrated*, the authors surmise that no one is born with a gift. They believe that any success is acquired by applying three principles: You love to do what you're doing; you are willing to personally commit to the time necessary to improve and evolve; and you practice with laser-focused purpose.

The concept that hard work beats talent was exemplified by undersized All Pro wide receiver Wes Welker. For Welker—who lived by the principle "Dominate every day"—getting great was nothing more than a math problem. He knew if he outworked peers who were considered better than he was by a certain factor, then he would eventually catch and pass those who were bigger, and thus perceived to have more of an "upside." Welker's only lament was that there wasn't more time in the day to outwork others and catch up faster.

I knew that I could run in the same race with some of the best athletes in the world by working hard and by sheer will and determination.

—◦—

The terrain in Mile 8 serves as a precursor to the hills that lie ahead in Newton. There are four separate humps within the mile as the runner rides up and down this undulating stretch. At the 7.3-mile mark, the runners enter into Natick, which sits at the base of a sneaky little knoll known as "Heartburn Hill." American champion Greg Meyer, who won the race in 1983, notes that this rise makes "an impression on the runners." He further observed that this point of the course provides the runner with an opportunity to conduct a self-assessment. Meyer said that for some runners, this inventory of their physical state will be reassuring, while for others, it will be disconcerting. "You'll have a good idea at this point if it is your day or not," he said.

For the first time, the course requires you to dig in and start to get after it. For miles you have been granted a magic carpet ride of downhills, but now it's time to draw upon the moxie that you will need to run the race on this day.

In a 1911 *Boston Journal* article, a reporter profiled the type of runner that should be allowed to run Boston: "Only men rich in grit and muscle are fit for it." Back in 1899, the same paper said about the race, "It is a mere test of endurance or brute strength." By running the Boston Marathon, runners find out if they have the grit, muscle, and makeup to discover who they are.

While running through Mile 8, I realized I'd now run farther than I had ever run in a race before. Champion runners Johnny Miles (1926) and Fred

Cameron (1910) won Boston despite never running more than ten miles in a race. Now that I was on the course, I would feed off their examples, knowing that just because you hadn't done something before doesn't mean you can't do it now.

At this point of the race, there was no need for the creative part of my brain. From here on in, it was going to be nothing but hard work that would get me to the finish line.

Over the history of the race, hard work has been a hallmark of marathon runners, from the leaders to the back of the pack. One runner who had the hunger to get to Boston was James Henigan of Malden. Throughout the 1920s, Henigan had run with the leaders only to have leg cramps sabotage his dream. But in 1931, nothing would stop him. When he was running the second half, his cramps came back. He immediately made his way to the side of the road and grabbed a stick, using it to lash his legs in an effort to work out the cramps before running on to victory.

Seven-time wheelchair champion Jean Driscoll would beat other runners in the weight room, as she was able to bench-press double her body weight. It was this hard work and strength that would allow her to push past competitors on the uphills. While they were trying to survive, she was thriving.

When Miki Gorman ran the Women's championship in 1977, she actually preferred to be challenged. "I love running. If it's easy, it's not fun."

People run Boston because it will change their lives. Runners discover things about themselves that they didn't know existed. But exploration is never easy. When President John F. Kennedy spoke about his motivation for the United States to go to the moon, he recognized that there is value in doing the difficult. There are rewards for challenging who we are. "We choose to go to the moon in this decade and do the other things, not because they are easy, but because they are hard."

～◦～

Natick, the fourth town on the route, hosts 16 percent of the course and covers just over sixteen square miles in area. Its population, just over 33,000, is almost doubled on race day; the marathon essentially consumes the town.

Natick is known as the "Place of Hills." John Eliot was granted two thousand acres here to resettle a group of Native Americans known as "200 Praying Indians." The town was situated on multiple water sources, including the Charles River and Lake Cochituate. The displaced Indians thrived until colonists realized the value of the location and took over the land by right of force.

At the end of Mile 8, the skyline of Boston is still just a dream to the runners, an oasis in the desert—a rumor. But every step brings them closer to the City upon the Hill.

I ran through the eighth mile with Boston on my mind, worrying about each step in front of me. Up and down the hills of Natick, I ran where Indians had once prayed, hunted, and lived.

Members of the Korean contingent (left to right), manager Sohn Kee Chung, Song Kil Yoon, Hann Kil Yong, and Choi Yan Chil, arrive at Logan Airport for the 1950 Boston Marathon. PHOTO COURTESY OF *BOSTON HERALD*

(Left to right) Michael "Rad" Radley, Rich Twombly, Jack Radley, and Michael Connelly are ready and raring to go as they pose on the morning of the race. PHOTO COURTESY OF BARBARA MULLIGAN

Running at a world-record pace in 1985 in his Prime Computer shirt, Geoff Smith screams in pain as his hamstring (and his record) both cramp. PHOTO COURTESY OF VICTAH SAILER/MCMANUS

Wheelchair competitors carefully navigate the treacherous Three Mile Island in Ashland during the 100th running of the Boston Marathon. PHOTO COURTESY OF FANFOTO

Jock Semple feels the wrath of Kathy Switzer's running companion, Tom Miller, in the 1967 Boston Marathon as Semple attempts to rip Kathy's number from her jersey. Women were not allowed to "officially" run the Boston Marathon until 1972.

Gérard Côté (left) and Tarzan Brown battle for the lead as they pass the Framingham train station in 1939.

In an effort to be recognized by the BAA in 1977, Bob Hall races toward the finish line while being urged on by his sister. PHOTO COURTESY OF THE BOSTON ATHLETIC ASSOCIATION

Team Hoyt: The father-and-son team of Dick and Rick Hoyt inspire all who witness their quest to meet the challenge. PHOTO COURTESY OF *BOSTON HERALD*

Almost ten miles into the race, runners can be tempted by the refreshing sight of Fiske Pond. PHOTO COURTESY OF THE BOSTON ATHLETIC ASSOCIATION

Runners in the 1996 Marathon pass through Natick Center. PHOTO COURTESY OF STEVE ROSSI

Desiree Linden offers her help to Shalane Flanagan in 2018, in the pouring rain.
PHOTO COURTESY OF VICTAH SAILER

The incomparable Clarence DeMar runs toward one of his seven championships.
PHOTO COURTESY OF *BOSTON HERALD*

Geoff Smith travels past the crowd of Wellesley College well-wishers.

Wellesley College students adding their decibels to the famous "Scream Tunnel."

The lead group of runners works its way through Wellesley Center and toward the halfway point in 1994. PHOTO COURTESY OF VICTAH SAILER

Mile 9

Risk and Reward

As I ran into Mile 9, I could increasingly feel the effects of an injury I had suffered to my iliotibial band during a run back in early March. The IT band is a tissue that runs from the hip to the outside of the knee; the result of my injury was intense pain in the outer left knee. Recovery had been slow and never quite complete, although not for lack of effort. At the time of the injury, I was four months into my training and had already undergone heart surgery in order to line up in Hopkinton. I was not going to let some knee soreness ruin my dream of running Boston.

From early March until the gun went off, I dedicated myself to remedying the ailment. I attended physical therapy sessions where therapists Sandra and Jennifer pushed, massaged, shocked, and manipulated the leg back into shape—despite the fact that my quad muscles were, in their words, "as tight as piano strings." After each session, I downed ibuprofen, iced my knee with bags of frozen vegetables, and devoured books and articles that dealt with strategies for coping with pain. One of my readings offered a method called "imagery." This theory called for the injured to concentrate on the pain and imagine that the area of discomfort is a square of butter sitting in a heated pan; remaining completely focused on the pat of butter, you are supposed to envision the pain melting away, as the butter does in your imaginary pan. It all seemed pretty hokey to me, as did the article that recommended you run tall and strong, not allowing the mind to acquiesce to the pain.

Gradually, my combined efforts allowed the knee to heal—somewhat. After multiple therapy sessions, I was finally cleared to test out the knee on a treadmill at the local YMCA. After tentatively mounting the machine, I cautiously ran my ten-minute miles, relatively pain-free. On the treadmill next to me, my good friend Jack Linso was busy covering his miles at a 6:30 pace. When I finished my workout, I dismounted and said good-bye. He returned the good-bye as he continued his sprint. While I worked my way behind his treadmill, still gasping from my exertions, I accidentally kicked out the cord to Jackie's treadmill, causing his machine to screech to a halt. Fortunately, Jackie wasn't catapulted across the room like a cartoon character. Feeling two inches tall, I quietly slunk out of the gym.

One week later, I stepped out onto my front porch with three miles on my mind. I did all the pre-run stretching as instructed, and then loped down the street for two blocks before folding up my tent and limping home. The pain was still holed up in the knee, meaning I now had to take the next and most drastic step. I had endured heart surgery and then flat-lined on the recovery table. I had trained for almost six months now. I had no choice but to take the next leap: I placed a call to Dr. Diane English, orthopedic surgeon extraordinaire, and asked for a cortisone shot.

Much to my chagrin, she agreed and told me to come into the office. Sitting in the waiting room, the last two words I wanted to hear were "Michael Connelly." When my name was called, my face went pale and my palms turned sweaty. The thought of a needle puncturing my skin and injecting burning cortisone into my body was not what I had in mind back in October. I walked forward with clenched fists and grinding teeth. The doctor rubbed the spot with an alcohol swab, inserted the needle, and it was over. I didn't cry, but I didn't get a lollipop either. It wasn't as bad as anticipated, and the results were promising. With just weeks to go, I needed to be patient while the cortisone did its job.

Five days later, I stretched out on the infamous porch and held my breath, wondering what the coming steps would hold. Slowly I ran down my street and hardly exhaled. A hundred yards became a half-mile, and then two miles, and then one more. Every time my left foot landed, I wondered if it would be my last step toward Hopkinton. About two blocks from home, I felt the twinge I had been dreading—the same place, the same pain. I cringed and tried to convince myself to keep running. I summoned up the imagery exercises that I had mocked earlier. To stop now would have extinguished any hope. There was no way I could stop running. "Stand tall! Be strong! Melting butter! Melting butter!"

After attempting the mental exercises, I realized that the whole imaging thing was a bunch of nonsense, except that it had diverted my attention for the last block and my house was in sight. I just had to push through the pain. Fifty yards, forty, thirty, ten, five, one—I made it! I collapsed on my porch as if I had found a life raft floating in the middle of the Atlantic Ocean. I knew that I would live to run again.

I picked myself up and proceeded to increase my workouts to ten miles. In my mind, I felt healthy enough to stand in Hopkinton and give it a shot. My last runs before the race were relatively pain-free, allowing me to cloak my physical weakness with a false sense of bravado. But no matter how much I tried to fool myself, there was no denying that I would enter the race grossly underprepared. I had never run more than eighteen miles in my entire life; the race on Patriots' Day would exceed that distance by eight miles.

This is the risk I'd accepted. Now I was nine miles into the race, and my leg was beginning to talk to me. Starting back around Mile 6 the injury had flared up, resulting in very limited extension of the knee. My left leg had to stay straight, leaving my right leg with a lot of responsibility. The course was conspiring with my wavering confidence to open a space of doubt in my mind—an unhealthy incubator for rambling thoughts. I didn't need an abacus to figure out that I had almost seventeen miles left.

I tried to keep in mind that injuries, colds, and other restricting ailments were just part of the game. In the months before a marathon, all runners push their bodies close to the point of breaking (or beyond it) as they build up the endurance to run twenty-six miles. Inevitably, the immune system weakens and the chances of sickness and injury climb. Toeing the line in Hopkinton at less than 100 percent is the norm. Many other runners were also doubting their fitness or engaging in denial. I had to focus on one thing: survival. Suck it up and grind it out. No one wanted to hear about why I couldn't run. I either had to do it, or not do it. Never mind the bullshit!

For the previous three miles, the runners had been treated to a pancake-flat course, allowing them to settle into a consistent pace with limited downshifting or upshifting. Mile 9, however, hits the runner like a sneaky uppercut. The mile starts on the crown of an incline only to dip before jumping up again. There are inclines at the beginning and again toward the end of the mile. Here the route passes by a combination of commercial enterprises on the left and wooded lots and a residential stretch on the right.

For the wheelchair competitors it's between Miles 6 and 11 where the game of cat and mouse is played out. Drafting and false surges are all part of competitors' strategies that are played out between Hopkinton and Boston.

In the ninth mile, the runners run by a park named in honor of Natick resident Henry Wilson. Wilson was the vice president under Ulysses S. Grant in the 1870s, just two decades before the first Boston Marathon. Wilson was a passionate advocate of the antislavery movement. Prior to serving the president, he was a senator representing Massachusetts. He authored several pieces of legislation to earn rights for black citizens, which Abraham Lincoln signed into law. Wilson's position on abolition infuriated the opposition and caused both a Southern senator and a congressman to challenge him to a duel. Wilson would die in office as the sitting vice president, lying in state in the US Capitol Rotunda before being carried back to Natick, where he was buried.

The moderate ups and downs of this mile are a test for your legs. Not too demanding, but a good opportunity for you to let the engine out a little bit and let your legs do the work. Of course, every mile matters, but this is one of the miles on the course where you can take in the scenery of the waterways, and rest your anxious mind that has been in overdrive since the gun went off over an hour ago.

It was just this type of running that I loved during my training. One of the wonderful aspects of running is that while it strengthens you physically, it also offers you the opportunity to experience catharsis. Until I'd started my journey toward Hopkinton six months prior to the race, I hadn't realized that training runs would almost always include movement in the spirit as well as the body. The simple act of separating myself from the distractions of my daily grind gave me the chance to release whatever needed to be released. With sneakers double-knotted and water in hand, I welcomed the chance that each run offered. Out on the road, I found a respite from the day as I ran in my solitary world.

Off the porch and down the street, it would take a mile to get the blood flowing to the muscles and the breathing settled. But once you arrive in that zone of being fully within yourself, you're provided with a unique opportunity to reflect in peace. Running becomes effortless; the machine-of-the-stride is almost self-propelling, allowing you to separate the physical from the mental. Your feet move as if you're suspended in a sleepwalk: no conscious steps, no thoughts, no intentional focus. It is out on the road that you come to realize more about yourself. It's within this feeling of lightness that your running switches to autopilot. Each step seems to correspond with a contemplation. Whether the subject is past, present, or future, I would always come to realize a little more about myself. Running can be liberating, cleansing, and thought-provoking. Questions that stymied me before a run—as an employee, a father, or a husband—always seemed clearer from the perspective I gained on the road. The very process of removing oneself from the stressors in life allows for regeneration. The runner wakes from slumber or stretches after a run, somewhere between refreshed and reborn.

Clarence DeMar used to run back and forth to work to prepare for his seven championships. During these runs he felt that he could get lost in the symphonic cadence of legs and arms working in perfect movement together. It made him feel like he could run forever. DeMar would say of this state, "[A] real marathoner delights in the exhibition of making his legs move in a kind of mechanical rhythm and seeing the miles drift by as though he was under the influence of mental anesthesia."

John "The Elder" Kelley would talk about the ease of running when you get in a groove: "If a guy hits the right stride, he could run all day like an auto." In the book *Born to Run*, runner Ann Trason speaks of the sensation of "breaking through" in her runs. Author Chris McDougall writes about the simple joy and Zen-like state Ann achieves in running: "Relax enough and your body becomes so familiar with the cradle-rocking rhythm that you almost forget you're moving." Trason even finds "that soft, half-levitating flow" a romantic thing.

Olympic swimmer and 2013 Boston Marathon competitor Summer Sanders spoke of the altered state that occurs out on her runs, in which her breathing calms and she undergoes a transformation in her mind: "I don't know if it's the endorphins or the power of reflection, but at some point in my run, I have this amazing creative release where there is great clarity on life or work, allowing me to run in a state of both happiness and excitement. It's at this moment that I could run forever."

This state of athletic bliss can make you feel like you're running to the simple beats of a 1970s soft rock song (one by Bread, or Seals and Croft), with each foot barely touching the ground before floating effortlessly up and then back down again.

Sadly, this state is not eternal; instead, it's a brief wonderful part of your overall run. Up ahead in the Marathon, mayhem awaits. You will have to draw upon those training runs that sucked. The runs that hurt—where you hated every step, and had to fight through. That's the type of dirty, roll-up-your-sleeves running you will have to do on this day to reach your goal.

Running Boston requires an all-out commitment to preparation. Lawrence Sweeney of the *Boston Globe* wrote prior to the 1920 race, "To endure hardships of such a grueling grind, a competitor must be well knit, have a full development of chest power, and a muscular and nervous system that come only of maturity."

To be "well knit," one must not just log miles, but log miles relevant to—and reminiscent of—the Boston course. The undulating course is so topographically unique, it's almost impossible to simulate—not only the uphills of the race, but the critical downhills as well. It is this rolling topography that inevitably impacts the runners, causing them to spend the final hours of daylight on Patriots' Day lamenting their lack of planning and preparation, promising that it will be different next year. Next time, they will train on a route that incorporates downhills; or they will spend less time on a track and more time on uphills, or at the very least, they will push the incline button on the treadmill; or they will commit to running corners on tangents. This is what makes Boston unique: Its subtle nuances just can't be duplicated.

Running Boston isn't a run in your local park with the dog. Boston is serious business, with grave risk biting at you throughout the course. Like climbing Mount Everest, the danger comes with a wonderful reward, and sometimes tragic consequences. The risk of running twenty-six miles has been debated for decades.

In a 1912 newspaper article in the *Winnipeg Tribune*, titled "Marathon Races Are Barbaric," a reporter notes, "The lesson seems to be that the distance is too great to [be] run by a human being at high pressure." Two years earlier, the same paper had printed a similar article with the headline "Race Over Marathon Route Nothing Short of Mankiller."

As far back as the 1898 Boston Marathon, doctors have been concerned with the impact that such a challenge could potentially have on runners. Following the second year's race, reporters noted that "runners were examined for the effects of the hard run upon their hearts, lungs and blood. In addition to a sport the race served in the cause of medical science." Every year until the race got too big, doctors would examine every runner's heart, weight, and feet prior to the race to ensure they were worthy of the challenge.

Medical exams before and after the race couldn't account for the long-term impact long-distance running can have on athletes' bodies. Incredibly, four of the first ten winners of the Boston Marathon were dead within just years of their victory. John McDermott, the winner of the inaugural race, ran that day with lung disease and never recovered. This threat inherent in marathoning prompted *Boston Globe* reporter Lawrence Sweeney to pen a piece that questioned the whole purpose of the event, titled "Why Run a Marathon?"

A study conducted by cardiologists Dr. James O'Keefe and Dr. Carl Lavie suggested that running both fast and far is not only counterproductive but categorically dangerous. "Running too fast, too far and for too many years may speed one's progress toward the finish line of life," they wrote. Their research showed that running more than twenty-five miles a week and/or over eight miles per hour actually neutralized the benefit of exercise.

In the 1920s a popular Boston runner named Bill Prouty used to run the Marathon every year, but instead of taking the train to the starting line, he would run from Boston to Hopkinton and *then back* in the same six hours. Prouty would die at age forty-two—while running. Though some runners live a healthy and full life, sadly, there are those whose physiology makes running a perilous, if not fatal, activity.

Runners by nature want to push, to challenge, to do more than just be average or sit on the sidelines. It was Clarence DeMar who was told by his doctor never to run another step; he ignored his doctor's warnings and went on to win six more Bostons. DeMar's story was so inspiring that a high school student, Wendell Powers of Medford, went for a run after the 1924 Boston Marathon, trying to emulate his hero, only to drop dead in front of his house. This is why only 1 percent of the world has ever run a marathon—it's difficult, dangerous, and, some would argue, simply not necessary.

In 2002, Cynthia Lucero was running Boston as a celebration. She had received her doctorate the week before, and her family was at the finish line to rejoice in her accomplishment. She had written her thesis on the healing powers of running a marathon.

Lucero was prepared to run, but had overhydrated for her first Boston Marathon. Running through Cleveland Circle, the volume of water that she had drunk started to have the reverse effect, practically drowning her brain cells. With her parents and the finish line just four miles away, Cynthia tragically dropped to the ground and died.

Cynthia was the third participant of the Boston Marathon to die as a result of running the race. In 1973, forty-four-year-old Harold Gale of Hartford, Connecticut, was running late in the race when he was overcome by a cardiac event from which he would later die at the hospital. Twenty-three years later, sixty-one-year-old Swedish runner Humphrey Siesage would also die of an apparent heart attack, after crossing the finish line.

In 1908, the *Boston Globe* warned runners that "water is almost fatal to a runner's chances, and only the inexperienced ask for it during the run." Two decades later, however, in 1927, it was reported that Clarence DeMar drank "gallons" of water before what would be his fifth Boston victory. Before I ran the race in 1996, I drank water nonstop for hours before the gun was fired.

In his book, *When Bad Things Happen to Good People*, Rabbi Harold Kushner writes about the randomness of life and how it is impacted by God's gift of free will that was bestowed not just upon his people, but also upon the Earth itself. In 1940, a twenty-six-year-old man from Gardner, Massachusetts, Oliver Wiljakainen had a heart attack in the twenty-third mile and was rushed to a city hospital. In 1990 Robert Muratori unknowingly suffered a heart attack in Framingham, yet still finished the race.

From the very first marathon, the journey has been associated with both tragedy and joy. When the Greek courier Pheidippides arrived in Athens, history's first long-distance runner dropped dead—right after he had delivered the message of Greece's victory over Persia. Inspired by his courageous run, people have followed in his footsteps ever since, risking all in an effort to realize a variety of things—honor, fulfillment, satisfaction, wealth, glory, and camaraderie.

So, enjoy this mile, but be ready, because there are storm clouds ahead. Toward the end of Mile 9, the runners make their way through the Speen Street intersection (named after John Speen, a Native American who first built on this land in the early 1700s) and bend left. At this point, runners move past Fiske Pond on their right and Lake Cochituate, at the end of the mile. Trees that protected runners from the right give way to the waterways that expose them to all weather conditions, including beating sun, crosswinds, and, in some years, driving rain or snow. The sight of water after running through primarily residential or commercial areas can be soothing. This is one of those miles that you might feel indifferent to on the macro level, but you have to remember that your focus has to be on the micro. Pay attention to each step, celebrating your footfalls as you get ever closer to Boston.

To be successful in my mission going forward, I realized that it would be necessary to adjust my competitive instincts. As I ran down the road, I intended to shift my focus to make sure I competed against the course and not the other athletes around me. It was imperative that I concentrate on making my challenge singular, while ignoring my surroundings. To accomplish this task, I drew on the advice my father once gave me: "Don't concern yourself with being the fastest. Your only goal in life should be to maximize your God-given talents, and never settle for anything less."

My father's sentiment was supported by an anecdote in the book *The Greatest Salesman in the World*: "I will climb today's mountain to the utmost of my ability, yet tomorrow I will climb higher than today, and the next will be higher than tomorrow. To surpass the deeds of others is unimportant; to surpass my own deeds is all."

If the runners can push through, the ten-mile mark is up ahead. Compared to the sparse gatherings that saluted them along Mile 9, they are in for a giant welcome.

Mile 10

Open Race

After leaving an open area at the end of the lake, where the runners are exposed to the random weather of April, the course works its way up a slight incline for two-tenths of a mile, toward the protection of West Central Street. Uta Pippig enjoys this part of the route. "For some reason, I look forward to this small hill," she said. "I don't know why. Maybe it's the way it twists back and forth. But I know it's up ahead, and I am excited to get there."

At the top of the hill, West Central Street (still Route 135) straightens and begins to move through the residential portion of the Henry Wilson Historic District. Here, magnificent trees line the road on both sides, providing the athletes with a natural protective tunnel as they parade toward Natick Center. Over the years, nature has ravaged the trees with ice storms and disease, but they endure, rising dramatically toward the sun, their tops meeting over the road like a marine honor guard crossing swords at a wedding.

In 1909, Lucy Child, a resident of Framingham, aptly described the site as "a row of stately trees which fling their arms across W. Central Street, forming a green roof in the summer and a brown arch in winter." In the late 1800s and early 1900s, this segment of West Central Street was used for buggy rides on spring and summer afternoons; in the winter, the street was scraped, rolled, and roped off so that the affluent could race their horse-drawn sleighs here each afternoon. The sleigh rides of the early 1900s were competitions that took place on the same streets as the Boston Marathon. The winter events depended upon the elements, including snow and freezing temperatures. The Marathon, however, never has the luxury of waiting for appropriate conditions. Often, the weather joins forces with the course itself to stretch the challenge of the 26.2 miles.

Mile 10 continues through the intersection with Taylor Street, just past the half-mile point. The Edward Wolcott estate, on the left side of the road, sheltered runaway slaves in the 1800s. With twenty-one rooms, the mansion was the most impressive property in the town, but its real stature is due to the tunnels that ran from the rear of the estate to the Boston & Albany train tracks, one hundred feet away. Fugitive slaves who jumped from passing trains and made their way underground to the estate would receive food and shelter here before continuing on to Canada.

Over the history of Boston and its race, both institutions have been a beacon of tolerance and inclusivity. Since the Boston Marathon began, the race has been considered "open" to all. And because of this openness, all races, tribes, and nationalities, all types of abled runners—and later, all genders—have been welcomed.

The Marathon itself is an integrated entity in a host city that has been perceived by some to be unwelcoming to others. Boston has a unique history with both tolerance and, for a brief period, intolerance. It's known as the "City upon a Hill" because one of the founding fathers, John Winthrop, believed in the city's soul and felt that it was worthy of the world's attention.

Even though Boston was known for its broad-mindedness, the city would be ripped apart in the 1970s when forced integration of public schools would forever tarnish its reputation. To this day, Boston is considered by many (who don't have all the facts) as a city where intolerance is practiced.

Throughout the mid-1800s, abolitionists, including William Lloyd Garrison, Wendell Phillips, Henry David Thoreau, and Lucy Stone, would convene in the Marathon town of Framingham to rally, strategize, and raise funds for their cause. During the nineteenth century the city was known as the hub of abolitionists. William Lloyd Garrison wrote the antislavery newspaper the *Liberator* for thirty-four years. The all-black troops from the Civil War, the 54th Massachusetts Infantry Regiment, were led by Bostonian Colonel Robert Gould Shaw, for whom the local school was named—the very school where Rad, Richie, and I played basketball and made our vow to run Boston together.

It was in Boston and its outskirts where Harriet Beecher Stowe wrote *Uncle Tom's Cabin.* It's where Frederick Douglass, Harriet Tubman, Martin Luther King Jr., Malcolm X, Louis Farrakhan, William Monroe Trotter, and President Barack Obama (a Harvard alum) all once resided.

In the 1970s, the busing conflict frayed the fabric of Boston. Everyone who lived in the city was impacted by those days of fear and distrust, including me. On bus rides to school, my school bus was pelted with rocks. Once, on the Orange Line subway, a wronged black man pointed a gun in my face because I was white. It was a sad time in our city. Happily, Boston has since found its way back to its roots as the world-class city it has been for most of its four-hundred-year existence.

Like its host city, the Boston Marathon has been open to all races from the very beginning. In newspaper accounts, the descriptive terms and euphemisms used were acceptable to the readers and consistent with the vernacular of the times.

In 1901, the *Herald* reported that one of the participants of the race, William Davis, was a "full-blooded Mohawk Indian" and "[the] most picturesque figure."

In 1907, Thomas Longboat of the Onondaga tribe was a celebrated runner. His arrival was the most anticipated in the race's eleven-year history. The hotel he stayed at in Ashland was surrounded by the curious. Prior to the race, in which he would set a world record, the *Boston Journal* wrote about Longboat: "A descendant of a real old American family, his name is not on the rolls of blue books nor upon social registers. He is, however, a Native American, and a representative of the men who owned and populated this country at the time that [the] first marathon was run in Greece, in the year 490 BC." After his win, it was written, "Longboat's victory makes him the greatest of marathon runners. The Redman never has been the equal of the Caucasian in physical strength or endurance, and Longboat, lean and lithe, is the rare exception of his race."

That year it was reported that the crowd was diverse, and representative of New Englanders. "From start to finish the running of the race was watched by crowds of every nationality and creed, [of] every nation in life, from the millionaire automobilists to the day laborer." The crowd that day in 1907 not only cheered the "Indian," but also the "colored runner," Delliam Whiting of Yonkers.

In 1919, "colored" runner Aaron Morris finished sixth, becoming the first African-American runner to finish in the prizes. Three years later, second-place finisher, Native American Al Smoke, was described as "bronze as they come."

In 1936, Tarzan Brown would become the second Native American to win the Boston Marathon, one year after finishing the race in bare feet. On his shirt, the runner from Rhode Island wore a patch depicting the founder of the state, Roger Williams, who was expelled from Massachusetts for preaching dogma that included, "Colonists have no right to Indian lands."

In 1947, Suh Yun-Bok from South Korea was the first Asian runner to win at Boston. Bok had avoided serving in the Japanese military during World War II. Four years later, Japanese runner Shigeki Tanaka, from Hiroshima, was the first from his country to win Boston. Even though America was just six years removed from losing sons in the war with the country he came from, the crowd was warm and welcoming to the winner. In the *Boston Traveler* the next day, a reporter posed the rhetorical questions, "Who would have dreamed an hour after Pearl Harbor that Americans would ever cheer another Japanese?" In the *Dallas Morning News*, the headline read "Jap Runner Cops Marathon."

Tanaka's win is what is special about the Boston Marathon: A simple road race brings people together and allows us to see each other as individuals. In a later edition of the *Boston Traveler*, a reporter pondered, "One would think that man, given only 12 miles of life above his head, would husband it and spread it jealously about the earth. Walls fall, cities rise; Tanaka proved that. But it may not be thus forced unless we can learn the art of living together."

Sometimes change and acceptance is slow—like a marathon. It takes time to understand how people, perceived as being different from us, are not all that different after all. When runners come to Boston, they carry with them the same goals, dreams, and sense of purpose. The roads from Hopkinton to Boston provide runners with a forum to see their true selves—to realize that the more we are different, the more we are the same.

I couldn't be prouder to be from Boston. It's one of the most beautiful cities in the world, with exceptional educational institutions and a collection of hospitals that attracts the best and the brightest. The neighborhoods on their own have sometimes separated one from the other, but when they are all connected, they form a magical mosaic that honors John Winthrop's prophecy, of why "the eyes of all people are upon us." And this is never truer than every third Monday in April.

———

At the Forest Street intersection on Mile 10, runners pass another house connected to a dark chapter in American history. Major Daniel Henry Lawrence Gleason lived at 71 West Central Street, on the left side of the road, after serving in Washington, DC, during the Civil War. Gleason is famous for his intimate connection with the assassination of Abraham Lincoln. When

Gleason was working in Washington, one of his associates attended secret meetings where a plot to kidnap President Lincoln was discussed; one of the individuals present at those meetings was John Wilkes Booth. When he learned of the plot, Gleason warned officials, but to no avail. The kidnapping plan turned into murder, and after the assassination, authorities turned to Gleason for help in hunting down the culprits. With his assistance they tracked down Booth, but the others escaped. Gleason died in Natick in 1917.

My spirits rose slightly at the sight of the Mile 10 demarcation visible in the distance, such a critical juncture in the race. Although this milestone was another benchmark on a long list, my excitement was tempered by the fact that the race wasn't even half finished yet. Nevertheless, it was an opportunity to take satisfaction in my efforts while still focusing on the challenges that loomed ahead.

Many recreational runners call it a day here at the ten-mile mark. In 1927, 23 percent of the competitors walked off the course rather than keeping on and fighting the sun. A good number of the early participants enjoy the pageantry of the start, got in some exercise, and then dropped out after ten miles for a beer and some chicken wings, rather than a PowerBar and sixteen more miles.

At house parties and celebrations taking place on the town common there are always signs and shouts of encouragement to take one's mind off the grind of the course. At the end of the mile, I saw a sign on a front lawn that read "Shortcut to Boston," with an arrow pointing toward kegs of beer—an enticing offer to surrender and enjoy the day with a red cup of cold beer.

Champion Rob de Castella used to say, "If you feel bad at Mile 10, you're in trouble. If you feel bad at Mile 20, you're normal. If you don't feel bad at Mile 26, you're abnormal."

Running through Mile 10, the runner is treated to a calm stretch of the course, bordered on both sides with aesthetically pleasing houses and seasoned trees that might provide some shade for the runners.

As I made my way toward the end of the mile, I could see two rising steeples in the coming town center of Natick. It's the type of sight that reminds you that you're not running alone.

Thank You for Your Service

The beginning of Mile 11 starts at the intersection of Route 135 and Route 27. In the old days there was a water trough at this intersection for horses to refresh themselves. For the runners, this juncture is literally a crossroad. After running ten miles, runners will ask themselves the question they have been asking all day—what I've been asking myself—"Can I get to Boston?" For those who waver, the Natick town common is a good place to call it a day.

As soon as the runners enter into Mile 11, they can see the steeple of the First Congregational Church rising above the treetops of West Central Street, leading the athletes into the town center. On the steeple's face sits a clock, and this is where the runners are exposed to truth. From a runner's very first race, it has been the tick of time that has played the role of judge and jury. Time doesn't lie. Fast or slow, paced or reckless, the clock gives testament to the runner's performance. This is why Bill Rodgers always looked forward to Natick. "There are two things that excite runners," Rodgers said. "They are people and clocks—you've got both here."

Two-tenths into the mile, the runners cross the Route 27 intersection and arrive at the Natick Common. It was here that the Great Fire of 1874 destroyed half of the town center in just six hours, including the post office, the Congregational Church, the fire station, and the brand-new shoe factory. For years, this point not only served as an ideal viewing location for fans of the race, but also as the second checkpoint (prior to their movement to more appropriate locations on the course).

Like Hopkinton, Natick Center has a village-like feel to it. It's the small-town America that you see in pickup truck commercials or in country music videos. There is a soldiers' monument on the lawn to honor the eighty-nine Natick soldiers who died in the Civil War. The common is a great meeting place for families. It's usually busy with a concert on the bandstand, mothers with babies, and teenagers staring at their cell phones and taking selfies.

At this point West Central Street becomes East Central Street (but remains Route 135). Both sides of the road offer welcome and much-needed fan support. Runners might not feel worthy, but by this point in the race they are starting to crave the shouts of encouragement to assure them they are "looking good," to urge them to "keep going." The presence of the spectators and their supportive tone is like an emotional water stop.

Early accounts of the race spoke to the supportive and enthusiastic crowds in Natick, including "Natick women and girls [shaking] American flags hysterically."

Moving through Natick Center, the race route continues flat and straight with a slight bump at the 10.4-mile mark. On the left side of the road, a new police station, fire station, and library represent the contributions of Natick's taxpayers. Halfway through the mile, the runners pass by the front stairs of St. Patrick's Church. It is here where babies are carried to their christenings, brides beam the smiles of newlyweds, and caskets are carried—better known as, "hatch, match, and dispatch."

Runners work toward the end of the mile where Nick's, the popular Natick ice-cream and hot-dog place, used to stand, on the right. Nick's was best known for its Saturday-night gatherings of classic 1950s automobiles, especially Corvettes. For years the Boston Marathon marked opening day for the ice-cream establishment. Outside, they would dress the place up for the big race with balloons and American flags. If you were in need of ice cream some Saturday night, you could drop by (preferably not in your minivan).

Past a tricky little intersection with Union Street on the right, runners veer left and continue through the final tenths of the mile. On the right, the runners pass the courthouse and, at the 10.7-mile mark, the Natick Battalion Armory. The Armory was built to honor the veterans of the Spanish-American War. It was during that war in 1898 that the BAA and those who supported the race had to decide whether it was appropriate to run the second annual Marathon with war imminent. This would be the first time in the race's history that the world around the Boston Marathon would impact the race—but it would be far from the last. The race *was* run that year, with officials realizing the power and importance of the Boston Marathon. Running Boston, even as war was on the horizon, demonstrated to people that although citizens respected those about to enter the fray, life must go on, and that the race could serve as a galvanizing force for the community.

Fortunately, the Spanish-American War was over in just three months, with the Americans scoring a decisive victory. Fifteen years later, the Boston

Marathon, like the rest of the world, would again suffer from world conflict on a much grander scale. In World War I—dubbed the "War to End all Wars"—American soldiers went to Europe, including 168 members of the Boston Athletic Association, who knew that war took priority over all. "We believe that the entire energy and resources of the organization should be concentrated on the task of winning the war," the BAA announced. Winner of the 1915 race, Edouard Fabre, regretted winning because he was then obligated to run a race in San Francisco instead of being able to enlist in the British Army.

As the war waged on, the death toll touched every corner of the world. In all, sixteen million people perished, including 1914 Boston Marathon champion James Duffy. The *Globe* wrote, "As Pheidippides gave his all for his country, so too have marathon heroes of later years laid down their lives for the honor of their countries, and will continue to offer and sacrifice their youth—their lives."

The BAA was so concerned about the overwhelming effect of the war on the community that there was a heated debate about whether to run the race in 1917, the year America entered the conflict. Opinions focused on both respect and security concerns, and the organization issued a statement to explain their reservations and contemplated canceling the race "because of the tenseness of the American situation at present [and] because of the trepidation with which the flower of American manhood looks out upon the future."

The race went on that year, and was won by Boston's adopted son, William Kennedy, who before the race implored American runners to "[e]ndeavor this year, above all others, to prove to the world that America is supreme in all branches of endeavor." The newspaper would write the next day about the runner who ran to victory with an American flag around his head. "He won a remarkable race," the paper reported, "and carried Old Glory to one of the most popular victories achieved in this or any other country."

The question of whether to run or not was again debated in the following year, 1918. This time, the BAA changed the tradition of making it an open race and instead dedicated the marathon to the American military by organizing a twenty-six-mile relay race for sixteen service teams. During the run, participants carried batons with a message inside that the runners read to the crowd at the finish line. "We will fight to the limit, and we expect you to buy [Liberty Bonds] to the limit."

The winner that day was the Camp Devens team, who ran in their "khaki suits and leggings with government-issued shoes," beating the Boston Naval Yard in their "spic and span white suits."

The Allies were victorious in Europe, and those who were fortunate to survive the trenches, including runners Chuck Mellor, Frank Zuna, Clarence DeMar, and William Kennedy, would come back to win Boston. As did runner Richard Conboy, who would endure to run future Bostons, but with a hole in his face from where a bullet had exited after going through his mouth.

After the war, the Natick Armory was named after hero Michael Perkins of South Boston. Private Perkins was awarded the Medal of Honor for acts of valor during the campaign in France, in which he attacked a German bunker single-handedly. With grenades, he gained entrance to a machine-gun nest where he overwhelmed twenty-five German soldiers with a knife, taking out their seven machine guns.

The men returned home to America, believing the world had been freed from tyranny. Sadly, the war to end all wars didn't end all wars. In 1941, America once again went to battle in Europe and Asia, and again the Boston Marathon community was committed to the cause. Larry Brignolia donated his Marathon championship statue of Mercury, which he had received for winning the 1899 race, for scrap metal. In 1942, the race was moved to Sunday by Governor Saltonstall, "to keep war work proceeding without moment of slow up." Jock Semple, Gérard Côté, Johnny "The Elder" Kelley, and countless Marathon personnel and runners fought for the Allies, while the Women's Defense Corps used Patriots' Day to put on demonstrations on bomb drills and air-raid preparation.

Despite the war, the race continued. Canadian army soldier Gérard Côté took a leave from his duties to fly across the world and win his third Boston Marathon. Prior to the 1943 race, the runners were led down the course by an armada of army vehicles (each of which had their cost publicized to justify the $13 billion loan the government had taken out for the war effort). Two years later, in 1945, John "The Elder" Kelley returned from the war and won his second Boston, the same year his brother was killed in Japan.

In 1947, Francis Austin from Quincy would run the race after recovering from wounds suffered when his B-29 plane was shot down. Over two decades after being wounded, war hero Jimmy Demtralis would run Boston in 1967 with shrapnel still in his body.

While serving in Europe, Bill Fitz of Milton dreamed of coming home and doing the most Boston thing possible—run the Marathon. It was a dream of his, and war had a way of compelling people to make promises. So, when Fitz returned home, the six-foot-three veteran enrolled at Harvard University, playing first base for the school's baseball team. Except on Marathon

Day, when he told his coach he had a promise to keep. The paratrooper ran the 1946 race and then returned to the Harvard campus to pinch-hit in a game on the same day.

In the 1950 race, three Korean runners finished 1-2-3. Two months after the race, the Korean War commenced. Prior to the 1951 race, Korean runners were told they were forbidden to run, and Ki Yong Ham was not allowed to defend his championship. On race day that year, the crowd was diminished, as many people were at home in front of their televisions, watching General Douglas MacArthur speak to the American people about the war in Asia.

Six years later, Billy Cons came to run Boston, considered a dark horse to win the race. Cons was the recipient of a Purple Heart and a Silver Medal for actions in combat during the Korean War. After his platoon was ambushed, his leg was riddled with machine-gun bullets. He crawled one and a half miles to safety, where he argued with surgeons to not amputate his leg. Five years later, in 1957, he was leading the Boston Marathon, only to fade later in the race. He still finished ninth.

In the 1960s America was once again at war in Asia. It was in Vietnam that Eugene Roberts stepped on a mine and lost his legs. In 1970, Roberts became the first wheelchair competitor to run Boston. Before running the Marathon, Robert had only completed one mile in his hospital-issued chair. During the 1970 race he wore a T-shirt that read "Jesus Saves." When he was confronted with the hills of Newton, he left the climb "in God's hands." As he made his way across the course, fans, who were taken by his efforts, joined him for the march into Boston. When he got to the finish line, he got out of his chair and pulled himself across the finish line, singing "Praise the Lord."

Pat Messore would come home from Vietnam and fulfill a dream, like Harvard baseball player Bill Fitz. He would run Boston after reading about the race while fighting in the jungles of Southeast Asia.

Tragically, Boston Marathon runner Andrew Bacevich was killed by a roadside bomb in Iraq, in 2007. Twelve years later, a veteran of the Afghanistan conflict, Micah Herndon, would run Boston to honor his three mates, killed in the vehicle he was riding in at the time when they came upon an improvised explosive device. As he ran down Boylston Street, their three names tattooed on his hand, his legs gave way and he fell to the pavement of the Boston roadway. Desperate to fulfill his promise to honor his fallen friends, he started to yell their names over and over again: "Ballard, Juarez, Hamer—Ballard, Juarez, Hamer!" Hearing their names inspired him to start crawling, elbow over elbow. Little by little, he chewed up inches of the last pieces of the course until he approached the finish line. When he crossed over, fulfilling his dream, the Boylston crowd went wild.

After he had been looked after by medical staff, he would say of his courageous run, "The pain I was going through was nothing compared to the pain they went through."

~ — ~

I am humbled by those who have sacrificed so much in defense of American freedom. I grew up in a home that respected flag and country. My father was a marine, an experience that positively impacted who he was. We boys all knew the Marines' Hymn—"From the Halls of Montezuma to the Shores of Tripoli." My uncle Al fought in World War II and came home to join the Boston Police force. My great-uncle Thomas Crosby would die from complications related to his service (in the South Pacific), as would my godfather's son, Lieutenant Colonel James Walton, who was killed in Afghanistan by a roadside bomb and is buried at Arlington Cemetery. Our next-door neighbor was a hero in Vietnam, while, sadly, the name of another neighbor, Paul Reid, is etched on the Vietnam Veterans Memorial Wall in recognition of his sacrifice for God and country.

Like the Marathon, war has always orbited around the Connelly family, which is true for all American families. When a family friend came home from Vietnam, my parents brought the six Connelly children to Logan Airport to greet him. We stood there at attention with little American flags in our hands. When he walked through the door, we waved our hearts out. We didn't know at the time that while he had returned physically, emotionally he would never come home.

My sisters wore POW bracelets with the names of American prisoners of war on them. At St. Theresa School, we prayed for Henry Kissinger to be blessed with wisdom and compromise at the Paris Peace Accords. And when peace was reached and the treaty was signed, we Connelly children stood on our front steps and listened to the church bells ring, signaling peace.

At the end of Mile 11, the course rises just a little bit. Not a problem, but still, anything that causes you to have to do a little more will only diminish the fuel you have left in your tank.

Practice Not Quitting

NBA executive Pat Williams is the father of eighteen children, fourteen of whom are adopted. He has worked for the Chicago Bulls, the Philadelphia 76ers, and Orlando Magic in some capacity since 1968. But despite his demanding schedule, he has made time to run several Boston Marathons. When asked what he got out of running the race, he answered, "It's practice at not quitting."

In the twelfth mile, I was starting to wrestle with doubt. I had been running for almost two hours, and I wasn't even halfway to Boston. Shakespeare wrote that "Our doubts are traitors, and make us lose the good we oft might win, by fearing to attempt." This trepidation was the source of an involuntary debate going on in my head: Could I be successful on this day? It was the type of tug-of-war that made me aware that running a marathon is not a mere physical endeavor, but also a mental debate. A debate in which doubt and your fragile confidence are combatants in a battle where doubt tries to force confidence to crawl up into the fetal position and quit.

While I was starting to doubt my ability in 1996, back in 1971 Colombian runner Alvaro Mejia ran in a similar state of apprehension. He would say after the race, "Five or ten occasions I thought seriously about quitting." He didn't quit, and went on to win the world's greatest race.

During this stretch of course, I decided to change my goals. Instead of running to Boston, I changed my mission to making it to the Scream Tunnel at Wellesley College, in the next mile. I went from big picture to short film. Down the road, I would refine my purpose even further to simply taking another step.

In his book *Man's Search for Meaning*, Viktor Frankl chronicled his captivity in German death camps. "Those who know how close the connection is between the state of mind of a man—his courage and hope, or lack of them—and the state of immunity of his body will understand that the sudden loss of hope and courage can have a deadly effect."

Following the 1995 race, a *Boston Globe* article discussed this phenomenon of the tiring runner and the corresponding effect it has upon his mental well-being. Within the piece, runner Joe McCusker spoke to the sense of dread that overwhelms hope. "It's like *The Old Man and the Sea*," he said, referring to the classic Hemingway novel. "He thinks he got a big marlin, but he doesn't have the marlin, because they keep taking bites out of it . . . that's what the Marathon does to you. Little bites all over."

It is during these moments that runners need to remind themselves why they toed the line thirteen-plus miles earlier. Everyone has a personal reason for going out to Hopkinton on the third Monday in April. Some run to win; some run to be part of the 1 percent; some run because the course "is there"; while others run for a cause, to honor a friend, or simply to pay homage to the world's greatest race.

At heart, the runners run because their souls tell them they must run. Therefore, the question intrepid runners must ask themselves is a simple one: What possessed me to travel to the starting line this morning? It's here, during these moments of doubt, that they must examine *why* they began to run in the first place. It's within the answer to this question that they will find the motivation to push forward.

The motivation to continue to run can be found within the original decision that compelled the runner to first start running. Because in that instance, when the desire first bubbled to the surface, the runner saw the world with his or her legs and not just his or her eyes.

"Why run?" is not just a question for the doubting amateur; the elite must ask it as well. The two greatest champions in the history of the race, Clarence DeMar and Bill Rodgers, nurtured their craft of running because of something more elemental: They had to get to work somehow. Rodgers grew up running, but returned to his gift when his motorcycle was stolen and he had no other way to get to his job. While DeMar and Rodgers ran to their places of work, Alberto Mejia of Colombia ran *after* losing his job as a metalworker. After getting laid off, he had nothing else to do, so he trained with laser focus in the weeks leading up to his 1971 Boston championship.

Others run because they are physically required to do so. Quite literally, they run to live—or to live the way they want to. Gayle Barron, winner of the 1979 race, had only been running for ten years when she captured the championship. The only reason she started to run was that she liked to eat and couldn't continue as a newscaster if she didn't find a way to neutralize the calories.

While Barron ran to maintain her physical status for her job, Elijah Lagat of Kenya had to lose weight to live. He had never been interested in running until at age twenty-five, his doctor told him he had to lose twenty-five pounds or die. He ran, and won the 2000 race.

Others use running as a desperate attempt to save their spiritual and emotional well-being. For some, running can be an outlet that separates them from the mental traps that restrict—and sometimes paralyze—their lives. Back in the 1970s, chain-smoking Patti Catalano decided to turn her life around while sitting in a drinking establishment where she had turned to escape the shackles of a harmful family life. It was in running that she felt free—that she found purpose and direction. Catalano would go on to become one of the greatest female runners in American history. She won the Honolulu Marathon three times, finished second in Boston three times, and set American records in almost every running discipline—including the marathon.

The commitment to reverse the course of one's life is a process that requires muscles besides those found in one's legs. In 1989, New Zealand runner John Campbell confessed that he had lost his way. Depressed over failed business ventures and a crumbling marriage, he realized that his life was in flux. "My life was in shambles, I was going nowhere," he admitted. Campbell turned his attention back to running with a renewed focus. In 1991, he came to Boston and posted a Masters (ages forty to forty-nine) record of 2:11:04. He is considered by many to be the greatest Masters runner of all time.

Physical and emotional limitations have provoked some to take to running; they do it to stop the spiral of life and its offerings. These runners run in search of catharsis and release. Professional race-car driver Michael Waltrip spends his workday traveling at death-defying speeds in a million-dollar vehicle, sometimes separated from his competitors by mere inches. Turning or braking at the wrong time could have fatal consequences. So, when he searched for an outlet to take him away from NASCAR, he found running. In 2000, he decided to run the Boston Marathon just hours after being part of a multicar pileup at Talladega. Waltrip ran to help deal with the pressures of drafting, hairpin turns, and extremely perilous speeds. It was in the rhythmic steps of solitude that he was able to decompress from the pressures of a hectic life.

Nine years later, another runner was determined to run Boston and find peace of mind. Like Waltrip, Patrick Harten was also desperate for quiet solitude. He had to run Boston, or run somewhere—anywhere. An air traffic controller at LaGuardia Airport in New York, Harten was compelled to run because of the stress of his job. His decisions on the job can have massive consequences.

A normal day's duties for an air traffic controller are stressful enough, but on January 15, 2009, Patrick Harten took a call from the pilot of US Airways flight 1549—Chesley B. Sullenberger. "Sully" Sullenberger was the pilot of a flight leaving LaGuardia Airport in New York that struck a flock of Canada geese, causing both engines to fail. The last thing Sully said to Harten that day was, "We're going to be in the Hudson." And into the Hudson River the plane went. Through Sully's heroic efforts, the plane slid along the winter whitecaps from the river, coming to rest and allowing all 155 passengers to survive.

Harten would be party to one of the greatest flying feats of passenger flight history. Although grateful for the magic of his pilot, he was nonetheless traumatized as a result of witnessing what seemed like certain tragedy. He would be obligated to speak to Congress about that day. "I believed at that moment," Harten told the congressional committee, "I was going to be the last person to talk to anyone on that plane alive.

"It was a traumatic event for me, initially," said Harten, who turned to running as a means to cope with stress. "As I've processed it, now I appreciate it for what it was: a miraculous event with a happy ending."

In 2009, the air traffic controller submitted an application to the Boston Athletic Association to run the Boston Marathon. Upon being granted entrance, Harten had one more request of the BAA: He wanted to run with the race number 1549, in honor of the US Airways flight that had landed so softly in the Hudson River. The number was granted, and Patrick Harten ran Boston in 2:47:19. When the air traffic controllers' union heard of their member's run, they wished him good luck, good-naturedly teasing him to "watch out for the water stops."

Running allows people from dangerous and stressful walks of life—air traffic controllers, race-car drivers, working mothers—to carry on. Rather than getting on the couch in a therapist's office, the runner takes to the road.

Mile 12 continues through Natick, past a mostly residential neighborhood with the occasional business mixed in at the start. Along this part of the course, house parties are popular, and the fans are polite. The twelfth mile is relatively quiet, but more demanding than appearances would lead the runner to believe. The homes comprise colonial, gambrel, and split-level houses occupied by middle-class families. The crowds are somewhat sporadic, but well-meaning; the runners get a push forward as the spectators look up from their hamburger or hot dog to wish them well. With more significant miles still ahead in the distance, runners might be lulled into a sense of indifference—until they discover that Mile 12 is more than just the relaxed flats of Framingham. They are wise to heed Jim Knaub's maxim: "There is no such thing as an unimportant mile."

To make it to the final stretch on Boylston Street, runners must respect each step along the course. Even during the quiet moments, when the ranks of lawn-chaired grandparents thin out and the screams of beer-slugging college kids temporarily subside, the runner's mind drifts away from the sights and sounds—even from the running itself. At these times, the race seems more like a daydream than a concentrated effort.

For the first third of the mile the course jumps around and slides to the left. Now is a good time for runners to test-drive those muscles in their legs to make sure they are ready for the rising hill outside of Wellesley College.

At the 11.4-mile mark, the course bids adieu to Natick and enters the affluent town of Wellesley. Here, the runners are guided east by the same train tracks that escorted the founders of the race a century ago. The course dives down for a tenth of a mile. In an 1898 account of the course, the papers would say that the "route through the Wellesley and Newtons is the ideal of suburban scenery." The runners will run through the fifth town along the course for 4.21 miles, or 16.07 percent of the race.

It was here in the Wellesley section that one of the 2018 women favorites, Desiree Linden, was herself wrestling with doubt. Over the past year, her spirit had been compromised as she grappled with the why's of running. Approaching Patriots' Day, she was prepared and willing, but that was before she showed up to the starting line to face the worst weather in the history of the Boston Marathon. The weather was so unbearable that it was more than enough to shake the firmest resolve. Wind chills were below freezing, and over a half-inch of freezing rain was splashing down into the faces of the runners throughout the race, thanks to thirty-mile-per-hour headwinds. It was the type of day that challenged the 1897 decree: "The race will run—rain or shine."

Struggling with fluid intake and a fickle mind, Linden spent the first eleven miles trying to decide whether she was going to finish the race or not. Her legs were sore and her heart, indifferent. In recent years, marathoning and long-distance running had been a source of great frustration in her life. In 2011 Linden was leading Boston with just yards to run when Caroline Kilel of Kenya passed her on Boylston Street, to beat her by just two seconds. Linden would comment about the race's outcome: "[I'm] pretty pissed."

Over the next six years, there had been a number of second-place finishes, only adding to the thirty-three-year old's exasperation. In 2017, Linden walked away from her livelihood, saying about the sport, "[I] hated everything about running."

But Linden soon realized that failure was part of the process. After a run where she didn't accomplish her ultimate goal, Desiree was philosophical. "Did I fail? Yes, but it's okay. Live and learn, go back to work, and try again."

President Teddy Roosevelt would have appreciated Desiree powering through the storm. In 1910, he honored those who at least tried in his famous "Man in the Arena" speech:

> *The credit belongs to the man who is actually in the arena, whose face is marred by dust and sweat and blood; who strives valiantly; who errs, who comes short again and again, because there is no effort without error and shortcoming; but who does actually strive to do the deeds; who knows great enthusiasms, the great devotions; who spends himself in a worthy cause; who at the best knows in the end the triumph of high achievement, and who at the worst, if he fails, at least fails while daring greatly, so that his place shall never be with those cold and timid souls who neither know victory nor defeat.*

Failure is part of every success. Without accepting that failing is part of the process, one would never be able to push forward and learn from past mistakes. Winston Churchill recognized the value of disappointment when he said, "Success is the ability to go from one failure to another with no loss of enthusiasm."

In his memoirs, horror writer Stephen King shares a time in his career when he confronted failure head-on. Day after day he was receiving rejection notices from publishers for his story, which would become known as *Carrie*. Fed up, he was walking the train tracks near his home one day when he found a giant rail spike. He picked it up and brought it home with him. He then grabbed a mallet and walked into his bedroom and, to his wife's dismay, hammered the spike into the wall. He had decided that he would puncture a hole in every rejection notice and slide them down the spike. When there was no more room on the spike, he would give up on writing.

Every morning he would wake up to see that spike and the mounting notices. It was a tangible source of motivation. He increased his intensity. He would write better and target publishers that were open to his unique brand of writing. Failures helped him channel his energies to improve his craft. He would eventually convince a publisher to take a chance on him. He would dedicate his first book to his wife, Tabitha, to compensate for the hole in their bedroom wall. He would go on to sell 350 million books.

Desiree banged the spike into her wall and came back to Boston in April of 2018. She had "failed" before, but was now ready to succeed. That was until the wintry weather greeted the runners for the April race. The Michigan runner had hoped to be the first American woman to win at Boston in thirty-three years, but as she ran, her hands and legs were freezing. She was worried about muscle pulls and the potential of an embarrassing outcome. From Natick to Wellesley she was running with fellow American, and one of the favorites to win the race, Shalane Flanagan.

As they ran together, Linden suggested to Flanagan that she wasn't planning on finishing the race. It wasn't her day. But she also felt that if she wasn't going to win, maybe she should help a fellow American, so she said to her running partner, "Hey, I think I'm going to drop out today, so if you need any help with anything, let me know. I'm happy to block the wind—whatever it may be."

Flanagan was shocked. As they ran up the surprisingly challenging incline at the 11.6-mile mark, Flanagan spotted a row of Porta-Potties on the side of road and elected to break off from the lead pack to relieve herself. Seconds later, she exited the portable bathroom only to find that Linden had slowed her pace to stay with her American friend so she could help her get through the wind and back to the lead pack.

But then something happened. The pause had rejuvenated Linden. She found her second wind, and started to push. Her stride had shifted from ambivalent to purposeful. She was tearing up the pavement with each step. She was running with an attitude her coach would have called "I've got nothing to lose." This made her dangerous and unpredictable. She found herself running with the lead group, and before long, she was making her way down Boylston Street in her yellow-striped rain coat.

This time she wasn't being chased by the Kenyan but instead was all alone. A loneliness that elite runners dream of. Within steps of the finish line she dabbed at her eyes with her right hand, then her left. Desi was awash in tears and rain and joy and fulfillment. Her past failures would make this success even more special.

After years of missed chances, teasing finishes, and uneven passion, Desi was now breaking the tape at the Boston Marathon. She was adding her name to the list that includes the likes of DeMar, Benoit, Ndereba, and Kelley. She had made history.

By agreeing to run on that ugly April day, Linden had risked failure. She had risked the pain of piercing an already-tender ego. She had already suffered painful losses, but by continuing to put one foot in front of the other, she proved that her resolve was stronger than her doubt. She washed away the pain of 2011 and wrote a chapter on resilience. As she ran through the falling rain with purpose, she validated what champions have known in Boston for over a century: If you push past doubt, you can do anything.

Linden would speak to the process of failures and success. "If you do it long enough, you go through the highs and the lows—just like life. We celebrate the good days. We remember the tough days. It's all part of history."

In the book *Epiphany*, author and marketing guru Roy Williams talks about using past failures to his advantage. "I actually had a competitive edge in the real world because things didn't intimidate me. I realized that I just wasn't frightened by things that scare other people."

At the finish line, Desiree's husband, Ryan, hugged her, cried with her, and shared in the moment. For the runner's loved ones, there is no distinction between being a supporter and being an enabler. The significant other serves as trainer, motivator, psychiatrist, and coach.

Joe Smith's wife performed these roles on the morning of the 1942 Marathon. With the race due to start in just hours, Joe Smith was allowing doubt to creep into his being.

The race was being run on a Sunday so workers in the war factories could watch the race. Smith had the day off from delivering milk and decided to hide in bed. He hadn't trained well through the winter, and didn't think he would be able to run even six miles. That was until his wife, Isabel, came into the bedroom and demanded that he get up and run the race, saying, "Joe, nobody thinks you will win the Marathon, but you can fool them all. Give them something to remember you by." She ended by saying, "I'll be at the finish, and I won't be surprised to see you come in first."

Smith showed up at the starting line and set off on the sound of the gun. Because he had such low expectations, he started slow. But as the race wore on, he was getting more and more comfortable. As he got closer to Boston, the leaders were coming into sight. He decided to not worry about the finish line but instead focused on passing each runner who ran in front of him. "The thing was getting to be a game. See a guy and catch him and forget all the others."

Smith would pass every man in front of him. As he ran down Exeter Street to the finish, he still didn't believe he would win. When he broke the tape, Isabel jumped out of the crowd and gave him three kisses that made the men topped in gray fedora hats blush. After the race, Smith would say of his wife, "Only person who knew I could win was my wife."

Whether waning heart or frail mind, the runner is left to his or her own devices when it comes to deciding whether to continue to run or not.

No runner was stronger mentally than Clarence DeMar. He was a God-fearing, hardworking American who ran back and forth to work for his training. DeMar won his first Boston Marathon in 1911, and his seventh at age forty-two, in 1930, a staggering nineteen years later. Following one of his races, the *Boston Globe* wrote of the two-time Olympian, "[He ran] like a running brook." Like a brook he would run Boston thirty-three times, finishing every time, including a seventh-place finish when he was fifty.

DeMar might not have had polish, but he had plenty of substance. His grind-it-out running form made up in effort what it lacked in style. With his left hand held out at his hip, pawing at the air as if it were a personal trigger to pronate forward, he ran with upright rigidity, symbolic of his uncompromising personality on the road. It was this type of running that endeared him to the locals who lined the sidewalks, unable to leave until DeMar had passed by.

After winning Boston for the first time, DeMar's doctor told him that the stability of his heart was tenuous, so he gave up running his hometown race for eleven years. It wasn't until 1922 that DeMar dared risk defying his doctor's advice. But when he did, he continued right where he'd left off, breaking the tape in Boston. His victory was saluted around the country, the *Herald* calling it one of the greatest achievements in the athletic history of the world.

When past winner Mike Ryan was asked how DeMar had succeeded in his comeback, Ryan pointed to both his physical and mental approach: "[DeMar] proved that there is a great mental side to athletics in addition to the physical test. He won the race primarily because of hard, concentrated work on the road, but that alone never would have prevailed had he not been assisted by the mental energy he exerted at times during the heart-breaking grind."

So, as Joe Smith did in 1942, and as champion Desi Linden did in 2018, I ran up the side of the rising slope of Mile 12, trying my best to drown out the voice of doubt whispering in my ear.

In the book *The Greatest Salesman in the World*, the idea of pushing past doubt is central to success. "I will never consider defeat, and I will remove from my vocabulary such words and phrases as quit, cannot, unable, impossible, out of the question, improbable, failure, unworkable, hopeless, and retreat; for they are the words of fools. I will avoid despair, but if this disease of the mind should infect me, then I will work on."

—◆—

As I ran the last part of Mile 12, into the affluent town of Wellesley, someone yelled out that Uta Pippig had won the Women's race. Almost instantly the group of runners in my pack started chanting, "Uta, Uta, Uta." Ever since Uta had first run to Boston, she had embraced the city and the city had embraced her right back. Her beautiful spirit and smile had melted the community. Uta was making history on the streets of Boston. Little did any of us know when we were chanting her name how much she had struggled to earn her third title that day.

It was inspiring for us, but at the same time, somewhat demoralizing to know that we hadn't even reached the halfway point, and there were runners already in Boston with medals around their necks. With more than fourteen miles to go, it was best not to focus on the fact that some fellow competitors were relaxing while you still had over two hours of work in front of you.

As an athlete who had worked hard to prepare for the event, I found it difficult to comprehend that there are athletes who can run so fast for so long. I didn't know whether to respect or envy their superhuman ability. Either way, it was never more apparent than at this point in the race that the light of the Lord's gracious hand shined on the 2:20 marathoners, while a cloud hovered over the sweaty non-endorsed plodders somewhere back in Wellesley. (In later conversations with the champion, Uta, she would say of back-of-the-pack runners like me, "They do something I could never do—running for four-plus hours is an accomplishment by itself.")

By the time you reach the thirteen-mile mark, the anticipated struggle is slowly becoming a reality. The route is increasingly hilly, and the tough half of the course still lies ahead. So, as your head begins to droop just a notch, you gladly come upon this oasis of sound.

At the end of the mile, as runners collectively run toward Mile 13, they all start to hear the first faint echoes of a faraway din. Over the collective drumbeat of thousands of footfalls, up ahead I could hear what I'd heard so much about—the Wellesley College Scream Tunnel. Veterans of the race know that they are just yards away from the rallying cries of the women of Wellesley College, and the much-needed boost their support and enthusiasm bring to the runner.

However, it can also add a distraction.

John "The Elder" Kelley, local hero and patriarch of the Boston Marathon, always warned of the need to stay focused at this juncture of the race. With the impending excitement in the next mile, he believed it was essential to stay within your game plan and not push yourself too early. He knew this from personal experience that may have cost him two championships: "Running past the girls at Wellesley College, your mind tells you one thing, but your legs do something different. I was always impatient both in life and in running, and it cost me dearly later in the course."

As the course moves into Wellesley, the road widens, and the speed limit goes up to forty-five miles per hour. The road drops for two-tenths of a mile until the mile mark, then rises over what is one of the most trying inclines on the course. Fortunately, you won't know you are running uphill, thanks to the women of Wellesley College.

MILE 13

The Boston Marathon Community

Each April, people from every corner of the globe travel thousands of miles to run twenty-six. Nowhere on the face of the Earth do more people from more diverse backgrounds gather for a one-day event. The Boston Marathon is a celebration of tradition, a celebration of health and fitness, a celebration of life. From Hopkinton to Boston, the spectators and runners are provided a stage to act out a play that runs the gamut from Shakespeare to Will Ferrell (runner of the Boston Marathon). Tragedy, triumph, love, frustration, and comedy are all components of this road race.

The Boston Marathon is life itself. For over a hundred years the mecca of all running events is a metaphor for the world around it. As the world has evolved, the Boston Marathon has evolved with it.

The twenty-six miles of roads, sidewalks, and bridges are nothing more than a backdrop for athletic conquests and failures, weddings, inebriated college students, and overpriced vendors—all of whom play an intricate role in molding this race and its legacy.

The Boston Marathon's ultimate purpose is as distinct as the people who embrace it. Whether your goal is to run, to barbecue, to say hello to your neighbor, to gather with your family, or to delay studying for college finals, the race is a willing partner for all who come to celebrate.

In this sometimes cynical and unfriendly world, people are more likely to keep their heads down as they hurry by than to offer a hello and a smile to a passing neighbor. This is not the case with the Boston Marathon—which is one reason the event is so special. If only for one day, the runners give each other reassuring smiles, the fans genuinely wish the competitors well and inspire them to go faster, and farther, and the volunteers freely give immeasurable support to the athletes.

As I was running by a table manned by volunteers, a runner came by and grabbed a desperately needed gob of Vaseline. As he moved on, he yelled, in thanks, "I love you!" The volunteer shouted back, "I love you too!"

As I took in this scene, I couldn't help but smile at the sight of people happily giving their time to pass out water and assist the runners with whatever needs they might have. This simple story captures the essence of the Boston Marathon. It's so much more than a laurel wreath and splits and the turn onto Boylston Street. In its purest form, the race has the capacity to break down the hard borders of nations and identities and allow total strangers to realize what they have in common is stronger than what makes them different. From Hopkinton to Boston, each runner is woven together by the thread of collective purpose: They are all there to run the world's greatest race. In a cold world where the line between what separates seems so defined, so final, it's on Patriots' Day that the line begins to fade. In the back of the pack, two runners who would have never met otherwise may forge a profound bond—despite the fact that they might be from different countries, belong to different religions, and speak different languages—all because they ran the Boston Marathon together.

When President Obama spoke at the services in Boston after the 2013 terrorist attack, he reflected on the special nature of the Boston Marathon community:

> *Even when our heart aches, we summon the strength that maybe we didn't even know we had, and we carry on; we finish the race. We finish the race, and we do that because of who we are, and we do that because we know that somewhere around the bend, a stranger has a cup of water. Around the bend, somebody's there to boost our spirits. On that toughest mile, just when we think that we've hit a wall, someone will be there to cheer us on and pick us up if we fall. We know that.*

The slow, arduous incline toward Wellesley College continues from the previous mile into Mile 13. The slope is the most difficult ascent on the route—so far. In total, the rise in the route continues for the better part of a mile.

In 1904, it was said that the runners "could recognize Wellesley College by the lofty spires." This hilly terrain, which tests the quads and spirits of even top athletes during the race, prompted the most prolific landscape architect of his time, Frederick Law Olmsted Jr. (son of the famed designer of Central Park), to bemoan that the location was problematic because of the "complex topography."

Wellesley College was founded in 1870 as a "Seven Sisters College," to serve as a "female seminary . . . [to] prepare women for great conflicts for vast reforms in social life." In the first years of the institution, 704 students paid $250 to attend the school. Currently, there are 2,350 undergraduates from 62 countries who pay $73,148 a year to live and learn. The school is ranked in the top five nationally for liberal arts schools, according to *US News & World Report*, boasting such illustrious alumnae as former first lady and secretary of state Hillary Rodham Clinton, journalists Diane Sawyer and Cokie Roberts, former secretary of state Madeleine Albright, and Katharine Lee Bates (class of 1880), author of "America the Beautiful."

In the late 1800s, there was a four-story factory situated near the Wellesley College campus. Town benefactor Horatio Hollis Hunnewell did not feel that industry was good for the image of the town, so he simply bought the factory and donated the land to Wellesley College for dormitories. Currently the college is the town's largest employer, with over 1,200 workers. Despite its educational mission and prestigious history, Wellesley College is best known to marathoners as the high-water mark on the course in terms of shrieks and screams.

If there was ever a segment of the first half of the course where a runner needed distraction, this is it. Some runners climb with their heads hung low and spirits starting to melt. Thankfully, the runner discovers this oasis of relief at the gates of Wellesley College.

When the runners arrive, they realize that the legend of Wellesley College is not hyperbole; if anything, it's understated. It is here that the past quiet miles turn into a tsunami of well wishes, screams of encouragement, and pleas for a kiss.

At the very first Marathon in 1897, the papers would say of the school's spirit, "The pretty college girls at Wellesley, who had assembled along the highway to cheer on the tired runners, had flaunted their dainty kerchiefs and class colors in the faces of the heaving, panting leaders." Ever since that first greeting, the young ladies from the dorms of Pomeroy, Munger, and Shafer have welcomed Boston Marathon runners. In 1899, the papers referred to the students as "fair belles" or "fair maids of Wellesley . . . pretty girls all gowned in fashionable and varicolored gowns." Since that first race in 1897, the women of Wellesley College have hurried through lunch in order to stand on the old stone wall to encourage, inspire, and deafen the passing athletes. Runners need to stay disciplined in this stretch, known, for obvious reasons, as the "Scream Tunnel."

From the first runner to the last, the women scream their love. This choir of primal yells can be heard from miles away. They offer good tidings, kisses, and unconditional support. Runners finish this section completely oblivious to form, splits, or terrain. They are so appreciative that one year, a runner kissed as many fans as he could and then reversed his course and returned to the beginning of the Tunnel to do it all over again.

The women of Wellesley epitomize the unique contribution the crowd makes to the race. For more than a century—beginning with the very first year when they lifted winner John McDermott up on their shoulders—the race has served as a platform for the love affair between fans and runners. The fans are sincere in their adulation, and the runners, sincere in their appreciation. Italian champion Gelindo Bordin, who won Boston in 1990, called the Boston Marathon his favorite race. "As a total experience, it's unparalleled," Bordin said. "The history behind it; the level of competition; the educated fans; the festivities of the day."

Four-time Women's champ Catherine Ndereba agrees. "Boston is my finest and my favorite milestone. I like the people and the atmosphere down there because they are very friendly . . . the fans are very welcoming."

Boston Marathon fans are not only educated on the event and the sport, but also very protective of *their* race. Their attendance is not random; it's not impulsive happenstance that brings them to the side of the road. It's not because they saw helicopters overhead and heard sirens down the way. Boston fans come to watch the race because it is a New England rite of passage. A fan that stands on the side of the road quite possibly could be the fourth or fifth generation of that particular family to do so—like the Connellys. At each race, a fan could be standing alongside multiple generations, including parents and children.

The Boston Marathon isn't a road race for people with short shorts and sneakers; it's a family heirloom. It's a part of the community's identity. Year after year, decade after decade, generation after generation, families line the streets on both sides. Parents bring their kids out to the course to expose them to a positive and traditional pastime—a baptism in the waters of the Boston Marathon. When one lives in these parts, the Boston Marathon is a way of life. Marathoner Pat Williams is amazed each year to see the same faces in the same spots. He wonders, "Could these families lay claim to a piece of the roadside as a function of squatters' rights?"

New Englanders are traditionalists with parochial allegiance to any possession they perceive as theirs. In fact, the obsessive ownership and passion that fans feel toward the race occasionally causes them to give the impression they are more than just fans.

For months leading up to the race, locals have been forced into hibernation by blizzards and storms. Being trapped in the house by the sadistic blasts of a winter nor'easter means that by the time Patriots' Day arrives on the calendar, the antidote for cabin fever is the Boston Marathon. The fan base is sincere not only in their love for the race, but also in their actual role within it. From offering words of encouragement to opening bathroom doors in Hopkinton, from screaming out how much farther a runner might have to go to cooling warm runners with garden hoses or slices of oranges—all of these actions speak to the fan's role in the race. This is not a parade that they are passively watching; the spectators are part of the race, earning the undying appreciation of the runners. It is an impressive display of goodwill in its purest form—people caring for others without previous acquaintance.

Whether the marathoners want it or not, this is what Boston is all about. Runners, officials, fans, and the terrain of the city itself—all have a role to play. Every year following the race the *Boston Globe* is inundated with letters to the editor from runners who are desperate to thank the million-plus fans who lined the course and served as that extra motivation the runners so desperately need in their battle to run Boston.

Following the 1967 race, runner Bill Taylor wrote to the *Globe:* "To the people who lined the way from Hopkinton to Boston, for all the refreshments and sincere moral encouragement given all the runners—I was very much impressed and felt like a hometown boy." This sentiment was echoed in another note to the *Globe* from "Forty Runners from Northern California": "We wish to express our heartfelt thanks to all of you from all of us. You spectators of this race make it what it is, simply the finest race ever . . . Your cheering was an inspiration, to say the least. We couldn't have done it without you."

Some fans are so supportive, their help sometimes goes beyond just a well wish or slap on the back. In 1976 a runner ripped his sneaker running through Wellesley. A fan, seeing him in distress, took off his own sneakers and gave them to the runner. One year later, Vince McDonald was running a sub-three-hour marathon when a fan came out of the crowd and handed him a beer, which he proceeded to drink. After the race, McDonald would say, "The people here make the race. Don't let them change a thing." The encounter is so heartwarming that it once provoked a runner in the 1930s to ask, "Is this heaven?"

———

When I ran past the tunnel, I actually got emotional. The women were so sincere in their support that I felt unworthy of their regard. They didn't know me, but they treated me like a friend. They were new friends that made a difference in my quest. When I came out the other end of the Tunnel, I was sad to leave the warmth of their embrace, but I was also re-dedicated. I now needed to honor their kindness by working harder as I continued my way down the road.

I had arrived at the gates of Wellesley College more than two hours after the wheelchair competitors had passed. I didn't expect much at that time of the day, but I still looked forward to passing the area that veteran runners had talked so much about. As I came upon the campus, I was amazed to find the place still packed with enthusiastic college students. The cheering was unbelievable; it made me wonder if Wellesley applicants had to send in recordings of themselves screaming along with their transcripts and SAT scores. To maintain such a level of volume for so long must be nearly as challenging as running the race. This great outpouring of passion truly lifted my spirits. I felt I owed it to these women to keep working hard. To stop now would be to betray their trust and let them down; the only way I could repay them was to dig in and concentrate on putting one foot in front of the other.

In the closing tenths of Mile 13, the competitors bid the students goodbye, hopefully with renewed strength and commitment in addition to smiles on their faces.

———

With the train tracks still on the left and the grounds of Wellesley's campus on the right, the runners continue uphill until they are welcomed through the gates of Wellesley Center, where the course flattens out. Here, the echoes of exultation still reverberate and the cheers continue to inspire, with the understanding that this is not just a physical endeavor, but a spiritual one as well.

Wellesley is an aesthetically pleasing town. The center serves as a stark contrast to the hollowed-out factories back in Framingham, where the roads in 1898 were described as dusty, as opposed to Wellesley. This is where the shouts of "Run!" are replaced by golf claps from the town's citizens, who are wearing the latest fashions. For the other 364 days of the year, Range Rovers and Mercedes pass through these streets, as shoppers with bags in in their hands and discretionary income in their pockets poke in and out of places like The Cheese Shop, London Harness Company, and dueling cafes selling lattes and finger sandwiches. The town's main thoroughfare is the home of the affluent and the commerce hub of the wealthy.

The runner must be conscious of an important change to the course here. Between the quaint brick- and stucco-faced buildings, the town has made the streets pedestrian-friendly by extending walkways and thus compressing the race route. In the previous mile, the course provided runners with four lanes on which to spread out, but now, as they enter Wellesley Center, they'll be unceremoniously forced to squeeze into two. Three-time winner Uta Pippig reminds herself when running through Wellesley to run with caution. "As you move past the halfway mark, the road narrows," she explains. "It's not a concern, but I am aware of it."

Since the early 1800s, this town has leveraged its capital to its advantage. The Wellesley Historical Society contains many accounts of the town's history. One from the 1800s noted the town's ability to use its considerable wealth to its advantage by claiming, "Wellesley was getting a reputation as a town that gets what it wants. Might was right. There was no problem too big [that it couldn't] be solved with money." The town was named after Isabella Pratt Welles, wife of the town's largest benefactor, Horatio Hollis Hunnewell. Along with his wife's maiden name, Hunnewell also gave Wellesley a great deal of land, and financial support.

After passing the boutiques and cute eateries, the course drops down and slides left at Tutto Italiano, where Rob Palizzolo makes the best Italian sandwich around. Soon, the runners will pass the library and the town hall, coming to a fork in the road. Here, at the end of Mile 13, runners will turn onto Route 16, the first time they will not be running on Route 135.

MILE 14

Not Alone

The town of Wellesley is indicative of the diversity of the route that hosts the race as much as the runners represent the diversity of the global population. On the course, however, there is no class system based on wealth—just a hierarchy of speed, endurance, and experience. Those familiar with the route know that Mile 14 is not focused on deciding between Wyke Farms Cheddar and Rouge River Blue, but instead for checking off another significant benchmark on their run. It is here, in the back side of Wellesley Center, that runners cross over the literal halfway point of the course.

As part of our training during the winter, the four of us ran the New Bedford Half Marathon down the southeast coast of Massachusetts. On a gray, freezing day, we ran alongside the Atlantic Ocean, the route ending with a sadistic, steep hill. For me it was another milestone in my effort to run Boston, and I was now able to put a 13.1-mile run on my résumé. When I stepped across the finish line that day, I was exhausted. On the forty-minute car ride back to Boston, I felt completely spent.

Now, as I crossed over the halfway point in Wellesley, I said to myself, "Shit—I have to run two New Bedfords back to back without stopping."

It was never-mind-the-bullshit time; this is what I'd signed up for. Back to one step at a time. On a positive note: Every step after the halfway point means that the finish line is now closer than the starting line.

While the halfway benchmark can provide some runners with a surge of renewed energy, for those with tiring legs and slumping shoulders, the halfway point can be a source of discouragement. After all, half of the course still lies ahead—and it's the more difficult half, filled with miles of uphills and downhills, not to mention the cumulative effect of the miles already run.

Moving left, the runners pass in front of St. Paul's Church, which sits on the right. The church was founded back in 1906, the year a little-known runner named Timmy Ford (see the "Mile 18" chapter) would shock everyone by breaking the tape in Boston.

When champions John "The Elder" Kelley and Alvaro Mejia ran past St. Paul's, they always blessed themselves in gratitude while humbly asking for intercession. In 1982, Sister Madonna Buder passed St. Paul's as the first nun to run the race. She spent the twenty-six miles praying the Rosary repeatedly, saying, "Prayers are free flowing . . . and the rhythmic Rosary provides a mental block against the physical exertion."

The Boston Marathon is a celebration of health and fitness for individuals that have been blessed to be able to participate in an event of such vitality. The very fact that the runner can run, whether in sneakers or in a wheelchair, means that God has shone the light of fortune upon him or her. It's a reminder that running provides the individual an opportunity beyond listening to a music playlist and banging out miles. Being out on the road grants the runner a chance to talk with oneself, perhaps align with one's inner self.

All along the course, the runner moves past houses of faith: Catholic, Protestant, Jewish, Hindu, and Muslim. As you pass these houses of faith, it is important to keep in mind that although you run alone, you don't have to be by yourself.

The second half of the race will present fierce challenges—daunting hills and sharp corners and perilous train tracks. Miles known by the monikers "Haunted" and "Hell's Alley" await the vulnerable. It behooves competitors to not attempt to conquer these beasts by themselves. To move forward during the solitary miles ahead, you are best served by connecting with your spiritual side. It's in the monotonous routine of setting and raising your feet thousands and thousands of times on this day that you have the opportunity to become reacquainted with your blessings.

Many people run marathons because they have questions. Questions about themselves—their lives—their purpose. The race is a living metaphor. It's where character is formed, and souls are strengthened. At runners' lowest moments—whether in the race or in life itself—knowing there is an entity looking out for their best interests can only help them continue forward.

In 1985, Joe Michaels ran Boston after surviving seven heart attacks, carrying with him the philosophy that helped him to endure in life as well as on the course: "The secret to life is hope."

When former Boston mayor Ray Flynn arrived at the top of Heartbreak Hill, his running partner Donald Murray said to him, "This will be the closest you'll be to God all day." Flynn, who served as the ambassador to the Vatican, and was blessed to meet two saints along his journeys, responded, "How can't I make it to the peak after that?"

As I crossed over the halfway point, it was time yet again to conduct a physical and emotional assessment. I still had 13.1 miles to run, which included four hills. It was apparent to me that I would need to seek help in order to realize my dream of running all the way to Boston on this day.

When college football coach Dan Mullen completed his own appraisal of his run back in 2016, he looked back and recognized a distinct difference between the first and second half. "I enjoyed the first half a lot. I wasn't smiling as much the second half of the race."

Distance running provides athletes with a chance to do something they can't do during their busy lives—have an honest discourse with themselves. They can ask themselves questions and then answer them without risk of judgment. Within the run they have the chance to recognize their personal limitations, both as athletes and as human beings. This, in turn, allows them to assess how to improve or remedy what has distracted them in their quest to be their best in all facets of life.

There are no boundaries within these private conversations. For some, they can be personal, with just themselves, while others may extend the dialogue beyond earthly confines to include a higher being. In the form of prayer or meditation, you can give thanks, seek guidance, or ask for inspiration.

These moments can also include interaction with loved ones who have passed and who may offer intercession. After all, no one has greater perspective than those who were enlightened in their final moments while the final candle flickered. As life faded for those who are gone, they lived anew, even if it was for a brief moment. Through the lens of true understanding they saw the miracle of life in every snowflake, raindrop, sunrise, and breath. Runners can draw upon this strength when their quads tighten and their breath shortens. This is the power of running. It's not miles and hills and oxygen intake—it's exploiting the run in a way that allows you to be the best person you can be.

From my earliest memory, whenever I was participating in an event of consequence, my father always sent me out the door, whether with baseball glove or book bag in hand, with the same advice: "Do your best and say a Hail Mary"— an approach that four-time winner Catherine Ndereba employed. "I think I've done everything I'm supposed to do, and the rest I leave to God," she has said.

I was brought up in a Catholic home. All six of us went to St. Theresa School in West Roxbury. I was an altar boy, as were my two brothers. We went to Mass as a family each Sunday and said grace before dinner at the dining-room table. God was important in our house. He was a part of the family. We knew that having a spiritual entity in your life means that you are never alone. You have a partner there to listen, intercede, and even sometimes to carry you. So, when attempting something beyond your abilities, it is essential to incorporate something beyond your physical self into your endeavor. If you have limitations, then you have to figure out how you're going to stretch yourself beyond established restrictions. In my case, the best way to push forward when I was pressing against the margins of my ability was to include heavenly entities in the undertaking.

When I ran Boston, I ran each mile interacting with friends and family that were no longer walking on this Earth. My engagement with my heavenly friends included reflecting on warm memories of times I spent with them, along with appeals for help. These conversations not only served to cure my loneliness but also provided me with confidence. I knew that each friend or family member I was conferring with had my best interests in mind, and that they were in a position to influence the outcome of my efforts while also advancing who I am as a person.

Surrounding these petitions to my friends were desperate Our Fathers and Hail Marys, including self-serving petitions to the Almighty to help me keep putting one foot in front of the other. Interfacing with heavenly entities also served another purpose: It shifted my attention from the monotony of tens of thousands of steps to a focus on happy thoughts. During difficult stretches, when answers were scarce and the running was tough, I would routinely find myself reciting verses of my favorite poem, "Forgive Me When I Whine," in order to maintain a proper perspective.

> *Today upon a bus I saw a lovely maiden with golden hair;*
> *I envied her, she seemed so happy and, Oh, I wished I were so fair*
> *When, suddenly, she rose to leave, I saw her hobble down the aisle;*
> *She had one foot and wore a crutch, but as she passed a smile.*
> *Oh, God forgive me when I whine;*
> *I have two feet, the world is mine . . .*
>
> *With feet to take me where I'd go,*
> *With eyes to see the sunset's glow,*
> *With ears to hear what I should know,*
> *I'm blessed indeed, the world is mine*
> *Oh, God, forgive me when I whine!*

One person I called upon and talked to throughout training runs, and especially on this day, was my father-in-law, Tom Concannon. Tom was a simple man. And when I say simple, I mean it in the most complimentary manner. He lived his life, took care of his family, and didn't let others bother him. If they weren't his type of people, he paid them little attention. He didn't waste negative energy—unless he was complaining about those "bums," the Red Sox.

Tom was born and raised in Connemara, Ireland. He was a good man who raised two children, including his daughter, Noreen. In July of 1987, on the family farm back in Ireland, I proposed to Noreen on the shores of Galway Bay. She agreed to be my wife, and we planned our wedding for July, in the coming year. Tom was there to share the joy of our engagement.

Later that year, on St. Patrick's Day, the Irishman was diagnosed with terminal stomach cancer. Doctors gave him four to six weeks to live. Both Tom's physician and our priest pleaded with us to move up our wedding date so Tom could be present to see his only daughter exchange wedding vows. We vacillated on the decision until Tom made up our minds for us. He assured us that he would be there. So, we kept the date and said our prayers.

As the days passed, Tom's condition worsened. Jaundiced, unable to eat, he was slowly withering away in front of our very eyes. But somehow, on our wedding day, Tom put on his tuxedo and walked his daughter down the aisle. It was the greatest tangible example of love I had ever witnessed. Those steps, with his daughter on his arm, will stay with me forever. They were steps filled with love and courage. Everyone there was in the presence of a miracle. It was through God's direct intercession that Tom was allowed to defy the hand of death to see his daughter to the altar.

Viktor Frankl would say that our life has purpose up to our final breath. "In accepting this challenge to suffer bravely, life has a meaning up to the last moment, and it retains this meaning literally to the end. In other words, life's meaning is an unconditional one."

Two weeks after his courageous walk, with his daughter on his arm, we were back in the church and Tom was again traveling the same aisle, sadly, this time, for his funeral. We sent him off that day.

Here, at Mile 14, I found myself drawing upon the strength my father-in-law showed on our wedding day. The steps he took down the aisle that day defied medical science. I talked to my father-in-law throughout the race and asked for his intercession, hoping to emulate his will, strength, and courage so I could keep pushing forward.

Just as I feel a spiritual connection with my father-in-law, Viktor Frankl spent his days in several concentration camps, sustaining his connection with his deceased wife. "More and more I felt that she was present, that she was with me; I had the feeling that I was able to touch her, able to stretch out my hand and grasp hers."

This is how I feel about my friends who are no longer with us. Especially on this day. I knew they were with me. With Tom and God and the Blessed Mother on my side, my odds of success were greatly enhanced.

For years people have run to honor the memory of loved ones.

In 2018, Conrad Roy Jr. ran Boston to honor his son. Conrad Henri Roy III killed himself in the infamous tragedy in which his girlfriend encouraged him through texts to complete the act. His father ran to raise awareness and funds for a cause committed to preventing suicide.

In 2014, Meb Keflezighi won Boston with the names of those who had died in the previous year's bombing written on his bib. After he won, he would articulate his feeling that there was a force involved beyond his legs that brought him to the tape in Boston. "I strongly believe that there was a higher purpose at play that day, that the stars were all aligned for me. This was the moment I had prayed for."

In 2008, Laura Dempsey ran for her late friend Laura Linehan, who died from liver disease. "I had her in my mind the whole time. In some ways it was very motivating, and in other ways it was sad. She was with me every step of the way."

In 2003, Ted Williams's daughter Claudia signed up to run in memory of her father, after he passed away. It's likely she recalled his words from 1959: "It takes real guts to tackle the job of covering twenty-six miles."

In 2002, veteran marathoner Tom Frost stopped at the base of Heartbreak Hill for a moment of silence. It was on that very spot in years past that Tom's daughter Lisa used to stand and cheer for him. On September 11, 2001, Lisa Frost perished on United Flight 175. On race day in 2002, Lisa was running beside her father.

Also in 2002, Boston police officer Henry Staines ran Boston to honor his dear friend, Jerry Dewan. Jerry was a New York fireman who participated in the greatest rescue mission in the country's history. On 9/11, Jerry and his brothers answered the call in New York. Jerry and Henry had pledged to each other to someday run the race together. Henry made good on that pledge. As he ran the final steps of Boylston Street, he held his friend's helmet, found by his side at Ground Zero. When Henry crossed the finish line, he looked up to the sky as his running partner said, "Jerry is watching us right now; you did it!"

In 2001, Korean runner Lee Bong-Ju ran with a heavy heart. In the months leading up to the race, he had lost his father. He didn't know how he would run Boston without him. Finally, he relented and arrived in Hopkinton. Suffocated by the memory of his earnest dad, who had worked at his rice farm up to his dying day, Lee took the first step toward Boston. As he ran, he sensed his father's presence. He said, "I felt him when I needed encouragement and confidence." When Lee crossed the finish line as champion, he would later say in profound reflection, "I felt that my father was with me today."

Race director Dave McGillivray runs the twenty-six miles every year after he has finished officiating the event. He runs in honor of his grandfather, who encouraged him to someday run the Marathon. Dave said of his grandfather, "He is there in spirit."

Viktor Frankl spoke of this type of bond, and the responsibility of the surviving member of the relationship to sustain the connection. "They must not lose hope but should keep their courage in the certainty that the hopelessness of our struggle did not detract from its dignity and its meaning. I said that someone looks down on each of us in difficult hours—a friend, a wife, somebody alive or dead, or a god, and he would not expect us to disappoint him."

Seven-time champion Clarence DeMar set prayer as his life's foundation. A daily Bible reader, DeMar was once asked how a person wins the Boston Marathon. "It isn't the personality," he replied. "It isn't the runner's appearance; it isn't his ability; it isn't his clean living. It is the practice, nine times out of ten. It is prayer, and it is his determination, drawn on some latent ability, that decides the winner in a marathon race."

———

As I ran through Wellesley, the road was small-town simple. Up and down, with shops on each side. By this point of the day, I hadn't eaten in almost six hours, and I was burning carbs like crazy, despite my humble split times. My stomach was starting to clamor for sustenance. With the clock now pointing toward late afternoon, the oranges offered by well-meaning fans were starting to warm. I had tried orange slices during training runs but had sworn off them because of the acid's effect on my stomach. Prior to the race, I had reminded myself to limit food and fluid consumption to items that were acceptable to my system.

But here, almost fourteen miles from Hopkinton, I was starting to get desperate. Strangely my mind began to pull up random files that existed somewhere deep in my subconscious, as it would throughout the second half of the race. Spying the volunteers' table up ahead with the oranges, my brain selected the file titled "Bataan Death March," the horrific incident that took place in the Philippines during World War II. Seventy thousand American POWs were forced by the Japanese to march seventy miles in 100-degree temperatures, with almost no food or water. During this sadistic parade, the prisoners were told that if they attempted to obtain water, they would be executed. Nonetheless, many risked the consequences and tried to quench their thirst. Approaching the oranges, my subconscious deemed my situation to be similar to that faced by the POWs—although of infinitely less importance, of course.

I stuck out my hand.

Needless to say, the warm oranges didn't cure my ills. To the contrary, they triggered bouts of queasiness that would be intensified over the next miles by every roadside cookout. My stomach churning stomach, I tried to distract myself by searching for my college friend Jimmy Delaney, who'd told me he would be waiting in Wellesley. Jimmy and I played baseball together at Bentley College. I hadn't seen a familiar face since my sisters' back in Ashland. I was starting to get desperate. This lonely run was getting to me. Although the odds of finding him were slim, I needed to see him. The effects of the Wellesley College Scream Tunnel were wearing off.

MILE 15

Overcome

Wellesley, the fifth town along the Marathon route, is such an idyllic place to live that it used to be known as "Contentment." Years later the name of this utopian enclave was changed because the town's most prominent benefactor wanted to name it after his wife, Isabella Pratt Welles.

A 1906 article said of the town, quite optimistically: "Pleasant paths for long, lonely strolls. . . . Wellesley, a residential village with no manufacturing, has long been noted for its pure water and invigorating air. It is believed that this fine village is absolutely free from all evil influence which tends to corrupt youth."

Prominent Wellesley citizen Isaac Sprague hoped that his town would comprise a citizenry of note. "A beautiful town attracts a certain type of resident, one who has not just great wealth, but also the intelligence and wisdom needed to run the town and help [it] thrive and prosper."

Mile 15 continues through a pleasant commercial section, with shops on either side of the route. On the left, the train tracks continue to shadow the runners. Up ahead is the Wellesley Hills train station and the local post office, on the left. After the depot, a variety of commercial buildings and businesses lead up to the Unitarian Universalist Society Church and the sixty-five-foot Wellesley Hills clock tower, built with famous Wellesley fieldstone back in 1928. The structure is well considered by the townspeople and those who judge buildings of note, and thus it is listed on the National Register of Historic Places. In years past, the bells of the tower were rung to greet the runners. This is one of the many traditions that have fallen away because of the current size of the Marathon; the field is now far too large to continue to sound the chimes. It would be impractical to keep ringing the bells as forty thousand runners made their way past.

The tower is one of four prominent clocks along the course, joining those found in the Ashland clock tower, the Natick Congregational Church steeple, and Newton Town Hall, ahead. But no form of time is more impactful than the shadows that start to slope farther away from you as the sun begins to fall and you realize that you have been on the course for a long time.

As this mostly level mile ends, the runners approach a multi-street intersection surrounded by places of business. At this segment of the route, the wheelchair competitors need to be cognizant of a change in the surface that might cause their wheels to jump and their spinning to have increased resistance. The unevenness of the road surface only adds to the challenge and necessitates that runners in wheelchairs exert additional energies just past the halfway point of the race. Eight-time champion Jean Driscoll spoke of the distinctive tarmac in this mile. "For some reason, you can't stroke as fluidly at this section," she says, "so you have to bear down more than you should through a level stretch."

With eight separate towns from start to finish on this point-to-point course, the route has different pavements, sewer systems, and road design; this makes each town, each mile, each stretch of ground separate and unique. The smart runners know this, and prepare for it. The importance of every step and spin from Hopkinton to Boston is not just a cliché—it's the difference between finishing and not.

Throughout the run, competitors are going to be confronted with a variety of obstacles and challenges. When you sign up to run Boston, your perception might be that the test is to run on smooth, unobstructed pavement from Point A to Point B. But that's not the case with this race. For over a century the Boston Marathon has been a virtual haunted house for runners.

Edgar Allan Poe once wrote, "Never to suffer would never to have been blessed." The glory of running Boston comes not from completing the smooth miles on the course, but from dealing with the hills, train tracks, potholes, and dogs along the way. The torment allows the earnest runner to look back at the route from the finish line and feel that he or she has traversed a course of consequence. Conquering the challenges only enhances the fulfillment you will feel if you can make it all the way to Boston.

Nana Kenny talked about the journey everyone travels, her message less about destination than the route we take. She used to say that when you looked back upon your life, you would be surprised by the twists and turns and obstacles you faced. She said it was these detours and diversions that ended up serving as our life's crossroads, determining who we become.

Nana Kenny knew about adversity; she lived through typhoid, two world wars, the Great Depression, and the loss of her father. She learned how to overcome from her amazing mother, Mary Downey.

Both sides of my family came from Ireland. In the years leading up to the twentieth century, my great-grandmother Mary Downey came to the States from Ireland, traveling alone in the bowels of a Cunard steamship. My Nana Kenny would write: "My mother left her home in County Roscommon at the age of eighteen. She had visions of life in America which promised work, money, possibly a husband and a home of her own."

Mary Downey married a hardworking gentleman named Thomas Crosby. Thomas, my great-grandfather, worked fourteen-hour days on the coal wharves of Boston. One day he was burned badly in an explosion at work. Soon thereafter he went about forming a union with his friend, John Lucey. As the unionizing of workers was gaining momentum, he was invited to meet with management. He left one morning for the meeting wearing his Sunday-best black overcoat with a velvet collar and a derby hat. He never came home that night, reportedly killed and thrown into Boston Harbor, his body never found.

Great-Grandma Crosby would work long hours to keep her eight children under one roof. During the day she would scrub theater floors by hand, only to come home and iron the laundry that she took in. My grandmother would write of her mother's pride in her work, saying, "Her laundry was beautiful to see."

Here I was worrying about hills and water tables in my "self-actualization" run of Boston when just generations earlier, my ancestors literally lived at the bottom of Maslow's pyramid. Great-Grandma Crosby was fighting every day to keep her family together, fed and clothed, and on the intended path toward realizing the "American Dream." Every time she went without, she allowed me and my siblings the opportunities that we now enjoy. I run on this day by the grace of God and the love and sacrifice of all those who came before me.

My obstacles on this day were many. But no runner in the history of the Boston Marathon was confronted by more challenges—beyond running—than Clarence DeMar. These hindrances just made DeMar's accomplishment that much more impressive, considering he was also battling a cardiac condition. According to the newspaper reports, DeMar needed to run the first part of the course in order to get his heart functioning properly—all the way to the Wellesley Hills clock tower. "His heart is not acting normally until he has run fifteen miles or so. Once he has covered that distance successfully, he is fit, and heaven only can help his rivals."

DeMar seemed to be the target of outside elements that led him to battle forces beyond those of his fellow runners. During his thirty-three Marathons—in which he won seven, finished second twice, and finished seventh (when he was fifty years old)—he had been hit by cars, bikes, and fans, and at one point he was attacked by a dog (which he proceeded to "drop-kick" off the road).

In 1922, DeMar was cut off by a car and almost knocked into the crowd during a race that featured so many cars on the route that the papers would say the next day he was "lost in blue and black smoke from the autos, oil and petro." One year later, a car swerved into DeMar's attendant (on a bicycle), who ricocheted into DeMar, ripping his sneaker from his foot and forcing him to run with his sneaker dangling from his bare foot for the last three miles of the race. In 1942, a well-meaning fan assumed the champion would appreciate a cool bath. When the fan threw water on the lead runner, DeMar stopped long enough to punch out the spectator.

Over his many runs, DeMar had been known to throw his share of haymakers at fans. Years later, he was asked about fans that intrude upon the runners' quest to reach Boston. "Many people—I'm afraid—think that I have a nasty temper while I'm running. That's because I wanted everyone to know that I don't want to be encouraged or interfered with."

Since the first Boston Marathon, entities beyond the race itself have served to inject themselves into the race's story, sometimes even impacting the race's outcome. In 1897, winner John McDermott had to navigate through a funeral parade to get to the finish line. At the 1908 race, officials were concerned with the treatment of horses pulling fans desperate to stay up front, with the leaders. "Police officials are to make special attention of reckless drivers of carriages who beat their horse to make them keep up with the runners."

By 1917, cars had become so prominent on the course that it was rare a race could be completed without a fan or competitor being hit by a distracted driver. In that year, officials lashed out at careless drivers: "Numbers [of] instances of interference with runners by the greatest hogs in the world—the motor cars."

Tarzan Brown in 1936 and Stylianos Kyriakides in 1946 were both nearly killed by cars while in the lead, almost costing them their lives along with their historic runs. In 1938 five reporters were traveling in a car at such a reckless pace—trying to keep up with the leaders—that their car flipped over, almost killing them. (They later showed up at the finish line looking like battle-wearied soldiers.) Three years earlier it was said that the "dust and fumes from the cars was choking." It was so difficult and dangerous for the runners that Lieutenant Governor Edward Barry had promised to present legislation that would consider the race a "state institution," giving public officials the right to ban cars from the course.

The most famous incident of interference occurred in the 1907 race. Race favorite Thomas Longboat was running with a slight lead through Framingham when he spied a freight train pulling across the route. Longboat decided to make a run for it and attempt to beat the train. In full sprint, Longboat sacrificed his legs and wind; with nineteen miles still to run, he knew that if he could beat the train, victory would be his. If he didn't make it, he would have expended significant fuel for nothing, most likely wasting away on the course's later hills. Of course, he also risked the possibility of being hit by the train. The sprint was more than one hundred yards, prompting one of his competitors to mock, "That crazy Indian; he won't finish the race."

When Longboat arrived at the tracks, witnesses report that the locomotive had beaten the Indian and the trailing cars were now blocking the course. Not discouraged, Longboat searched each car until he found an open door. He then jumped into the car and out the other side.

Decades later, in 1973, marathon spectator Harry Augusto, who had witnessed the event, recalled the bold maneuver: "I was fourteen at the time, and the fact that I saw Tom do this has always stayed with me. I was amazed he took the chance he did."

Longboat was now the only runner on the Boston side of the train; on the other side of the tracks stood 113 impatient challengers, including the two pre-race favorites. Frustrated and growing stiff as they stood there, Longboat's competitors were forced to wait for the train to pass while the Canadian took advantage of his good fortune (and brave move), running through the day's snow to the finish line.

The *Globe* wrote the following day, "Longboat's victory makes him the greatest of marathon runners. It is the more extraordinary that he competed with 101 white men, [only] 52 of whom finished."

In 1933, runner Joseph Faultstick was run over by a streetcar and knocked out of the race. In 1960 and 1982, sadistic fans came out of the crowd to punch runners in the lead pack.

But there was no force more problematic than dogs.

In 1929, two-time winner Johnny Miles was bitten by a dog as he ran in the lead.

In 1947, a fox terrier knocked down Korean runner Suh Yun-Bok as he ran through Newton. The impact from the clash caused Yun-Bok's sneaker to rip and lace to come undone. Despite having to deal with a bleeding knee and an untied sneaker, the suddenness of the dog's intrusion had shocked the runner, giving him an immediate rush of adrenaline that he used to propel him on to victory.

In 1959, runner Jack Dwyer actually carried a billy club throughout the race to fend off snapping dogs.

Unfortunately, in 1961, no one in the lead pack had a billy club. That year a rogue dog actually determined the outcome of the race. For more than fourteen miles a vicious black beast had been stalking the leaders. Up and down hills, the dog shadowed the lead pack, plotting when to attack the men in short shorts and tank tops. When they came to the border of Wellesley and Newton, the dog shot left across the course, crashing into John "The Younger" Kelley. The leader was knocked off his feet and pushed to the ground as the sadistic dog disappeared into the crowd.

Kelley was covered in abrasions on shoulders and elbows. The press bus was bearing down on him when English runner Fred Norris stopped to pick Kelley up before he was crushed. Unfortunately, the time lost trying to gather himself would cost him the championship, as he finished seconds behind the winner. After the race, Norris was asked what type of dog it was, to which he responded, "a son of a bitch."

Police did their best to keep dogs and cars off the road, but sometimes the police themselves were the problem. In 1982, Women's wheelchair champion Candice Cable would say after the race, "The race was real scary with all of those police horses out there." It was the same year that Alberto Salazar and Dave Beardsley battled for most of the race into Boston only to have police on motorcycles bump into them as the officers battled to inject themselves into photographs.

While I didn't have to worry about dogs or cars on the road, every step mattered. I didn't have a single footfall to spare. I knew from my training runs that once I started running, I was incapable of stopping and then restarting the engine. For me, it would be like pulling the cord on a lawn mower with no gas in the tank. Because of this, even though I had overindulged on water before the race, I'd decided not to make any bathroom visits on the course.

Despite my best intentions to maintain the same cadence from Hopkinton to Boston, it wasn't meant to be. When I was scaling a hill on Mile 21, I saw out of the corner of my eye that a young toddler had broken loose from his distracted parents. It was apparent that our paths were going to intersect. Even though it would have been a good lesson learned for the child, I elected not to run him over like an NFL linebacker, instead rearranging my steps to avoid the rogue rug rat, which of course forced me to deviate from my intended course. Although this amounted to just ten steps out of fifty thousand or so I took that day, they were the most difficult.

Uta Pippig said about winning her second Boston, saddled by blisters, "This is sport, and anything can happen. It would be no good if you had absolutely no problems. It would be too easy."

The runners work their way across a bridge that travels over Route 9. At the beginning of the bridge, there is a slight bump, which forces the runners to pick up their feet and the wheelchair competitors to cross carefully. On the left sits the Wellesley Hills Congregational Church; it was here in 1996 (during the race's centennial) that Knoxville runners Denise Dillon and Edgar Walters stopped in the middle of the race to exchange wedding vows, alongside family and a string quartet. At a local flower shop, Ed changed into a tuxedo shirt and Denise, into a wedding top. "To run this far was an effort," Reverend Craig Adams told the couple, "but the contest you face beyond the finish line is going to be even greater." The newlyweds kissed and returned to the course to finish the race.

As I ran through the back end of Mile 15, I approached one of the junctures on the course I wished I wasn't familiar with. The course moves through a neighborhood with quaint picket fences—like it came right out of the Bedford Falls set in *It's a Wonderful Life*. But the soundtrack for this mile shouldn't be a nice sing-along of "Auld Lang Syne," led by Jimmy Stewart; instead, it should be the score from *Jaws*, because *it's* coming, and there's nothing you can do about it.

Despite knowing what's ahead, the runners keep moving forward. Maybe it's the endorphins, or maybe it's just in the true runner's nature to run toward the storm. Perhaps the marathoner simply knows that the answers lie there. With head down and resolve in his or her heart, the runner keeps putting one foot in front of the other, into the storm.

As I ran toward Mile 16, I couldn't help but be consumed by fear. I was heading into, not away from, the hurricane that awaited me in the miles ahead. Knowing this, I could feel my mind shifting out of attack mode and into a state of reluctance—the kind I suffered when the alarm clock went off in the dark to let me know it was time to do some miles. Or the urge to plop down on the couch after work instead of changing immediately into shorts, T-shirt, and sneakers.

I was amazed by how this mind-set allowed me to validate the most absurd excuses on why I shouldn't run. Sometimes it was too hot; other times, too cold. Sometimes I needed quality time with my son; other times, I needed private time at the house. Or I needed to rest my weary legs, or save my fresh legs, or let my blisters die down, or avoid new blisters. Too early, too late, too wet, too dry, too many carbohydrates, too few, full moon, half moon, can't run on days that end with the letter *y*—you name it, I used it. Whatever the excuse, it was all too easy to persuade myself to grab the clicker and a spot on the couch instead of my Walkman and sneakers.

As I approached the end of Mile 15, I continued to put one foot in front of the other in a twisted suicide mission, directly into the eye of the Boston Marathon. How could I not? The answers lay ahead. Somewhere in the coming miles, fulfillment awaited. How could I pass up the opportunity to search the undiscovered depths of my soul? Six months ago, I had flat-lined. There had to be a reason why I felt driven to run Boston. I needed to go forward to find it. So, I ran.

Still, I was desperate for someone to pull me forward. I needed outside support to validate this bout of insanity. With just a half-mile left in the town of Wellesley I still hadn't found Jimmy. I longed to see a familiar face, so I kept looking.

Black Diamond

Professor Morrie Schwartz once asked rhetorically "If you only had twenty-four hours to live—what would you do?" I would hope that living life to the fullest, participating in life-changing events, and enjoying the company of family and friends would all be part of my final twenty-four hours.

In an effort to celebrate life and wring every drop out of my existence, I decided to say yes to friends Janet Hill and Kevin Marquis when asked if I would like to parachute. Like running Boston, jumping out of a plane was on my bucket list. I must admit that both endeavors require more courage, or foolishness, than other bucket-list items like seeing Mount Rushmore or attending a college football game at Clemson University.

On the morning we jumped out of the sky, Janet, Kevin, and I were required to watch a video about the jump before we boarded the plane. The very beginning of the video caused all the spit in my mouth to go dry. When the instructor hit "play" on the VCR, the first three words uttered were, "You may die."

From that point forward, the experience switched from fun to survival. I will never forget that feeling of standing at the open door up in the plane and looking out into the abyss, wondering why I wrote that bucket list in the first place.

Fifteen thousand feet later, I landed on the ground and hugged my waiting wife. I had done it. Check it off; no need to do that again. Like Arthur Roth, who won Boston in 1916, said after the race, "I am strong, and I feel great, but I fear that this ends my running career. I have got what I have been after all my many years and I am ready to hang up my shoes."

I needed to get what I'd been after all my many years—purpose, fulfillment, a life of consequence. For years my buddy Steve Alperin and I have had many a conversation about just this; sometimes enhanced by beer drinking, they were nonetheless sincere reflections that pose important questions: How can we best appreciate life? How can we take time to smell the daisies and appreciate our relative good fortune?

As part of this conversation, I always refer to my bucket list, formatted as an Excel spreadsheet. The list is fifteen columns wide and is broken into two parts. On the left side I have lists of where I want to go, what I want to accomplish, restaurants to eat at, concerts to attend, people to meet. The other half of the list comprises things I have seen and accomplished, favorite restaurants, noteworthy pieces of art I've seen, favorite disco and Irish songs, and best pints of Guinness.

Running the Marathon was on the left side, and it was my intention to cut and paste it over on the right side.

The Niagara River is a thirty-five-mile tributary that feeds water from Lake Erie into Lake Ontario. As the water flows from the source, it moves at a speed of one to two feet per second. When the current reaches the crest of the American Falls, the controlled streaming gives way to an awesome cascade of water that spills over the ledge at speeds of sixty-eight miles per hour, pouring more than six million cubic feet of water into the bottom basin every minute.

At the top of Mile 16, the runners travel the first third of the mile at an even pace, on a level course. It is here, like the movement of the Niagara River, where runners flow inevitably toward the coming falls. Running past the residential neighborhood, the athletes move forward in a state of either fear or denial. Either way, there is no turning back. The runner moves as if in a barrel, ready to go over the falls. From the crest of the mile to Newton Lower Falls below, the runner plunges one hundred feet, or 30 percent farther than the waters do at the American Falls at Niagara.

Runners can quickly assess their status in the early steps of this brief flat. While the first three-tenths of Mile 16 are almost as flat as a giant diving board, the last seventh-tenths are like a black diamond slope, reminding you that if you thought you were in the driver's seat, you're not; the course is in charge.

Runner Wolfgang Ketterle evaluates his condition at the beginning of the mile, switching from the physical to the cerebral. Ketterle, who has run multiple sub-three-hour marathons, uses the downhill to shift gears and extend his stride. If his body cooperates, he knows that he is positioned for a successful run. A professor of physics at Massachusetts Institute of Technology, and the winner of the 2001 Nobel Prize for Physics for his work related to ultracold atoms, Ketterle runs this section fast. When he submits to surges, it is not against other competitors, but instead to provide himself with data so he can be best informed on how to approach the rest of the race. If his body allows him to stretch out and open up the throttle, he knows he can cross the finish line in stride, leaving nothing on the course but his footprints.

Over the edge the runner goes. A third of the way into the mile, the runner falls like a character in a nightmare. Tumbling for over half a mile, each step will obligate the runner to place his or her foot on the accelerator and the brake at the same time.

Bureaucrats that oversee the running world have always looked at the downhills of the Boston Marathon as too easy. Thus, World and American records are not accepted when run on the Boston course. My guess is that these bureaucrats never ran Boston. Like anything, you must consider the context of the matter when making a determination.

Some running experts feel that the shifting muscle usage necessary to run straight downhill and then be confronted with four uphills makes this next five miles the most difficult stretch in the world, never mind the fact that it comes after already running sixteen miles.

Coach Bill Squires thinks that the downhill running is what makes Boston so trying. "Any really high-caliber athlete will tell you, the hardest thing is to brake. You know it in a car, but Boston would be better if it was flat. The downhills make you overrun. That's the reason why the eight Olympic champions have never won in Boston. They'd run the course like it was flat."

Grete Waitz, who won the New York City Marathon nine times between 1978 and 1988, pointed to the downhills in Boston as the most challenging aspect of the course. Struggling after the quad-crushing descents, she dropped out of the 1987 Boston Marathon with the lead, just a few miles away from the winner's circle. The experience gave her great respect for the course in Boston. "I never train downhill," she said. "No one I know trains downhill—we only train uphill. It can be hard to run downhill. Next year, I'll be ready." She never came back.

Dick Beardsley's opinion differs from track "experts," as well. In his mind, "What makes Boston difficult is the downhills. Your quads are basically shot and, all of a sudden, at 17 miles, for the next 3 1/2 miles, you've got basically continuous uphills. Then you've got that dive bomb off a hill coming off Heartbreak. It's got lots of extremes on it. Downhills and uphills."

The downhill at the end of Wellesley has always been a critical part of the race. Some runners who excel at downhilling will choose to push in this mile, and try to disrupt the tactical approach of their opponents. Four-time winner Bill Rodgers was a great downhill runner. In 1979, it was said that "[n]o runner alive can match Bill Rodgers running downhill. While other runners fight hills, supplying subconscious brakes to their legs. Rodgers flows down them."

Clarence DeMar ran the downhill in Newton with "chin up and chest out." Uta Pippig practically "fell" down the hill by relaxing every muscle and letting gravity do its work.

For me, it was more difficult. I'm a plodder who slams my feet down with each step. This only served to exasperate the braking muscles you need to run downhill.

At the end of the mile, you end up almost at sea level in Newton Lower Falls. That means from Hopkinton to Boston, you have now descended almost *five hundred* feet in your run, which is the height of many skyscrapers. For many this provides yet another opportunity to assess your condition. Two-time winner Tarzan Brown did just that in 1942, and decided it just wasn't his day. So instead of climbing the looming hill at the end of the mile, he walked off the course, dove into the Charles River, and went home.

As for me, I wasn't looking forward to the prospect of climbing after I'd just finished descending. The injury to the outside of my left knee was severely tested on the downhills. My inability to roll the knee normally made the 100-foot drop a painful undertaking. I had to extend my left leg straight out, like a peg leg, while my right leg did the rolling. By this point in the race, I had stopped checking my splits at the mile marks. Time was no longer a factor. From here on out, it was just a matter of survival.

When I reached the valley at Newton Lower Falls, I spotted a young girl with oranges on the right side of the course. I was once again desperate for some nourishment (even with the threat of the negative impact of the acid on my stomach), but I didn't want to waste the steps it would take to reach the side of the road. So, I yelled to her to throw an orange. She misjudged the distance and the orange sailed behind me. In dire need of something, anything, I threw my left hand behind me and made a behind-the-back catch that would have impressed my high school baseball coach.

I still had the four hills in Newton to run. I was starting to struggle. My wind was fine, but my legs were getting heavy, and my resolve, weak. I was starting to get desperate. This lonely run was getting to me. I needed to see Jimmy if I was going to be able to mount the hill that rose into the sky from down here at sea level.

The lead group in 1995 bids good-bye to Wellesley and enters Newton. PHOTO BY GEORGE MARTELL / *BOSTON HERALD*

Jon Anderson (left) and Tom Fleming (right) are escorted by the police and bikers during the 1973 Boston Marathon as they work their way up the overpass, which crosses over Route 128. PHOTO BY RICK LEVY

With white running gloves tucked neatly into my waistband, I approach the spot where my parents are standing. I had to figure out whether to keep running or to stop and assure myself of a ride home. PHOTO BY JOHN CONNELLY JR.

1972 Winner Olavvi Soum-
alainen takes the turn at the
Newton Fire Station onto Commonwealth Avenue.
PHOTO BY RICK LEVY

Women's wheelchair champion
Jean Driscoll moves toward her
seventh championship in the
1996 Boston Marathon.
PHOTO COURTESY OF FAYFOTO

In 1976 winner Jack Fultz
gets cooled down. The author's
grandmother, Catherine Connelly (in white dress), cheers
him on. PHOTO BY DICK RAPHAEL /
SPORTS ILLUSTRATED

With Heartbreak Hill in sight, and running gloves still in place, the author tries to put on a good face as he approaches his wife, son, and friends, waiting at the 20-mile mark. PHOTO COURTESY OF NOREEN CONNELLY

At the base of Heartbreak hill, the runners are inspired by the primal beats of an enthusiastic well-wisher in 1996.
PHOTO COURTESY OF FAYFOTO

A passionate spectator congratulates a runner after cresting Heartbreak Hill during the 100th running. PHOTO COURTESY OF FAYFOTO

John "The Younger" Kelley with the 1959 lead past St. Ignacius church, which stands on the Boston College Campus.
PHOTO COURTESY OF FAYFOTO

Running the greatest duel in the history of the Boston Marathon, Dick Beardsley (front) and Alberto Salazar battle each other, the crowd, a mounted policeman, and a number of police motorcycles in 1982.
PHOTO COURTESY OF ROBERT MAHONEY

Accompanied by the Green Line on their left, the 1996 leaders take another step toward the finish line in Boston.
PHOTO COURTESY OF VICTAH SAILER

Making their way down Beacon Street, friends Michael Radley and Rich Twombly move yet another step closer to the finish line. PHOTO COURTESY OF CAITLIN RADLEY

With the Citgo Fuel sign in the back ground, runners struggle up the last real topographical challenge of the race. PHOTO COURTESY OF FAYFOTO

Roberta Gibb runs through Kenmore Square during her landmark finish in 1966. PHOTO COURTESY OF THE BOSTON ATHLETIC ASSOCIATION

James Henigan, the 1931 winner, is surrounded by the entourage that always encircles the leader. PHOTO COURTESY OF *BOSTON HERALD*

Bill Rodgers runs up Hereford Street toward Boylston Street, and the 1975 championship. PHOTO COURTESY OF FAYFOTO

The crowd bends in an appropriate question mark to allow runners to turn from Hereford Street onto Boylston Street. PHOTO COURTESY OF FAYFOTO

Meb Keflezighi runs with the names of those who perished in the 2013 bombing on his bib. PHOTO COURTESY OF VICTAH SAILER

Champion John "The Elder" Kelley crosses the finish line in 1935. Note that officials never put the tape up and that Kelley dropped his aunt's handkerchief just yards before crossing the line. PHOTO COURTESY OF THE BOSTON PUBLIC LIBRARY PRINT DEPARTMENT

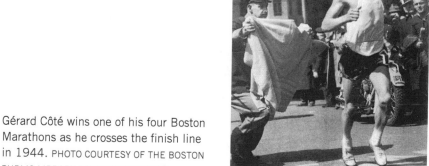

Gérard Côté wins one of his four Boston Marathons as he crosses the finish line in 1944. PHOTO COURTESY OF THE BOSTON PUBLIC LIBRARY PRINT DEPARTMENT

Uta Pippig breaks the tape with her third Boston Marathon championship in 1996. PHOTO COURTESY OF FAYFOTO

In an effort that exemplifies the battle of the Boston Marathon, a 1992 competitor refuses to be denied. PHOTO COURTESY OF JIM MAHONEY / *BOSTON HERALD*

Jessie Va Zant, Ollie Mannienen, Gérard Côté (winner), John "The Elder" Kelley, and Ted Vogel are more than happy to rest their sore and blistered feet following the 1948 race. PHOTO COURTESY OF THE BOSTON PUBLIC LIBRARY PRINT DEPARTMENT

Ellison "Tarzan" Brown proudly fashions his laurel wreath after winning the second of his two Boston Marathons in 1939. PHOTO COURTESY OF THE BOSTON PUBLIC LIBRARY PRINT DEPARTMENT

Work

You know those motivational speakers who profess that if you do something for work that you love, you'll never work a day in your life? Well, that's the type of bullshit line that makes you wish you'd skipped the speech and gone to the bar with the others in your group.

The chances of doing something you love for your occupation is the type of thing said by people with trust funds. The reality is that most people have no choice but to show up every day at a place of business they would prefer not to be at. You get up every morning, cut yourself shaving, throw on a wrinkled shirt, jump in the car with the gas tank on empty, and try to survive the commute to work. When you finally get to your place of employment, you've already put in a full day of stress.

Then you sit at your desk configuring how many months you have before you can take a distribution from your 401(k) and not have to pay a penalty to the IRS, who already have too much of your money. Eight and half hours later, you reverse your commute, wondering if brake lights are God's way of telling you to pause and start doing something that celebrates life. But before you do that, you must navigate the afternoon commute by avoiding texting drivers, sleepy truck drivers, and idiots who switch lanes because they want to test them all out.

Mile 17 is a seemingly never-ending upward slope with a bridge in the middle that takes the runners over the highway known as Route 128. For three decades, I have driven 128 to my ever-changing places of work. I have worked in banking ever since my father put a note on the kitchen table the day after Labor Day, 1986, which read, "Get a job!" In retrospect, I'm not sure what motivated me more—the message, or the anger in the dark underline, an effect that would make the most secure of handwriting experts shiver.

I landed a job in a field that dealt with math and numbers and decimal points, disciplines covered in my classes at Bentley College that I felt could wait for another day. And now I was paying my mortgage with those skills.

Over my three-plus decades in the industry, I have been challenged, and have challenged. I worked for a woman who had a coffee cup on her desk that read, "I have PMS—what's your problem?" I've been part of three layoffs, two mergers, and two bank failures, one of which included missing millions, an extended connection to Irish mobsters, screeching vans, government regulators with Uzis, indicted executives, and crying employees. I matriculated to another bank where I thrived, earning praise from the bank's board in the form of a plaque that read: "For extraordinary achievement, dedication, commitment, and leadership." Just months later my gutless boss couldn't summon the courage to stand up to a manic, manipulative chairman. Feeling unwanted, my team and I picked up and went to another bank that appreciated us. Before my first day there, my mother said to me, "Now, Michael, forget about that old place and look forward." I laughed and said back to her, "Mom, I'm five-foot-eight and Irish; I forget everything—except my grudges."

This is exactly why I ran Boston. It wasn't to prove that I could run twenty-six-plus miles. It was to prove to myself that I could run up any hill, around any pothole, through any weather. Running Boston was an exercise that I knew would help me as a father, husband, and banker.

I get it—work is a necessary evil. It makes the world go around.

After winning in 1933, Leslie Pawson's post-race comments captured the desperation of feeling like his job and feeding his family was more important than running. "I hope sometime to run in the Olympic Marathon for the United States, but if running interferes with my work or my education, why, I just will stop running." Pawson knew that running and working existed on different planes of Maslow's ladder.

But I realized that working five days a week for fifty weeks a year, for forty-plus years of your life, is the type of lifestyle that keeps actuaries rounding down on life expectancies. I didn't want my timeline to be determined by some accountant with a pocket protector. I was running Boston because I needed to accomplish things, see things, do things! There is more to life than work. As basketball coach John Wooden said, "Don't mistake activity with achievement."

On this day, I was not taking the ramp onto Route 128 North to my job. On this Monday in April of 1996, I took a vacation day, with the hope that I could change my life forever.

Other than the elite runners, most of the competitors who run Boston have full-time jobs. This means that to be able to stand on the line in Hopkinton, they have to learn how to juggle. Not three balls, but life. They have to find a way to keep earning a living while they train. Some bosses understand, and then there are those who just don't get it. That means long days, sneaking in a PowerBar at lunch and putting miles on your legs.

In the first half of the century, most of the runners were laborers without benefits. If they took off a day to run the race, they didn't get paid. William Kennedy won Boston in 1917 and was laying brick the next day in the Fenway area of Boston. Leading up to the race, he had trained at two in the morning while delivering papers, before going off to seek work in his trade.

Clarence DeMar was famous for showing up at work the night of his championship. He made $41 a week in 1924 as a printer. That was better than Doroteo Flores, who was making $7.50 a week in a textile mill in Colombia in 1952, when he won Boston.

In 1995, the *Boston Globe* provided statistics profiling that year's competitors. The analytics stratified size, age, gender, place of residence, and occupation. By far the most common profession of the runners was teaching. That year, 7.2 percent of the runners were leaders of classrooms. Over the history of the race, several teachers have stood on the winner's podium, including Clarence DeMar, John "The Younger" Kelley, Bill Rodgers, Amby Burfoot, Patrick McMahon, and Yoshiaki Unetani, as well as Greta Waitz (New York winner) and professor/author Erich Segal, who called running the Boston Marathon "an affirmation of life."

One other teacher who ran the race was Nicholas Franks, in 2014. Franks was the teacher of the smiling boy named Martin Richards who was killed by terrorists at the finish line in 2013. He was running to reclaim the race for Boston and to honor his student, saying, "This is my race."

Two-tenths into the mile, just past Gregorian Rugs, the five lanes become four, divided by cement islands. A sign on the right welcomes runners to Newton, the Garden City. Many Newton residents claim that the race should be called the Newton Marathon. By their calculations, Newton hosts a larger portion of the race (six miles) than any of the other seven towns. Within those six miles lie a hospital, two colleges, two country clubs, a town hall, and four hills. Arguably, more races have been won and lost in Newton than in any other town along the route.

One of the four hills stood in front of me. I looked up the hill, figuratively shook my head, and then got down to business by continuing to put my feet on the pavement. As I resolved to push forward, I heard the friendly voice of Jimmy Delaney running toward me from the side of the road, holding a green bottle of beer, a glow on his face. Finally, I'd met up with my college friend!

Jimmy and I have a special connection. We were both born on February 10. He has the warmest heart anyone could ever hope to find in a friend. Back when I fell unconscious during a game at Bentley College, it was his shoulder I passed out on in the ultimate "lean on me" moment. More than a decade later, here I was, leaning on him for support once again.

When Jimmy caught up to me, he was fired up. He asked me how I was doing as he ran with me for a hundred yards or so.

"I feel like shit," I replied, "but I'll do it!"

As he turned off, he yelled, "You're the man! Go get 'em!"

And with that, he was gone. He'd come at the perfect time. For one brief moment, I was reminded of all the good things in my life: friendship, good people, community. I ran up the hill over the highway thinking of the shepherd boy in Coelho's *The Alchemist*, whose quest for his destiny is aided by others, the way Jimmy just helped me to continue putting one foot in front of the other. "When a person really desires something, all the universe conspires to help that person realize his dreams."

Although I was psyched to see him, I was equally disappointed when we parted company. The pain and misery I was experiencing was made more difficult by the solitude of marathoning. It was a lonely pain. The struggle of a marathon is personal. Throughout the run, I wondered if the thousands of other competitors were feeling similar discomfort, or if for some reason, the course held a grudge against me and was saving its best shots for my run. Nevertheless, Jimmy had pumped me up enough. His encouragement was enough to get me over the hill to where my parents would be waiting.

In my estimation, this rise over the highway is the most demanding incline on the entire course. Like climbers on Mount Everest, who must ascend to base camp before attacking the peak itself, the runners must climb for almost three-quarters of a mile over the highway before being in a position to scale the hills up ahead. Heartbreak Hill gets a lot of attention later in the race. Fans and reporters hang out there, looking for people to cheer on, or to sadistically watch as some runners fade. Adding to the degree of difficulty is that there is no protection from the elements while on the bridge. Crosswinds can be fierce, and the sun on a hot day, draining.

At the end of the mile, the course flattens out and makes you wonder why people don't talk about the hill they call "Hell's Alley." According to the race administrators, this section of the course convinces more runners to raise the white flag than any other spot on the course. Runner Mark Coogan would say of this section, "Everyone goes into the Marathon with big dreams; [Hell's Alley is] the first place where your dream starts to get crushed."

It was while running into the fires of Hell's Alley, in 2013, that Olympic gold medalist swimmer and sports broadcaster Summer Sanders thought her dream of running Boston was going to be crushed. Summer Sanders came to Boston to fulfill a goal, to check an item off her bucket list, and to celebrate her fortieth year of life. Over the past mile Sanders had started to tire. Fortunately, she had coordinated with her mother prior to the race to meet her on the right side of the road in Newton.

As far back as Summer could remember, she and her mother Barbara had been one. Barbara was born with a competitive gene, but, as a girl, had never had an outlet in which to express it. In San Francisco, Barbara took up open-water swimming under the Golden Gate Bridge, without a wet suit—a dangerous activity that required her to swim fast. Barbara would pass on this strong will to her daughter, who would begin swimming at age three. Summer's journey culminated at the 1992 Summer Olympics in Barcelona, where she won two gold medals, a silver, and a bronze.

Now Summer needed her mother again. Scanning spectator after spectator, she started to panic that her mom wasn't there, or that she'd somehow missed her. Despite competing at the highest level of sports, at this point Summer was just another vulnerable runner in need of reassurance—a friendly face. As Summer struggled forward, her need to see her mother was satisfied. The very sight of her mother on the side of the road brought back all those memories of support and encouragement she'd provided at swim meets. Always there for her daughter, Barbara held up a green sign with the very words she'd uttered to her daughter before every swim meet: "Suck Their Eyes Out!"

Summer, overcome, stopped to hug and kiss her mom. Her mother's support reminded her that she could do it—that she could always do it. Both crying, they finally let go and parted ways. Although running a marathon is a particularly solitary pursuit, it often takes a whole family to make it possible. Spouses, children, and parents must sacrifice on behalf of the runner.

After reaching the crest of the hill, a fifty-five-foot rise in elevation over a half-plus mile, the runners work their way up to a cement island at a set of traffic lights. The road bends left and falls slightly downhill. Just after the intersection on the right is Newton-Wellesley Hospital. At the top of the seven-tenths-of-a-mile rise in the course, the route slightly drops as it moves past the hospital, which sits on the right side of the course. On hot Marathon Days, the hospital will be busy dealing with dehydrated runners and those suffering from sunstroke. It's such a chaotic day in the emergency room that the hospital elects to choose this day as crisis rehearsal for medical staff.

This hospital has profound meaning for me. This is where my son, Ryan, was born, giving my life eternal purpose and happiness. He was the first child of the next generation of Connellys.

As I ran up the hill over Route 128 (the image of the condensation dripping down Jimmy's beer bottle still fresh in my mind), I started to get excited about the prospect of seeing my parents a half-mile ahead. Here again, I felt a profound vulnerability that I never would have imagined I'd feel during a road race. The thought of briefly reuniting with my mother and father provoked powerful emotions within me. I felt childish for getting so sentimental, but the race is like a marine drill sergeant at boot camp at Parris Island. The roads and hills of Boston break you down to your core. The course's sole purpose is to test you to determine if you are worthy to be part of the fraternity/sorority of those who have run Boston. If you survive boot camp, then you can survive anything.

So, I ran with tears in my eyes, thinking of all the sacrifices my parents had made and the countless gifts they had bestowed upon me. Over thirty-some years they had firmly steered me through my childhood, tolerated me through the teenage years, and subtly guided me in my adult years, when I was too old to have my parents tell me what to do.

Six months earlier my father had sat in the hospital hallway with my wife and prayed for my recovery, just as my mom relied on the power of prayer to find solace and strength. Half a year after my heart had decided it preferred to restart rather than call it quits, I had been granted the wonderful gift of sharing yet another significant moment of my life with them. I was overcome by emotion, knowing that my new lease on life would be celebrated with the two people who had given me life to begin with.

Mom and Dad

Back on February 9, 1964, the Beatles appeared on *The Ed Sullivan Show*. More than 60 percent of all American TV rooms had the mop-headed four on their television sets that night. The band played five songs over the sound of girls hysterically screaming, the likes of which had only been heard before at Wellesley College on Marathon Day. They played the songs "All My Loving" and "She Loves You" and three other chart-topping hits.

In all, 73 million Americans stayed home to watch the Beatles that Sunday night, including every nurse from the maternity ward at St. Margaret's Hospital in Dorchester. My parents were waiting for my arrival that night. Now, thirty-two years later, they were once again waiting for their second son.

For miles I had been looking forward to seeing them. No matter how old you get, no matter how much you think you have all the answers—your parents are your anchor. They make you feel safe and let you believe that you are capable of anything. They provide you with the foundation on which you can build your whole life. Here, in my fourth decade, I was still desperate to see them.

My father was a two-sport athlete at Boston College, a marine, and later a chief probation officer before retirement. He is a loving amalgamation of Fred Flintstone, Ralph Kramden, and Archie Bunker. He taught his sons both to be polite and to get the first punch off; he taught us how to compete in the world. I can remember sitting in the TV room with him and my two brothers, watching a documentary on the Olympics. During the film, they showed a quote that appeared on the scoreboard at the Games: "It's not whether you win or lose—it's the way you play the game." My father, without taking his eyes off the television, commented on the quote in a fashion that would make Summer Sanders's mother nod in agreement: "Whoever said that never wore a jock strap in his life."

Now, mind you, he understood that everyone has limitations. Ultimately, he suggested that we focus on competing against ourselves. He told us there will always be someone faster, richer, stronger. He wanted us to be *our* fastest, and strongest. Similar to John "The Younger" Kelly, who won Boston in 1957 with the same philosophy, saying, "I run against myself. I am the only one I must control and guide. I must run correctly without giving too much regard to what others are doing."

My father married his high school sweetheart, Marilyn Kenny. Mal grew up in the same town as John "The Younger" Kelley in Arlington, Massachusetts. She might remind some of Laura Petrie (Mary Tyler Moore)—selfless, thoughtful, intelligent. She was old school, and new school. She minded the house and had a career. She helped us with our homework and got her master's at the same time. She wasn't June Cleaver. She had opinions and vacuumed (and assigned chores). But ultimately her primary focus was on raising her children. She used to get up thirty minutes early each morning to turn on the heat in the house and sit down for a cup of tea before six children came running down the stairs, looking for breakfast.

As the middle boy in a family of six, I knew that our middle-class resources would never provide for abundance. Yet we never lacked for food, or clothes, or hockey skates. My parents played a week-to-week shell game with their bank account, fending off the oil company to pay doctors—or convincing St. Theresa School to wait a week while they found a way to get the station wagon fixed. They always found a way. They were problem solvers who didn't always have the answers, but somehow always found a solution.

Cliché alert: While we weren't rich in material things, we had everything else. We had parents who cared and were always there, no matter if it was a cold hockey rink, a bad school play, or even a marathon where their son ran with great sincerity but not with the most expeditious gait. They were loving parents who provided the six Connelly children great advantages in life.

As I came upon where they were standing, I smiled the same smile I always smiled when I would see them at a game or when they pulled down the street to pick me up after practice. My parents returned the smile, and then my father stepped out on the course to take my picture, just as he had at First Communions, graduations, or important at-bats.

My parents were standing across the street from the Woodland Country Club, which for over a century has hosted golf tournaments and public celebrities like Babe Ruth, Groucho Marx, Bing Crosby, and Bobby Jones—all secondary to my parents, who celebrated their wedding reception at the club back in 1959.

Over the history of the race, parents have trained, inspired, and sometimes accompanied their children on their journey toward running Boston.

In 1906, little-known runner Tim Ford from Cambridge broke the tape, to the surprise of many. The *Boston Herald* described the scene at the finish line: "But when the indomitable Cambridge boy parted the tape, he had a full dozen yards to his credit. Bedlam broke loose. Thunderous were the plaudits and the tooting of automobiles. A giant policeman reached out to catch Ford, but before he had time to, an elderly man, who had been wildly twirling his hat, had the limp runner in his arms. His blue eyes closed for an instant, then opening again, he smiled feebly into the face of his father."

Ford's father looked at his son lovingly and said, "I'm proud of you." His son stood up and smiled as his father continued: "You've got the stuff in you and you have today well shown. Hurry home to your mother with the silver trophy, lad."

Tarzan Brown ran at the prodding of his mother, who beseeched him to "Run, my boy, and finish." His mother would die soon after the race. Brown won Boston wearing a shirt made from her wedding dress.

In 1917, William Kennedy ran one of the greatest races in the history of the Boston Marathon. It was in the middle of World War I, and he ran to represent his country. After crossing the finish line, he immediately wanted to share the moment with his father, so he sent a telegram to New York that read, "I won."

When twenty-year-old Johnny Miles won his first championship in 1926, the papers would say, "All he thought of was his dad. He thinks his dad is the greatest gent in the world." Miles would later say, with great affection, "All my success I owed to my father, who trained me."

As I came up to where my parents were positioned, it was a special but fleeting moment. While I ran past, I smiled and stood tall in hopes of disguising my discomfort: I was afraid that they would see through my ruse and demand that I end this foolishness. Fortunately, they understood the meaning of this endeavor. They knew I had to prove something on this day. My father gave me a thumbs-up, my mother waved, and once again, I was all alone.

As I looked back over my shoulder, I could see my mother had a concerned yet reassuring look upon her face, as if she was sending me off for my first day of school. My father put his thumb up again as if to say, "We're with you, and we're proud."

I continued down the road and started to get emotional. It was one of several times that I would break into tears on the course. Damn—they had done so much for me over the years. Sacrificed so much. Loved so much. I was so lucky, and I knew it. I wished I'd told them this more often when I was younger, when I thought I knew everything.

In 1923, George and Edgar McAlpine from the Dorchester neighborhood of Boston became the first father and son to run together in the same Boston Marathon.

On this day, I felt my father running with me every step. Tears running down my cheeks, I suddenly became conscious of a strange thought: If I wasn't going to finish this thing, I'd just lost out on a ride home. Oh, well . . . On I ran.

For the last half-mile, runners have had flat and relatively straight running, until you reach the 17.7-mile mark. These steps offer limited resistance and arrive at the ideal time for runners, who have been negatively affected by the schizophrenic topography of the course. For a half-mile, runners can recuperate and search for something beyond their second wind. After that, though, the hills await, as the *Boston Globe* warned back in 1909: "The long, hard, smooth hills in the distance have proved to be the undoing of many ambitious lads."

The course now leaves Route 16 and turns right onto Commonwealth Avenue. It's the first of five 90-degree turns on the course. There will be four more in the remaining miles. This one bends around the Newton Fire Department. Like staff at Newton-Wellesley Hospital, firefighters can be busy on hot days.

Bob Bright of the Chicago Marathon commented on the turn onto Commonwealth. "Boston traps you. You get sucked into it. Then that firehouse jumps out and trips you."

As you make your way onto Commonwealth Avenue, the first hill is right in front of you. It's like you took the wrong turn in a horror movie. DeMar said this hill was responsible for spoiling the hopes of many leaders in the race: "It was on this hill that many a likely winner had met his Waterloo."

It is amid these three hills that the back-of-the-pack runner begins to understand: The Boston Marathon course was designed with the world's greatest runners in mind, not ten-minute-milers with an item to cross off their bucket lists. In the running world, this stretch of the course is holy land, and should be approached with the reverence and care that this moniker implies.

Bill Rodgers has run all over the world, and sees the hills of Commonwealth Avenue as not merely unique; to him, this part of the course represents the apex of running. "This is the most significant stretch of course in the road-racing world," he argues. "The Fukuoka route [in Japan] has its spots, and other races have nice scenery, but there is no section that identifies the challenge and beauty of marathoning more than this section of the Boston Marathon."

The three hills after the turn at the Newton Fire Department are like the Giza pyramids of running. They stand on the horizon, tall and majestic, demanding a mix of respect, fear, and even wonder. The hills have been described in newspaper accounts over the past century in a variety of ways: teasing, topographically terrorizing, wicked, tortuous. The weak-minded runner advances upon this stretch with shaken knees and tentative strides; champions scale this three-headed monster like a warrior, as Tom Longboat did on his way to his 1907 championship run, despite the mockery of pre-race newspaper accounts that predicted he would go down in the hills of Newton.

John "The Younger" Kelley used the first, called "Carbuncle Hill," as his moment to strike in 1957, hitting it hard and putting a surge on the front pack, all the way to victory. Each individual competitor has to decide whether to attack on the hills or to conserve his or her energy. Wheelchair champion Jean Driscoll—with those "beautiful" strong arms, admired by President Bill Clinton—looks to the hills as an opportunity to knock out her competitors, pushing them past the point of no return.

Michael Spring used the exact opposite approach back in 1904. During his run, the lead runner had determined that the best use of his energies was on the flats and downhills, and thus he walked up any hills on the course. It's amazing to think that in 1904, the champion used walking on the course as a strategy, compared to 2011 champion Geoffrey Mutai, of Kenya, who *sprinted* over the entire course, averaging 4:42 miles for the entire race. Desiree Linden, 2018 champion, suggests that "You get your eyes up and attack what's in front of you."

My approach was the exact opposite. I kept my eyes directed downward, in front of my feet. I didn't want to be discouraged and see that my attack on the hills was more like the movie *Vertigo*. The more I ran, the farther away the peak seemed to float, like a kid's lost balloon. I used this same tactic whenever

I ran on a treadmill. I always covered the time and distance screens with a towel. Inevitably I felt I had gone much farther than I actually did.

Race director and annual runner of the race Dave McGillivray would say about the turn at the firehouse, "If you're worn out when you arrive, you'll be doing the 'survivor's shuffle' down Beacon Street—not fun."

When I got to the firehouse, I was already starting the shuffle. That meant Beacon Street was going to be a struggle. I was still pessimistic about the outcome, but I felt good enough to put my blinker on and take the right turn.

My months of mental conditioning were being severely tested, and so was my physical effort, a compromised knee that caused me to teeter on the cusp of failure. But my heart held strong, and I kept reminding myself of one common sentiment: "No one cares how far you ran or how long if it isn't 26.2 miles."

So never mind the bullshit, and keep running.

MILE 19

Nana Connelly

After discovering that Rad and Richie shared my dream to run Boston, I wondered how many others were curious about the annual April run from Hopkinton. I decided to start taking some notes related to training and, ultimately, about our Patriots' Day run. Soon my notes turned into an outline, which then developed into a manuscript. This idea—that "regular guys" like the three of us could turn from spectators to speculators—meant there were probably other fans of the race bewitched by the prospect of attempting the improbable.

During my research I discovered this was a valid assumption. Since the very first running of the Boston Marathon, race fans were naturally inclined to wonder if they too were capable of great things. In the 1897 *Herald*, following the first-ever running of the race, the writer spoke to this very supposition. "To see him [John McDermott] doing it would arouse notions in almost any robust soul that he, too, could go and do likewise."

Being a novice in the writing world, I just assumed that everyone shared my opinion. But that wasn't the case. Every day I sent out query letters to publishers, wondering if they would invest their resources in my premise. And every day I would come home from work and find a rejection notice in my mailbox. It didn't take long for my cheery outlook to mutate into one of utter frustration.

That was until one day, at a bookstore perusing the pages of a book about running, when I came across a photo of 1976 winner Jack Fultz running through Newton. And there, in the background, was Nana Connelly. I couldn't believe it! What are the odds that I'd pick up that book, turn to that very page, and see my beloved grandmother?

Nana Connelly had died ten years earlier and was dearly missed by all of us. Sunday dinner wasn't the same without her walking through the door five minutes late with a dessert in hand and a smile on her face. Nana was a special person for all of the Connelly kids. She was fun, and showed us how to laugh. And not just laugh in general, but also that it was all right to laugh at yourself—to not take yourself so seriously.

Nana hosted Thanksgiving and Easter. On Easter she would hang plastic eggs filled with coins from the shrubs outside for us grandkids. On Turkey Day, she would dress up like a Pilgrim. She loved the Red Sox and *The Lawrence Welk Show*. She drove a gold 1967 Mustang convertible; it wasn't unusual to see her pulled over by police for speeding, or for scooting through a yellowish-red light. Usually she would be sent on her way with a warning after lecturing the policeman about Mayor Kevin White's free spending of tax money.

Because Nana was so special to me, running in Mile 19 was emotional. It was in Newton on Commonwealth Avenue that we would stand with Nana and watch as she clapped or called out a name on a T-shirt for each runner. As I ran by where we always stood as a family, the race again shifted from legs to heart.

It was Nana Connelly who used to bring my two brothers and three sisters and me to watch the Marathon. Every Patriots' Day, Nana would squeeze the six of us into her convertible and treat us to a special day in the way only a grandparent could. We loved to take in the sights and sounds, and Nana loved watching her grandchildren as we stared in wonderment, adopting this special day as our own. Nana died in 1984, having fulfilled her responsibility as a Bostonian, passing the Boston Marathon tradition on from one generation to the next.

Of the five miles in this stretch of Commonwealth Avenue, this might be the easiest stretch of the leg. The mile starts at the top of "hill one" and then levels off and actually provides some easy descents, to let you flex your tiring legs. The course takes you past seven-figure Georgian homes. In the old days, affluent Bostonians used to take their vacation out west at Newton's parks and waterways. Some would take the streetcar, while others would drive their Stanley Steamer automobiles. One of the inventors of that model was Francis Stanley, who ironically died in his invention in 1918. Stanley is buried in the Newton Cemetery, situated on the right side of Mile 19. Also buried there is Red Sox great Dom DiMaggio; two Medal of Honor winners, Robert Hanson and Squire Howard; four congressmen; and Morrie Schwartz, featured in one of my favorite books, *Tuesdays with Morrie*.

As the course continues down toward Newton Town Hall, the road snakes back and forth as if built so drivers could have fun with their Stanley Steamers. As I ran, my mind continued to draw upon warm memories of my grandmother. I know she was with me this day. If she'd actually been on the sidewalk while I was running by, she would have broken into her big smile and definitely would have yelled out her favorite phrase from the 1940s, to express enthusiasm and approval: "Hubba, hubba!"

I never imagined when I'd decided to run this race that it would turn out to be such a poignant journey. It was drawing on every part of my being; my past, present, and future were all part of this run. The heart that I'd just gotten fixed six months earlier was now being tested, both physically and emotionally. Johnny "The Elder" Kelley ran Boston for the sixty-first time, at the age of eighty-four. He didn't consider himself old; he just saw himself as a runner.

Runners need to run. It's part of their DNA. They are like Sequoia trees that keep reaching for the sky despite the number of rings circling their trunk's marrow.

In the book *Born to Run*, author Christopher McDougall wrote of a man nearing the age of one hundred who was defying what the "experts" defined as protocol for a person of his age. In the book he insinuated that old people act old because that's what is expected of them. But not this man. "And if I really wanted to understand the Raramuri [tribe], I should have been there when this ninety-five-year-old man came hiking twenty-five miles over the mountain. Know why he could do it? Because no one ever told him he couldn't. No one ever told him he ought to be off dying somewhere in an old age home. You live up to your own expectations."

When Clarence DeMar won Boston at age thirty-three, in 1922, the papers called it the "greatest accomplishment in sports history." In the following day's accounts, they would say of his run, and his age, "As first-class long-distance runners are rated, he is an old man, and yet he has accomplished something that never has been done—he came back from oblivion."

In 1910, fifty-two-year-old Pete Foley of Winchester showed up at the starting line and was denied a number because of his "old" age, until he demanded that he be allowed to run. According to the *Boston Herald*, "It was decided that Foley should not be permitted to compete, but the old fellow pleaded so hard that the physicians yielded, for his examination was excellent." Foley would go on to finish the race, beating many runners less than half his age. Foley would run the race until he was eighty-five years old—without a doctor's blessing.

As the decades wore on, medical evidence altered perceptions of exercise and the "elderly." In 2018, over 9 percent of the runners at Boston were over the age of sixty, and seventy-four runners ran in the seventy-five- to eighty-year-old age group.

In 2019, seventy-one-year-old Gene Dykes ran Boston in a time of 2:58:50. Back in 1897, John McDermott won Boston's twenty-five-mile course in a time of 2:55:10. Meaning, if Dykes had participated in the first-ever Boston Marathon, he would have competed for the championship.

In an article in the 1917 *Boston Journal*, writer Bob Dunbar wondered, after seeing Foley run Boston, "Is marathoning running an old man's game? It is certainly a game in which mature strength and the knowledge born of experience proves mighty serviceable. They say there is no fool like an old fool."

In the Connelly house, all generations are valued. It was our ancestors whose pioneer spirit put us in a position to go to college, run marathons, and live fruitful lives.

In the book *Man's Search for Meaning*, Viktor Frankl would say of elders, "There is no reason to pity old people. Instead, young people should envy them." The author would write further, "Instead of possibilities in the future, they have realities in the past—the potentialities they have actualized, the meanings they have fulfilled, the values they have realized, and nothing and nobody can ever remove these assets from the past."

I interpreted seeing the picture of Nana in the bookstore that day as a sign. A message from her to keep plugging away. To be bold and keep pushing. So, I did. And eventually my first edition of this book was published in 1998. She would have loved this book, because she was a huge fan of the Boston Marathon. It was Nana Connelly who introduced me to the race that someday I would not only run, but would also write about, while fulfilling my responsibility of passing Boston heirlooms on to the next generation.

I aspire to have Nana Connelly's spirit. She saw the beauty in her grandchildren's eyes and delighted in the opportunities that waited for us down the road. She brought us to the Boston Marathon because there was joy there. Because that was where community was. That's where we would find people that were "Hubba hubba," and celebrated life!

The course for the next seven-tenths of the mile moves down and snakes left and right, with extended grass islands on the left. The first hill has been conquered, but there are still two more to go. The route levels off and then declines, as does the runner's pulse. The mile zigzags through a residential neighborhood and then continues past a set of traffic lights at the Chestnut Street intersection, and onward through to the right.

Three-time winner Ibrahim Hussein knew that to win Boston, he must win on the hills. To fail on Commonwealth Avenue would mean failure at the finish line. When asked about his strategy beforehand, he candidly answered, "I will sacrifice myself on the hills."

Across the street from the cemetery, a quarter-mile from the town hall, is Wauwinet Road, which marks the site of the old Wauwinet Dairy Farm. During the Great Depression, five hundred Jersey cows used to stop their grazing to cheer on Clarence DeMar as he ran past. At this point, runners know there can be no grazing; there are two more hills left to run, followed by what champion Rob de Castella would call the "second half" of the race.

MILE 20

Just Be There

When I was in college, my financial aid allowed for me to earn money from a work-study job. I signed up to be an apprentice carpenter. I didn't do much except carry tools or run for sandwiches for the guys. It was an interesting experience to work with these tradesmen. Some of them didn't have a high school degree, yet here they were, fixing problems that spoiled college kids couldn't figure out. Academically speaking, their résumés wouldn't impress anyone. But these guys were brimming over with common sense. It was amazing to watch them find solutions for every broken pipe or power outage. To this day, I marvel at the way they found a way to get things done.

One day I was working with George White, a husband and father, and the epitome of decency. While he was busy fixing something, our conversation slid to the topic of parenting and children. I expressed to him that I didn't want kids. He was surprised and asked why. My reasoning was sound. I said that I was a really good kid and wouldn't want to parent someone like me—let alone a kid who turned out to be an ass. He told me that I would change my mind when I got older. So, I asked him, "If I do happen to change my mind, what is the trick to being a good father?"

George gave me the best parenting advice I ever got. While I handed him pliers or snaked wires or something, he turned to me and said, matter-of-factly, "It's really pretty easy—*just be there.*" As simple as it sounds, in three words he summed up the foundation of parenting. Be engaged, participate in your kids' lives, support them, and let them know you're interested in their well-being.

So, years after graduating from college, I became the father of a baby boy my wife and I named Ryan. Ryan was everything to me. He gave my life so much meaning. He gave me purpose and filled my cynic's heart with joy. George White was right: Being a parent is a blessing. Ryan was truly a Godsend.

After Noreen's father died, I can remember waking up and remembering all over again that it wasn't a dream—he really had died. After Ryan was born, I would wake up each morning and be thankful all over again that I had this amazing young person in my life.

Every day was a gift. But no moment crystallized the joy of parenting more than one day when I met Noreen and Ryan for lunch. I was walking down the hallway and Ryan saw me coming toward them. He broke away from Noreen and ran to me, yelling, "Daddy!" He jumped up into my arms, and I can remember feeling an overwhelming sense of unadulterated happiness. I was the recipient of a miracle. Through God's grace, I had been blessed with someone who loved me unconditionally. It could only help me to have this kind of love in my heart.

This was one of the reasons I was running the marathon—to appreciate life. In the book *The Greatest Salesman in the World*, the author challenges the reader to take advantage of life. "I will live this day as if it is my last. I have but one life, and life is naught but a measurement of time. When I waste one, I destroy the other. If I waste today, I destroy the last page of my life."

After running through a mile in which my grandmother had distracted me from my slowing steps, now I was running Mile 20. If I could get through this mile, my three-year-old son, Ryan, would be waiting up ahead with Noreen. This wasn't Ryan's first Boston Marathon. He had already seen the race from my shoulder. He wasn't old enough yet to understand the effort the runners were putting forth, but I brought him anyway, to make sure I fulfilled my Bostonian obligation of introducing my son to the world's greatest race—and some ice cream.

When I was training for the Marathon, often I would break out the running stroller and take Ryan for a run. Sometimes we just ran some miles and came home, and sometimes we would run to the store for a treat, to thank him for being such a good training partner. During the runs we always listened to the Hootie & the Blowfish cassette, *Cracked Rear View*, especially the relevant song "Time."

The fact that Ryan got stuck doing training runs with me only served to deepen my resolve. Everyone was making sacrifices so I could run on this day. Although running Boston was mostly a self-serving endeavor, I still wanted to set an example for my son. Something real that I could point to and say, "You can do big things in life. It's okay to take risks and expose yourself to potential failure for the chance to realize something special."

The route now takes you down a knoll to the Newton City Hall, built during the Depression. The steeple on top of the hall has a large timepiece on its face, alerting runners to their tardiness. At this point, runners continue to assess their bodies and adjust their intended splits, rationalizing that the crowded start, headwinds, busy water stops, and weather are responsible for the slower-than-hoped-for times. They don't blame their splits on the sublime racecourse and its corners, climbing uphills, cascading downhills, uneven pavement, traffic islands, littered cups of drunk water, or deafening cries in the Scream Tunnel of Wellesley. But maybe to run Boston one needs this state of mind; the runner must believe what he or she needs to believe. It's kitchen-sink time—whatever it takes to move forward. If it's running in some state of denial, that might be the most rational approach, with two hills to go.

So, I ran Mile 20, home to the second hill on Commonwealth Avenue. After starting the mile in a descent, the runner crosses over the Walnut Street intersection. It is here that the John "The Elder" Kelley statue stands. The statue depicts young Kelley at age thirty-five, next to the eighty-year-old version of himself. The two images are running with raised hands, reminding everyone that age is only a barrier if you choose for it to be. Richie, Rad, Jack, and I used to stop here during training runs and leave our snacks and water at the base of the statue. When we ran the course after being dropped off up ahead, we would stop here for some replenishment and a source of motivation. It was almost like lighting a candle at the foot of a patron saint.

After passing the statue, it's roll-up-your-sleeves time, and time to fucking get after it. No other choice. It's time for the second hill. The rise is seven-tenths of a mile with seemingly no end to its gradual slope.

After Walnut Street, the runners are confronted with the most difficult of the three Commonwealth Avenue hills. In 1933, the second hill was described this way: "[T]he toughest climbing on the course [lay] ahead of them . . . the heart-wrenching hills of Newtonville and Newton Centre that kill the runners so."

This is where the racecourse morphs from Dr. David Banner into the Incredible Hulk. Many runners are quiet, well-mannered people who participate in the sport because their legs tell them to. But here at the twenty-mile mark, something changes them. This is when the memory of all they've sacrificed bubbles up and manifests itself into a fierce determination. This is where their legs and heart are tested to their natural limits.

Silver medalist John Treacy articulated the difference between the runners' demeanor before the race and at this crucial twenty-mile mark. "There is no animosity between the competitors at the starting line because we all understand the mortality of a marathon," he said. "There is no reason to get the competitive juices flowing at that point. The twenty-mile mark is where you evaluate and assess your competition."

If there is one mile that encapsulates the physical and mental challenges of the Boston Marathon, it is Mile 20. The cumulative toll of the previous miles makes the second hill, quite possibly, the most difficult of the three. The first hill gets attacked with great zest after the turn at the fire station. Running up Heartbreak Hill, the third hill, is the final battle in the war. Runners are so excited to run the iconic obstacle that adrenaline can take them over the summit. The second hill just plain hurts. This is why Jerry Nason named this hill "Withering Heights," as it "does all the work—Heartbreak [Hill] gets all the gravy."

At this point I was shocked to see how many runners were walking. The number was so great that at one point, a volunteer yelled out, "I only see one person running—let's go!" Luckily, I was that one person.

It is here on Commonwealth Avenue that the runner's story is told in the rising action, climbing toward the climax. The narrative is most profound in the arc, here in the belly of the race. Like any tale in literature that is filled with adventure, the real story isn't that the person arrived, but *how* he or she arrived.

It wasn't that *Apollo 13* splashed down in the South Pacific. It was that it traveled 200,000 miles *after the oxygen tanks exploded*. It wasn't just that Christ had died on the cross. It was also that he pulled himself up after his three falls, refusing to be denied his destiny.

It is on Commonwealth Avenue that each runner's story blooms. Whether the runner arrives in Boston or drops out somewhere along the way, it is usually because of what happened on these hills. Every year, reporters camping out at the hills of Newton, trying to chronicle what they witness here, craft lines such as, "The hills [are] the graveyard of many shattered dreams"; and "[the] topographical bludgeon which separates the men from the boys."

Halfway through the mile, the second hill ends. The now-level road serpentines back and forth until reaching the Centre Street intersection, where it straightens. At this point the residential neighborhood runs into a small commercial district.

As the end of the mile bends around, you can see the flags indicating the twenty-first mile. I was just steps away from seeing my son and my wife, so I made a conscious effort to perk up and put on my best face, and body language. I didn't want to scare Ryan the way Jimmy Henigan had unnerved his son back in 1931, when the local runner was hoping to finally win his first Boston. In past years, he had always competed in the front pack, only to agonizingly have to drop out seven straight times. In the '31 race, he was running in the lead when he passed his son in Kenmore Square. After he ran by, the Henigan son found a phone and called home, informing the family, "Pa's in front, but gosh, he's going awfully slow."

After leaving his son behind, Henigan had slowed to a walk. A fan became so concerned with the runner's appearance that he took it upon himself to shower him with cold water from a milk bottle. The press vehicle, which usually sped ahead of the runners to the finish line, decided to hover around the leader in hopes of capturing his inevitable collapse on film. This was not to be, however; Henigan would persevere on this day and break the tape, ruining the hopes of the photographers.

Gosh, I was going slowly like Henigan, but breaking the tape wasn't my goal—just finishing. And whether I finished or not, I'd already received my gifts from the race—one of the biggest, having time to reflect on my many blessings, especially my son, Ryan. During training runs leading up to Boston, I had constantly reminded myself to never take Ryan for granted. To this end, each year on his birthday, I play "Cat's in the Cradle," the tragic song by Harry Chapin about a father who misses out on the very best moments in his life—time with his son. I can never forget to act on George White's priceless advice, to "just be there." I knew if I could get to my wife and son, they would propel me forward and give me a chance of finishing.

With Heartbreak Hill just around the corner, runners tread water, hoping to stay afloat. Many will not make a conscious decision to continue but instead let the tide bring them forward.

MILE 21

Takes Two to Run

After Olympic gold medalist Frank Shorter suffered through the hills of Newton, he wondered, "Why couldn't Pheidippides have died at twenty miles?" But Pheidippides fought on, and so does the course of the Boston Marathon.

Mile 21 starts on some flats, with the infamous Heartbreak Hill standing proud in the foreground. After running twenty miles, this intimidating hill can make any runner hesitate and question his or her ability to move forward. This is the fourth hill in just under five miles. The accumulation of uphill running just keeps hitting you with body blows. Two-time winner Geoff Smith would say of this notorious ascent, "I've run up bigger hills, but by the time you hit it—it's a mountain."

During the race's infancy, *Boston Globe* writer Lawrence Sweeney described the hills in Newton as "heartbreaking hills." As the years went by, and the hills claimed more victims, race correspondent Jerry Nason built on Sweeney's description and formally christened the last and most treacherous of the three hills "Heartbreak Hill." "The big hill . . . has killed off many ambitious marathoners," the *Boston Globe* noted in 1925.

In 2007, after finishing second, two-time New York Marathon champion Jelena Prokopcuka of Latvia mixed up her words, but in doing so, got to the core of how she felt about fading on the third hill. She called it "Breakheart Hill."

I had now run twenty miles. Wow, two more than I'd ever run consecutively in my life. I was proud of myself, but was reminded of what 1986 winner Rob de Castella had said about Boston—that the first twenty miles is the first half of the race; the last six miles are the second half. This is because the runner traverses the course in two separate states of being. For the first twenty miles, the runner personifies the idealism of the Greek athlete, honoring the gods. In the last six miles, the runner moves as if he were the victim of the gods' wrath.

Oh, well.

I crossed over the Centre Street intersection and saw my family up ahead. I drew upon the suggestion of Clarence DeMar, "Chin up, chest out."

Marathon running is the essence of an individual sport. It's a selfish enterprise in which only you benefit while other people have to sacrifice. *Boston Globe* reporter Michael Madden wrote in 1983 about training for marathon and marriages: "Marriages hit the wall too often with marathoners . . . cause is rarely the other wife but usually the other life of training, preparing and dedicating a year." An article in the *Boston Herald* in 1978 seemd to share this sentiment, with the headline "[It] Takes Two to Run." The *Boston Herald* called marathoning "the Bermuda Triangle of matrimony." In 1936, longtime race participant Jock Semple, who later served five decades as a race official, was divorced from his wife. She had filed for separation, saying it was because Jock "[spent] too much time training for marathon races."

In 1924, Clarence DeMar was planning to give up running to concentrate on his marriage. "I'm going to settle down to make myself a good husband." DeMar would never settle down. Six years later, in 1930, he would explain his reasoning. "My wife has no objection to my running. In fact, she encourages me. Why should she object when it does not interfere with my business or my health?" DeMar would run all the way up to his death, three decades later.

Running marathons is a disease. Why else would people sacrifice so much, subject themselves to such pain, and force others to forfeit their opportunities so they can run? Even the doctor responsible for overseeing the Boston Marathon in 1919, Colonel Joel Goldthwait, indicated that running wasn't in one's best interest when he said, "[A] marathon cannot be termed an ideal form of exercise."

Despite all of these warnings, runners—like me—continue to toe the line in Hopkinton. I was able to do so because my wife gave me the opportunity, just as John "The Younger" Kelley's wife did for her husband, supporting him during his vulnerable days after devastating losses. After Kelley finally won in 1957, he would tell reporters that he couldn't have done it without her. "The encouragement of my wife Jessie helped carry me over the distance."

So far, the prospect of seeing my family had drawn me to this moment. If I just kept running, I'd see my family, who were waiting for me. So I ran, trying not to cry, reminding myself to "Run Tall / Run Strong!"

A tenth of a mile past the Centre Street intersection, I could see them up ahead. Ryan was in Noreen's arms. Just like he was the day he was born at Newton-Wellesley Hospital, along the Marathon route. Standing with them was my lifetime friend, Jay Parker, who was yelling "Here he comes!" Instantly, they all ran out onto the sidewalk. Jay gave me a high five and Noreen threw me a kiss. Although Ryan wasn't sure what I was doing, the mere sight of him filled me with joy.

Internally I was confused. I didn't know what I wanted to do. Should I quit after completing twenty miles, running nonstop for over three hours and fifteen minutes, thus assuring myself a ride home? Or should I keep going? My head said stop, but the nerve impulses being sent to my legs never picked up the phone—so I just kept running.

In 1936, Pat Dengis of Baltimore was running in the lead pack when he burst a blood vessel in his bladder. He kept on running until his wife, Eva, drove up beside him and forced him to quit the race and get in the car. At this point in the race, I almost wished my wife had channeled the spirit of Eva.

By the time I reached the base of Heartbreak Hill, my family (and my ride) had been left behind. I was alone yet again. As quickly as they'd appeared, they were gone. I was alone.

But then I wasn't. To my right on the sidewalk appeared Noreen, like a beautiful apparition, but real. She was running alongside me. She never looked more beautiful. She had never been more loving. It was the epitome of sincere care and love for another. Letting me run on this day was the essence of selflessness. While I'd been hanging out with Richie and Rad and Jack, working to fulfill my dream, she'd been home with a three-year-old, cooking dinner, cleaning up, reading bedtime stories.

In 1915, Clifton Horne's wife had followed him in a car until police forced the automobile off the road. Noreen wasn't being forced off the road, but she had to let me go on ahead, to fulfill my goal. "I love you!" she yelled. I mouthed it back.

I watched as my wife ran back to reclaim Ryan from Jay's arms. I was glad she was the woman who'd agreed to run beside me throughout life.

I continued to put one foot in front of the other. The sight of my family and my buddy Jay was just the injection of love I'd needed to face what now stood in front of me.

Heartbreak Hill.

On the left side of the road, a spectator was pounding a huge bass drum over and over again. The drumming seemed to keep time with my heartbeat;

I felt like a warrior being sent off to battle. I couldn't help but get pumped up as I prepared to attack the last of the three hills.

In all, the hill stretches nearly a half-mile. Jerry Nason memorably called it the "winding ribbon of Commonwealth Avenue that rises to the great tall towers of Boston College." During training runs, this is the spot on the course where I'd always faded and hit the wall. Not once did I make it over the hill. After his failed run in 1973, Bill Rodgers would call this slope a "bitch." I would agree.

In the book *David and Goliath*, Malcolm Gladwell wonders about the famous biblical encounter and submits that Goliath was wrongly deemed the superior of David, simply because he was bigger. "King Saul thinks of power in term of physical might. He doesn't appreciate that power can come in other forms as well—in breaking rules, in substituting speed and surprise for strength. In reality, the very thing that gave the giant his size was also the source of his greatest weakness. There is an important lesson in that for battles with all kinds of giants. The powerful and the strong are not always what they seem."

Heartbreak Hill stood in front of me, unapologetic. For years it had swallowed up runners and spit them out. I'd been betting on myself my whole life, and I wasn't going to stop today. The next steps I would take would be the most difficult physical act I had ever attempted in my life. But I was ready. In my head the ring announcer was yelling into the microphone, "Let's get ready to rumble!"

Some run, some walk, some crawl, and some surrender, but without doubt, all who dare to scale this "mountain" do so with respect. When wheelchair competitor Christina Ripp got to the base of the hill, she asked herself, "How am I going to get up there?"

Throughout this Himalayan-like passage—it rises ninety-one feet in all—there are different degrees of steepness. At one point the sadistic hill teases you with a flat plateau at the Grant Street intersection. But ten steps later, it's back to climbing. The crowd here is insane; some are here to try to pull you up with a virtual rope, while others are here to watch runners melt into the road.

For me, struggling up Heartbreak Hill didn't seem any harder than the steps on level ground. Every time I put my foot down was a painful experience. Each new step presented an obstacle as it arrived and became an accomplishment as it passed. The discomfort I was feeling was cumulative pain, deepening the farther I swam out from the shores of Hopkinton.

As I continued up the hill, at one point, I picked up my head to sneak a peek at the crest. While I assessed the situation, I noticed an older runner working it hard. Looking more closely, I saw that the man had one prosthetic leg. His effort inspired me and made me proud to be part of an event where courage was just as important as athletic ability.

Later that day, watching highlights of the race on the news, I caught sight of this man crossing the finish line. His success was a powerful statement about the will of someone who refused to be denied. It made me reflect upon my own physical ailment and how this race was a metaphor for our lives. Resilience, persistence, and a refusal to accept the limits life attempts to place on us—these traits serve us well not only on the road from Hopkinton to Boston, but also in our daily efforts to survive, and thrive.

Halfway up the hill, it seemed like days since Noreen had been running beside me. My parents were most likely home already, yet I was still in the middle of this chain gang, still plodding along. Other than the Scream Tunnel at Wellesley College, this is the second most rambunctious section of the course.

Up above are the echoes of celebration, but to be honest, I wasn't quite sure what I was hearing at this point. Twenty-one miles into it, my senses were becoming compromised. Peripheral vision was quickly diminishing, and my ears were ringing. Yells and cheers all seemed to funnel together into my ears, turning into what seemed like white noise. It's as if your brain has announced it's at DEFCON 1 and has elected to shut down all sensory neurons, committing all remaining resources to synapses in your legs and feet.

In 1956, the *Boston Daily Record* called the third hill "the boulevard of broken dreams" after Antti Viskari of Finland passed John "The Younger" Kelley on the hill, leaving him behind. Strangely, I was leaving many of the other competitors behind; by merely running, albeit slowly, I was passing hundreds of runners on the hill.

The fans arrive in droves here, both to support and to bear witness. It's not every day that you can see the human spirit emerging from the inner core of so many different people. It is here that one by one, the athletes dig in and push, plumbing unknown depths of will rarely done on such a massive—and public—scale. The crowds clap and yell and urge runners on, if only for the opportunity to share in the moment and perhaps take home with them validation of what's possible.

While some spectators may take pleasure in the inevitable crashes on Heartbreak Hill, most of the fans are providing invaluable support for the runners. With fans at the top pulling and fans behind them pushing, the runners move toward the peak of Heartbreak Hill. For five-tenths of a mile, it's all gritted teeth and clenched fists.

Finally, the crest of the hill is within sight. To the spectators, it appears that the runners' arms and legs have done all the work, but in actuality the competitors have relied heavily on one muscle—the heart.

And then finally, the *summit*—I had reached the peak. I had done it! I had won the famous battle within the battle. For years, I had read and witnessed tragic stories of wasted efforts and futile ascents. Now I had defeated the mountain. Instantly I felt like Sir Edmund Hillary. I had conquered the hill that had conquered so many. But now I own it!

I rejoiced in my accomplishment: Goliath had been slain. The scene at the top was one of elation; it was Mardi Gras, Times Square on New Year's Eve, and spring break, all rolled into one—the type of party where everyone is drunk but you. I was jealous, but I was fired up. The crowd saluted the runners for their efforts, and the runners showed their appreciation by throwing gloves and hats into the crowd in thanks. The display of adoration was so overwhelming that I moved to the side of the road to join the party and thank the crowd for their support. With my hand raised, I ran along the sidewalk, slapping palms. I realized the crowd had probably been drinking for more than four hours. One enthusiastic student almost knocked me back into Mile 15 as he reached back and crashed his hand into mine to congratulate me. (It's likely his blood alcohol was higher than my mile splits.) No doubt many of these fans would feel worse than me the day after.

The course now starts to fall toward Boston. The last three-tenths of the mile slide into Mile 22 and past the campus of Boston College. Up ahead, my brother Kevin awaits. He is going to run with me the last five-plus miles. It will be nice to have someone along for the demanding steps ahead.

Either way, the downhill of Wellesley, the rise over Route 128, and the three hills of Commonwealth Avenue are now behind the runner. But amazingly, the toughest miles still lie ahead. Runners need to keep their heads down, their feet moving, and their eyes peeled for the Citgo sign.

The Horror, The Horror

In 1963, the most talked-about Marathon runner in seven decades of the sport came to Boston. Abebe Bikila of Ethiopia captured the attention and imagination of the world after winning a gold medal at the 1960 Rome Olympics (the first African to win any medal) while running the twenty-six miles *in bare feet*. Before taking position in Hopkinton that year, he had run in four marathons and won them all, setting records in each.

After the starting gun, Bikila took off to the lead, as predicted, alongside his teammate, Mamo Wolde. The crowds cheered them wildly, as Bikila had become a global star who transcended sports. Their lead was wide and apparently insurmountable. Running in third place was Aurele Vandendriessche of Belgium, who was hoping to just maintain his position in the race when he rose over Heartbreak Hill and ran into Mile 22. From his lofty vantage point he could see the vista ahead, and, to his amazement, for the first time he could see Bikila and Wolde below. "I thought they were unbeatable," he said. "Now I ran to win."

Little by little Vandendriessche chipped away at the Ethiopians' lead, until he finally caught them and passed them two miles down the road. He never looked back. Bikila was so devastated about being passed that he began to walk, and ended up with a disappointing fifth-place finish. A reporter for the *Boston Globe* wrote the next day that Vandendriessche ran with great urgency, looking like an "MBTA bus driver late for lunch."

After conquering Heartbreak Hill, some runners, who aren't acclimated to the course, might run with the false impression that the race is over. Many of these runners trained under the premise "If I can run twenty miles, I can run twenty-six." Such speculation is foolhardy, however. "The great mystique of Heartbreak Hill is not getting up it," said the great Irish runner John Treacy. "It's getting down it."

For over a century, the back side of Heartbreak Hill has been a secret killer of both leaders and back-of-the-pack plodders, making athletes suffer the consequences of not running with proper respect, and forgetting Jim Knaub's adage: "There's no such thing as an unimportant mile."

This mile is so important that it has earned the nickname of the "Haunted Mile." It's haunted because people sometimes forget about why they are here. They forget that they came to run Boston, to be bold, and to impact their destiny. After climbing the summit of Heartbreak Hill, runners can be overcome by a false sense of accomplishment. They are so excited to have completed this dramatic part of the course that they might forget that their mission is to run all the way to Boston.

This is also the Haunted Mile because up ahead, on the right, sits the Evergreen Cemetery. Since the very first race in 1897, the burial ground has stood guard on Mile 22 to remind runners that their destiny lies in Boston, not at the top of Heartbreak Hill.

Summiting Heartbreak Hill means just one thing: You have fulfilled one of the requirements of your mission. It means that your opportunity to change your life is still alive. In *The Graveyard Book*, author Neil Gaiman writes about taking advantage of opportunities and not interfering with your own destiny. "You're alive. That means you have infinite potential. You can do anything, make anything, dream anything. If you change the world, the world will change. Potential. Once you're dead, it's gone. Over. You've made what you've made, dreamed your dream, written your name."

The hills may be done, but the race goes on. After the celebration at the top of Heartbreak Hill, the runners are once again alone. The athletes must immediately shift their attention from the excitement of running up Heartbreak Hill to the concern of running down it.

The descent in the first steps of Mile 22 mimics the landslide that the runners survived back in Mile 16 as they ran toward Newton Lower Falls. Once again, they need to mobilize leg muscles used in downhill running. This torment on the runners' legs prompted champion Rob de Castella to refer to this section of the race as "an anatomical challenge." Quads are put to the test as they work to simultaneously propel and brake, while feet must carefully avoid the water-stop litter that turns the pavement into slippery steps of wet trash. There are still more than five miles to go before the athletes earn the right to revel in their glory.

Because of the demands it places on different muscles, the Boston course is built for some runners and not for others. It's similar to a golf course that favors those who play a fade; players who hit the draw will likely be unsuccessful on this course. The great Frank Shorter realized this after melting at Boston, as described by Whitney Spivey: "Biomechanically, [Shorter is] not engineered to conquer the 480-foot net downhill course as quickly as, say, Bill Rodgers."

Shuffling forward, runners rappel down the hill. In a sort of tango, runner and racecourse serve as dance partners, but each is trying to lead and compel their will upon the other. Runners stride, brake, and contract their downhill muscles, feeling like the course is pulling away from each foot strike. It's not uncommon here for runners to see their fellow competitors walking, or even sitting.

With each mile the runner moves in a state of paradox. The satisfaction of crossing over mile marks is spoiled by the realization that each new mile only increases the degree of difficulty. The runner now understands the pleas of coaches and veterans who beseeched them to relax and go slow in the early miles. New Kids on the Block singer Joey McIntyre was advised by veterans of the race "to put on his smoking jacket and just chill" as he traveled through Hopkinton and Ashland. This is why worrying about running for a personal record is a form of psychological quicksand. This course hasn't existed for twelve decades by just letting runners go wild, oblivious to topography and history. The heart of this course pounds every Patriots' Day because it feeds off runners who think it will be easy.

At the beginning of the mile, my spirits were again lifted when I came upon my brother Kevin, who was standing with friends Tim and Mary Kate—both past survivors of the race. Tim and Mary Kate wished me well while Kevin joined me for the final five miles. As we took off, I was hoping he would say, "You look terrible—you have to stop." But instead he said, "You look great. Let's do it!"

Kevin's presence was advantageous for two reasons: I was desperate for the company, and I was starting to depreciate physically. In the previous miles I'd felt my senses diminishing. Now I could feel my head start to droop, and my arms that had been pumping miles ago were now dangling.

Kevin was fired up to join me, but would soon realize he'd have to run in low gear in order to stay in lockstep with me. Kevin and I have always been tight. We played Little League and hockey together, and we've been known to share a pint or two. It was awesome to be able to share this experience with him.

In 1936, defending champion Johnny "The Elder" Kelley was starting to hit the wall as he ran into Kenmore Square. Slowing to almost a walk, a car carrying his brothers Eddie and Willie pulled up beside the tiring runner. Willie jumped out and ran the rest of the way with his brother. The *Boston Herald* would say that Willie "wouldn't let Johnny stop." Kelley would finish fifth in 1936.

Like Willie Kelley, my brother was determined to help get me to Boston. Stride for stride he stayed with me, both encouraging me and lying to me, saying how good I looked.

We ran down the back side of Heartbreak Hill, passing the gates of Boston College on the right. Kevin was the captain of the baseball team at BC, and an all-conference catcher. A power hitter who was built like a fullback, he played for former Red Sox infielder Eddie Pellagrini in the manager's last year at the school. Ironically, my father had played for "Pellie" in his first year as manager at BC. Kevin was the fourth Connelly to play at the Heights, along with my father, my grandfather, and Uncle Paul, whose company Prime Computer had sponsored Geoff Smith.

The descent is almost a half-mile. At this point, runners must assess their energy reserves to determine whether they can push themselves, or whether they should just hold on for dear life. To the human eye the course here actually seems inviting—after all, the runner moves with the help of gravity. But at the Boston Marathon the most obvious is actually the most uncertain. Running hard and uninhibited will only hurt things. It's counterintuitive, like the thirsty boater drifting at sea who drinks the salt water; they soon find it only makes them thirstier.

This is the seduction of the course, or, as Bill Rodgers calls it, the "topographical trapdoor." After running four hills that are the equal of two miles in total uphill steps, runners may not notice that they have gone through a transformation. Whereas their strides were once intentional, signaled from the brain to the body, their legs now move in an involuntary, almost trance-like state, propelled forward by sheer will and the power of dreams. In Mile 22 the pathway of consent moves, from brain-to-legs to heart-to-legs.

Over the history of the race, more leads have been lost on the downhill past Boston College than any other mile on the course. It was this nearly annual tradition of champions' ambitions dying a sad death that prompted writer Jerry Nason to call this segment of the course "The Graveyard of Champions."

Many suspect that the spirits housed in the Evergreen Cemetery down the road are to blame for wreaking their demonic whims upon the runners. Whatever the cause, unexpected forces have influenced this section of the course. Menacing vehicles, illegal stimulants, and bizarre behavior have all conspired to turn Mile 22 into a diabolical vortex that sucks runners' dreams (and energy) into its whirlpool.

The runners' physical and mental exhaustion, the pull of gravity, the blood-alcohol level of the Boston College coeds, and the tricky islands that litter the road all add to the chaos of this mile. What was an open road from sidewalk to sidewalk is now compressed, as the public transport Green Line has train tracks that force runners to the right side of the road.

At the bottom of the hill, after Boston College, the route passes St. Ignatius Church on the right. It was here that textile worker Doroteo Flores of Guatemala was running in 1952 when he looked to the church for support. He had hoped that a win at the world's greatest race might help him to find employment or notoriety, allowing him to make a better life for himself and his family. With a prayer in his heart, the Roman Catholic had regained his stride and the will to win. "Coming over the hills I asked my God, 'How do I do it?'" After the race, the champion would say, in thanks, "He listened and gave me strength, and I ran with greater sense of purpose." After winning Boston in 1952, Flores's home country named the national stadium in Guatemala City after him.

Across the street is the Boston College Green Line train stop. The Green Line is famous for its deliberate pace. A writer once quipped, "A man was tied to the Green Line tracks. He died from starvation." In the old days, the train depot used to serve as one of the checkpoints on the course, selected so officials could jump on the train after the last runner had arrived and get into Boston with their results.

Across the Lake Street intersection, the runners pass St. John's Seminary, where in 1904 seminarians snuck out of theology classes to cheer the runners on. The runners now stay on the right side of Commonwealth Avenue, with train tracks shadowing the runners for the next three miles, all the way into Boston.

The Haunted Mile has always been a mystery. In the very first Boston Marathon, eventual winner John McDermott was running just fine down the hill. "McDermott's legs seemed to rise and fall like a phantom Greek," the paper reported. However, just a quarter of a mile later—in front of the cemetery, no less—he was afflicted with cramps, forcing him to come to a stop and scream at his attendant to massage his legs with pleas of "Rub!"

In the final steps of Mile 22, the runner will feel the effect of the hills and will need to push past the pain. Such was the case in 1901. Just feet from the mile marker, former champion Ronald MacDonald was confidently running, assured of victory, when he suffered a bout of discomfort. After running without aid or water to this point of the course, the Canadian called for his attendant, asking for refreshment for the very first time.

Back in 1897, runners lined up on a rural wooden bridge accompanied by attendants on bicycles, one assigned to each competitor. The runners were allowed assistance, but only if they came to a complete stop. Rules stated that the attendants were "allowed to give them a drink—lemon or brandy—on a sponge." The suggested honorarium for the attendants was twenty-five cents, even though the attendants sometimes added to the demands of the race. As one observer said, "They were more of a detriment than anything else, as they helped raise the dust." In addition, occasionally these attendants would focus not on their assigned runner but instead on the wishes of the gamblers who would pay them off if they could affect the outcome of the race.

One method used to affect the outcome—both positively and negatively—was the application of stimulants. In 1923, failing runner Albert Michelson was handed a flask by his attendant, who had been riding a bike alongside him throughout the race. The *Boston Globe* reported that the flask contained peppermint water and a pill of "unknown purpose." Whatever it was, it served its purpose, giving Michelson a second wind and a fourth-place finish.

Race officials were greatly concerned about the use of such stimulants and the influence of attendants on the race. Following the 1905 race, in which many runners suffered aftereffects of their run, Dr. Blake of the BAA was furious. "There were some who were in a bad way, but they can blame their handlers for this," Blake said. "These men were given whiskey on the journey, which is a very bad thing. It not only interferes with their running, but it acts badly on the heart. The men who did not take alcoholic stimulants fared the better."

Since the very first marathon in Athens in 1896—where runners drank wine at aid stations—runners have been using alcohol and other stimulants to refresh their minds and bodies. In the 1904 Olympics, gold medalist Thomas Hicks (who had placed second in that year's Boston Marathon) was given alcohol as well as drugs to stimulate him to victory. In fact, he was given so much brandy and strychnine (placed in raw eggs) that he started to hallucinate in the final miles, and almost died. After the race Hicks's attendant Charles Lucas boasted, "The marathon race, from a medical standpoint, demonstrated that drugs are of much benefit to athletes along the road."

Hicks would never run a marathon again. The medical field was so concerned about the impact of drugs and alcohol upon the Olympic champion that they recommended banning athletes from using either. The BAA went so far as to require applicants to divulge information about their alcohol consumption throughout the year on their application to run Boston.

Despite the pushback by doctors and race officials, many runners who were backed by the moneymen—mostly the gamblers and oddsmakers—ignored the wishes of the BAA. These differing perspectives were illustrated prior to the race in 1908, when the *Boston Globe* wrote, "The use of drugs is forbidden, and runners resorting to them [are] disqualified." But, being realists, they also wrote, "Stimulants must be figured on, and much depends upon the way they are handed out."

Drugs and alcohol have always been part of the sports world—with both enhanced and diminished results. Gamblers proved they would go to any lengths for money. In 1890, Boston boxer Johnny Murphy had his food poisoned prior to his bout, rendering him defenseless in the ring. Marathon runner Robert Fowler was aware of the risk of someone slipping him drugs on the course, and was mad at himself when, running with a significant lead, he accepted an orange from an unknown attendant at the Yonkers Marathon and collapsed to the ground. He would lie unconscious for five hours. When he awoke, he would blame himself. "I've been in the running game long enough to know better than to accept nourishment from a stranger," he said.

So, in 1901, as Ronald MacDonald ran through the final steps of Mile 22, knowing that "victory would be mine," he didn't account for the intrusion of the wicked. When he asked his attendant for refreshment, he was only concerned about ridding himself of the uneasiness. The attendant, unknown to MacDonald and dressed in army garb, poured the contents of his canteen onto a sponge. The attendant then strangely poured the remaining liquid from the canteen onto the street and disappeared.

MacDonald squeezed the liquid twice into his mouth. Immediately, his stomach and head felt the effects. He pushed forward, only to collapse to the ground, his throat burning from the unknown fluid. For hours he would lie unconscious. When he finally awoke, he would explain what the attendant had done. Immediately, Dr. Thompson, a supporter and the runner's physician, ran out to his carriage where the sponge was still sitting. Holding the sponge up to his nose, the doctor discovered that it had been saturated with chloroform. The following day's headline read "MacDonald Collapses after Plucky Race—Ugly Rumors as to Cause."

Some would theorize that the cause of MacDonald's collapse wasn't the solution on the sponge but instead was actually Dr. Thompson himself, and his overuse of stimulants on the runner. Dr. Thompson disputed this account, claiming that someone had intentionally handed MacDonald a sponge with chloroform. "It couldn't well have been an accident," Thompson said, "when there was so much money up on the race."

With his dream of a second laurel wreath stolen, MacDonald would take his doctor's side, claiming that Dr. Thompson had given him two strychnine pills to *counteract* the sponge, thus saving his life. Upon hearing this explanation, Herbert Holton of the BAA called the story "an excuse of a crybaby who was trying to cover up the disgrace of letting down the number of American bettors who had put their trust in him"—a sentence that does a good job of explaining how much influence gamblers once had over the race. MacDonald would continue to defend himself, claiming, "I am the victim of one of the most despicable deeds on record."

Despite Holton's words of virtual approval to those who wagered on the race, the BAA feigned vocal opposition to gambling, dating back to 1911. The *Boston Globe* reported that "The Boston A. A. is to be congratulated on its determination to keep the great Patriots' Day Marathon a sporting event unaccompanied, if possible, by pools or gambling."

Leading up to the race, the four of us had agreed that we shouldn't do anything during the race that we hadn't done in training. We needed to eat the same snacks, drink the same fluids, and run the same pace. During long training runs, I found that I liked a mixture of green Gatorade and water to give me a little boost of sugar. And for snacks, I liked the salt I got on pretzels.

Of course, I didn't abide by this imperative. Earlier in the race, I'd accepted an orange from the side of the road, and the acid did tricks with my stomach the rest of the way in. Later, I decided to take some hard candy from a fan, hoping that the sugar would reenergize me. Of course, I almost choked on the candy and had to spit it out.

In 1915, Hugh Honohan was running with a half-mile lead on Beacon Street, Boston in his sights. As he ran toward Kenmore Square his body was disintegrating. His attendant made his way over to a drugstore and procured his runner a raw egg. At that point, Honohan was willing to try anything, and ate the egg. The egg didn't agree with the runner's stomach—immediately he was brought to a halt and was passed three times. His half-mile lead was gone, and he would have to settle for fourth place.

Favorite for the 1911 race, Alexis Ahlgren from Sweden took castor oil the night before the race and never got a wink of sleep, or the laurel wreath. In 1954, Veikko Karvonen of Finland had to battle through stomach pains on his way to the championship after he drank coffee with multiple spoons of sugar, as well as blueberry soda. Compare these stories with that of 1925 winner Chuck Mellor, who somehow managed to chew tobacco throughout his run, with no negative effects.

Kevin and I finished the twenty-second mile just before the course leaves Commonwealth Avenue for a time. Kevin had finished his first mile and was still fired up. Our mantra: Gotta get to Boston!

MILE 23

Duels

In high school, Rad and Jay and I had played on a basketball team for our local parish, St. Theresa. One night we were playing rival St. Gregory's of Dorchester and found ourselves trailing by more than twenty points. Late in the game, Jay got hot and we staged a furious rally that fell one point short. After the game we commented to our coach, Rick Kuhn, on what a great comeback we'd had. Rick looked back at us and rebuked our premise, saying, "It's only a great comeback if you win."

Rick, like Bill Olsen's grandfather, wasn't about the bullshit. Both men were all about results. The fact that I had run twenty-two miles meant absolutely nothing. I either ran the next four, or the day was a total loss.

At Mile 23, the course continues down Commonwealth Avenue, surrounded by nondescript apartment buildings on the right and train tracks on the left. Behind the apartment buildings sits the Chestnut Hill Reservoir, which could be tempting on a hot day. At two-tenths into the mile, the course takes its second 90-degree turn.

The runners will be required to turn right and run downhill yet again, for three-tenths of a mile. This is one of the five corners along the route where competitors must navigate according to their legs' capacity. Past the corner, the road brings runners toward the insanity of Cleveland Circle. On the left side of the runners, railroad tracks that carry trolleys are exposed and raised, and can be treacherous for wheelchair tires. On rainy days, they can get slippery.

As you run down the hill, your raised vantage point allows you to look down into the chaotic intersection of Cleveland Circle that sits below. If the party at the top of Heartbreak Hill was an uninhibited party, Cleveland Circle is sheer bedlam. The intersection has six different entrances. Some are just for trains, but all of them add to the danger of this crossroad.

In 1976, Jack Fultz ran into Cleveland Circle with the lead but turned prematurely onto the wrong side of the road; fortunately, a fan yelled that he was on the wrong side of Beacon Street. Jack turned around, jumping over the train tracks again onto the eastbound side, and headed off to victory.

Although this descent can be worrisome, if approached properly, runners can take this opportunity to relax, let go, and actually add to their pace. It was here that three-time champion Uta Pippig liked to take advantage of a course that too often takes advantage of the runner. "I look forward to the right turn which moves you down to Cleveland Circle," she said. "If you let yourself go just a little bit, and don't push too hard, you can really fly."

The chaos is magnified for the wheelchair competitors, who fly down the hill at speeds close to thirty-five miles per hour, only to be faced with both a turn and the tracks. Racers are advised to start braking early so that they can safely travel the bend and cross over the tracks. But it's difficult to convince world-class competitors in the middle of a world-class event to slow down for safety's sake.

When you get to the bottom of the hill, you'll have to mind your angles and pace, as the course elbows left in yet another 90-degree turn. What makes this turn one of the most treacherous locations on the course is that you have to control your speed coming down the hill and navigate a radical turn laced with train tracks.

Jim Knaub would suggest that you should just attack them; it's either your day or it's not. But after a Boston winter, where frost heaves and snowplows have taken turns raising rail levels and the pavement around it, it's probably best that you proceed with caution. Taking an aggressive approach here has claimed its share of victims, including the leader in the 1980 race, George Murray, who caught his wheel as he attempted to cross the tracks, costing him the championship. The same thing happened to Jean Driscoll in 1997, during her run to become the most decorated champion in Boston Marathon history.

With Boston in the distance, Jean and Australian Louise Sauvage were locked in one of their classic head-to-head duels. As the two raced down the hill into Cleveland Circle, Driscoll caught a wheel on an exposed track, sending her to the ground with a flat tire. Her rival Sauvage rolled by, looking back at Jean almost apologetically. Nonetheless, Louise went on to victory, and Jean would have to settle for second place after completing the course on her flat tire. After the race, when she was asked what happened, Jean replied: "I had a great race until I met Cleveland Circle."

One year later the two competitors would wage yet another battle. As they approached the fateful tracks together, Louise suggested to her contemporary, "Take it easy here." After safely crossing over the tracks, Louise then offered, "Let's go!" From 1990 to 2001, Jean and Louise won every Women's championship. Their rivalry was competitive, but friendly and professional. The same cannot be said for every duel between runners.

Although Knaub, Fultz, Driscoll, and Sauvage were warriors of the sport, in 1962, the greatest competitor that these parts have ever witnessed came to Cleveland Circle on Marathon Day with his teammates, to be honored for their contribution to the city of Boston. On the night before the race, center Bill Russell led the Boston Celtics to the NBA championship. The future Hall of Famer scored thirty points while collecting forty rebounds in a Game Seven 110–107 victory over the Los Angeles Lakers. The following morning the Celtics climbed into convertibles in Cleveland Circle and prior to the race were saluted by Boston Marathon fans all the way to the finish line.

Being a great competitor means your will is greater than that of the person next to you. Running side by side with a challenger or in a lead pack late in the race is not for the faint of heart. You must bring all elements of yourself to the race, including legs, heart, brain, and even your primal self. It's in the midst of such a duel that you have to concern yourself with someone other than yourself. You need to be a processor of information—both yours and theirs.

Marathoning is akin to a giant poker game taking place on the streets of Greater Boston; a player endeavors not to fold, but instead to flush his or her competitor with a full house. The game is full of fake surges, risks, smarts; it's the ultimate battle of wills. Some competitors like to take the measure of their opponent across the felt table, while others would prefer to silently hold their hand and hide their intentions behind mirrored sunglasses. In the marathoning game, as well, the stakes are real; the consequences of victory or defeat are significant in both prestige, and—in these days of prize money and sponsorships—lucrative.

By assessing your competitor's "tells" in a duel, you can assess strategy and approach after determining if they are fading, bluffing, or soft in big moments. Are they willing to sacrifice all on the streets of Boston, or will they "fold" upon a surge? You need to be able to play your hand and be "all in."

The proper approach to running within a lead group depends upon the individual and his or her personal makeup. Some runners like to run out front and set the pace while others like to glide along from behind and bide their time; the front-runners shield them from the wind and relieve them of the psychological burden of having to wonder what lies behind. In 1937, leaders Walter Young and John "The Elder" Kelley tortured each other by switching leads sixteen times before Young from Canada would beat Kelley to the tape.

Whether you run from behind or from the front, both approaches require a distinct strategy. Either way you must have great resolve. When Meb Keflezighi ran with the lead in 2014 on his way to victory, he said of his competitors, "If they're going to come, they're going to have to earn it." While Irish runner Andy Ronan, who came in third in 1991, liked to run a race like an Irishman—with reckless abandon. "I'm here for it today, and if he's going to beat me, he's got to work for it."

Champion Joe Smith was a proponent of keeping his eyes forward when he was leading a race, and just worry about the course. "If you look back, you're done," he said. Three-time winner Robert Kipkoech Cheruiyot agreed with that sentiment: "When a lion is chasing an antelope, he doesn't look back. He has to eat."

In 1988, Juma Ikangaa looked over the wrong shoulder on Boylston Street, only to have Ibrahim Hussein sneak by him at the tape, winning the race by one second. After the race Ikangaa would talk about second-guessing and the inevitable sleepless nights that followed, while lamenting, "I didn't hear his shoes."

It is unnerving to always be the prey. The challenger runs from behind with a clear view of what lies ahead, while the leader runs, wondering not *if*, but *when*. Amby Burfoot, the 1968 winner, compared the security of the pack to "a comfortable, cozy nest," and hated running with the lead. Amby Burfoot was in front in 1968, but he wasn't able to enjoy it. "I couldn't see Bill Clark, but I could see his shadow out in front of me," he said. "It was like a ghost or a spirit haunting me. I was trying to get away from this guy. He wasn't there, but his shadow was; I couldn't get away from [it]. I was running to get away from this apparition."

Uta Pippig doesn't care whether she runs in a pack or by herself. "I am confident in my abilities and what I can do," she says. "Although, if in a pack, I respect everyone in that group. I feel solidarity with the other runners. I appreciate the physical and emotional investment that they have made in order to run in this race. Although I might not know some of the runners in my pack, I must respect them, because at that moment they are the same distance from the finish line as I am."

While the lead pack is sometimes an amicable group, sometimes team-mates/countrymen will use the lead pack to bully rivals. In the 2000 contest between Ethiopian runner Gezahegne Abera and multiple Kenyan runners, the race depreciated into an elbow-throwing death match that included both real blood and "bad blood." When the second-place Abera lost by less than a second, he claimed that the Kenyan runners had "ganged up" on him, pushing and shoving him throughout the race, and then working together to beat him at the end.

This type of aggressive team running was reminiscent of the Japanese runners in the 1950s and 1960s who would use manipulation, and, sometimes, intimidation by running alongside competitors from a different country as a whole. They worked together to eliminate that runner from contention by circling the other competitor and forcing him to run at their pace, in isolation from the freedom of the course. Eventually, the victim of the Japanese team would be forced to drop back.

Gamesmanship and intimidation can also backfire; it depends upon your opponent. Some competitors are fueled by the intensity of the competition—challenges actually help to propel them forward—while others might cower in the safety of trailing runners. Aggressive manipulation is tricky, and it behooves one to know the intended target. Whether to run, to bait, or to stay back are all calculations that a potential champion must assess during his or her run. It's not who is the fastest; it's who *gets to Boston* the fastest. It's while a runner appraises the other competitors that the physical joins forces with the cerebral. While the legs beneath the runner turn, the runner must switch his or her focus from the road ahead to the runner nearby.

In 1987, two-time champion Geoff Smith decided he would run up next to leader Toshihiko Seko and test him with some gamesmanship. As they ran shoulder to shoulder, Smith looked into Seko's eyes and smiled at him. Seko ignored the look, turned away, and ran on to victory. Smith, the eventual third-place finisher, said later, "I guess I shouldn't have smiled at him."

In 1936, in the hills of Newton, defending champion John "The Elder" Kelley had closed a half-mile gap on the leader, Tarzan Brown. Kelley moved up to Brown's side, riding the momentum, and tapped him on the shoulder, saying, "I will take it from here." This attempt by Kelley to demoralize the Narragansett Indian actually had the reverse effect, serving as motivation for the tiring runner, propelling him forward to victory.

In 1903, the *Globe* reported that Sammy Mellor ran up to Canadian Jack Caffery, using both his running skill and his snarky side, to pass him.

"Mellor trotted over to Caffery and eyed him from head to heel. A few sarcastic remarks, and Mellor jumped in front."

Proper assessment takes insight, deduction, and a keen understanding of the tangible indicators that differentiate between fresh and tired, hunter or hunted. It could be the labored breathing, changes in the pigmentation of the skin, or something as simple as the alteration of one's running form.

Stalking one's prey takes the heart of a lion. To patiently sit in the weeds, figuring out exactly when to strike, is a skill that separates the hungry from the fed. In 1971, unemployed Colombian Alvaro Mejia ran Boston for the first time. For miles he ran on the back shoulder of pre-race favorite, Pat McMahon, constantly breathing on him to remind him that he was there. Mile after mile, McMahon ran, tortured by the knowledge that Mejia had 4:04 mile on his résumé, and could pull it out whenever he wanted—which he did, on Boylston Street.

In the 1940s, five-foot-three Canadian Gérard Côté won Boston four times. Côté was bold and brash, never afraid to challenge, annoy, or win. With his two gold-capped teeth, Côté loved to sport a smile of both confidence and insolence. Before one race, he was so sure of himself that he ordered brandy, wine, and cigars to be delivered to his Lenox Hotel room, inviting the press to his post-race victory party.

In 1948 Côté was thirty-five, and his better days were behind him. His legs were tired, but he still had guile. He spent most of the race running side by side with Tufts University student Ted Vogel. Throughout their run he kept telling Vogel not to worry about him (because he was an old man), but to focus on the runners behind them, who were coming up fast.

Côté knew that the legs beside him were younger and faster, but he was a Canadian World War II veteran, and had lived through the heat, sand, and pain of the African campaign; Vogel lived a life of homework, socials, and professors. Côté believed that he would thrive in conflict and Vogel would melt.

As they ran the hills later in the course, Côté went from running side by side with Vogel to taking position behind him, stepping on the back of Vogel's sneakers. To avoid this annoyance, Vogel would change his stride, forcing Côté to run in front, where the impish Canadian tormented his opponent by cutting back and forth and in front of him.

Still neck and neck on the back side of the hills, Côté took a cup of water and tossed it over his head, soaking Vogel, gradually sending the college student over the edge. Finally, after passing through Cleveland Circle, Vogel had had enough. He ran up to Côté and offered to fight him right there in front of well-mannered women in dresses and men wearing fedoras. "Look, Gerry—you do that once more, and you and I are going to square off right in the middle of the street." Côté loved it. He looked at Vogel and smiled at him, flashing his golden teeth. Having accomplished his goal, Côté ran off to win his fourth championship.

While the above examples personify the essence of athletic competition, there was no mano a mano moment like the race waged between Alberto Salazar and Dick Beardsley in 1982. In that year's marathon, the two runners ran side by side from Hopkinton to Boston, fending off each other, fans, potholes, buses, and policemen. In the end, the two went down as the authors of the greatest race in the history of the Boston Marathon.

What made the contest so special was that there seemed to be no strategy at work—just primal running. As one runner placed his foot down, the other did the same. Step after step after step, each man refused to allow the other to move in front. It was Ali vs. Frazier on the streets of Boston.

When they came into Wellesley Square, an intoxicated fan took a swing at the runners. His fist barely missed Beardsley and struck Salazar in the stomach, knocking the wind out of him. Salazar regained his breath and continued stride for stride with Beardsley, into Kenmore Square. Here another drunken fan grabbed at Beardsley's shirt, impeding his stride yet again. Beardsley shook the fan off just in time to be sideswiped by the press bus, which the runner pounded with his fist in frustration.

From Hereford Street to the finish, Beardsley was twice blocked by a police motorcycle, and was actually hit by one. As they made the turn onto Boylston Street, the crowd was brought to such a fever pitch that television commentators couldn't hear each other, so they all ended up yelling and cheering at the same time. Salazar seemingly had victory in hand, only to have Beardsley come back over and over again. Salazar finally went on to win the race by two seconds, with a time of 2:08:52. After crossing the finish line they turned and hugged, holding each other up like Rocky and Apollo Creed at the end of their first fight when Apollo said, "Ain't gonna be no rematch." To which Rocky responded, "I don't want one."

Past the Circle, the course moves to the right side of Beacon Street and into the town of Brookline, the seventh municipality of the route. The race borrows the town on Patriots' Day for 2.25 miles of the race. Not incorporated until 1705, the village known as the "Hamlet of the Muddy River" had to petition the city of Boston in order to win its own identity. After much dispute, the villagers' request was granted, and the new town's boundaries were made to follow the natural line drawn by the Smelt Brook. The waterway (and border) ran through a 350-acre farm owned by Judge Samuel Sewall, who had inherited the property from his wife. Sewall was the judge who sentenced the Salem witches to death during the infamous trials of 1692.

In Mile 23, I felt like one of those witches on trial, subjected to forces beyond my control. I was in the physical and emotional fight of my life. Kevin and I survived the madhouse of Cleveland Circle, stepping over five separate sets of train tracks. As we turned onto Beacon Street, I felt the most subtle suggestion of a sea breeze, which meant Boston was getting closer. We were running east, toward the Atlantic Ocean.

The sensation that we were nearing Boston was exciting. But truly, I was more concerned with my next step. I'd now progressed from running in a perpetual state of discomfort to something that approached physical and mental distress. Any optimism that I'd fooled myself into feeling at the top of Heartbreak Hill was now a puddle of pessimism. I had never been more fragile mentally than I was in the first steps of Beacon Street.

The road is a two-lane thoroughfare with the Green Line train tracks running down the middle. These tracks carry the C train at a very deliberate pace. A runner who quits here and jumps on the train will soon realize that he or she probably would have arrived in Boston faster by running.

The route works its way straight, with a slight incline. This area is a mix of apartment buildings and businesses, the type of terrain that will allow runners with any pep in their legs to start passing competitors. Trailblazing women's runner Kathy Switzer found this scenario ideal. "When you are finishing strong, you can pick off as many as a hundred people in a very short distance. The people who are struggling seem like they are going backwards while you feel like the course is coming to you."

I wasn't passing anyone. Physically, I was a shadow of myself. I could no longer hold my head up, forcing me to rely on my brother to be my eyes. As I ran with my chin fixed to my chest and my vision locked on the pavement below, Kevin would alert me to walkers on the road ahead. Any attempts to drink were futile: Gatorade or water hit the back my mouth and came right back out. The sea breeze that had excited me earlier was causing the temperature to drop. Mylar blankets given to runners on the course were blowing in the wind and snapping me in the face.

As the elements swirled around me, Kevin continued to ask how I was doing, figuratively taking my vitals. At the 22.8-mile mark, I found I was starting to wander outside of my being, as if my mental side wanted to disassociate itself from my now-pathetic physical condition. My steps were now out of my control. They were being managed by some diabolical malware that had infected my hard drive, forcing my legs to take me to the end of this twisted journey under any circumstances. As my mind drifted, I found myself traveling back to a day back in February when I'd run around my block again and again and again, in a blizzard. I ran that day with my eyes fixed on the ground directly in front of me, placing each step with care. On each lap, I would follow my footprints from the previous trip around the block. If I lost sight of the tracks, it meant I had wandered off the sidewalk, into the street, and was in jeopardy of being crushed by a snowplow.

Now, some two months later, I once again found myself staring at the ground, blindly following the footprints laid down by Clarence DeMar, William Kennedy, Roberta Gibb Bingay, and hundreds of thousands of others who had sought private glory in the streets that led to Boston.

The Orbiting World

With the shadows of Boston's skyscrapers drawing nearer, the runners bounce down Beacon Street. Riding up and down small inclines and declines that rise and fall like waves, the runners move toward Coolidge Corner. Uta Pippig starts to get excited here: "For the first time in the race, you can feel the closeness of the finish line."

The course takes the runners down to the Washington Street intersection and continues to bend, with businesses and apartment buildings on the right and the snail-like Green Line train on the left. Three-quarters of the way through the mile, the runners pass through Coolidge Corner.

The corner takes its name from a local store owner, David Sullivan Coolidge. His general store—Coolidge & Bros.—was located on the corner of Harvard and Beacon Streets, a major thruway from the city out to the suburbs. In 1888 the street was widened to two hundred feet at the corner to accommodate an electric train, at the time, the longest continuous electric train route in the world.

The aristocrats of Brookline, who could afford to arrange their own transportation, had long been opponents of the train. One blue blood called it an "unpleasant mechanism of unproven worth; [a] vulgar common carrier." One wonders whether those aristocrats of Coolidge Corner would have turned up their noses at their latter-day neighbor, John Fitzgerald Kennedy, who years later would keep America from nuclear war with Russia and lead the charge to put a man on the moon.

It was in Coolidge Corner that the Kennedys and their grandfather, Mayor John Fitzgerald, known affectionately as "Honey Fitz," would come to watch the race.

Condominiums in this location can cost upwards of $3 million, while shop owners can pay dearly for the honor of leasing space in this busy corner of commerce. Despite the prices, Coolidge Corner is a melting pot. Visitors here are exposed to a great diversity of religions, cultures, and lifestyles, reflected in the variety of delicatessens and ethnic specialty shops, and the independent films shown at the historic nonprofit Coolidge Corner Theatre, established in 1933.

After the runners work their way by the corner at the intersection of Harvard and Beacon, the course moves downhill toward the end of the mile. In the early years of the race, affluent inhabitants of the Coolidge Corner brownstones used to sit in their windows and acknowledge the runners, as they did in 1902, when Sammy Mellor ran toward the tape. "Brookline's aristocracy leaned out of windows and waved lace handkerchiefs in the April breeze," the paper reported, "as the white shadow wended his way, acknowledging the salutation with a smile and nod."

Not to be outdone by the upper class, fifteen years later the laborers working on these urban estates took time from their honest day's work to cheer on their favorite runner—William "Bricklayer Bill" Kennedy. An actual bricklayer, Kennedy won the 1917 race, and was a consistent top-ten finisher during the 1920s. In the midst of his championship run, Kennedy was overcome by emotion as he ran through Coolidge Corner and was saluted by his brothers-in-trade, who took a quick break from their toil in order to clap their bricks together in an appropriate salute.

Falling just over two miles from the finish line, the crowds and chaotic atmosphere of Coolidge Corner have made this point an important benchmark in the race—as well as an obstacle to survive. At times, runners have been forced to run single file through the onslaught of well-wishers. As far back as 1907, the Coolidge Corner crowd was termed "a mob" by the *Globe*, which wrote: "From Coolidge Corner to Massachusetts Ave., the runners and attendants had to fight their way along practically, for they are mobbed. The police do everything in their power to keep the crowds back, yet each year the conditions become worse."

Greg Meyer compared the zeal of the populace in Mile 24 to that of a hungry reptile. As he ran toward his championship in 1983, the crowds from each side of the street seemed to meet in the middle of the road. When he approached them, he recalled, "They seemed to open up in front of me like a snake eating." As he passed through, he realized he could no longer see the competitors behind him because "the crowd reunited like a snake swallowing."

For many runners this wild environment can be frustrating. It was here where lead runner Clarence DeMar fell victim to the craziness in 1920 when a car drove over his foot at Coolidge Corner, ripping open his shoe. Others feed off the passion of the masses, as Gayle Barron did during her run to the wreath in 1978. "Back when I won the race," she said, "the Marathon was a personal event between the runners and the fans. I ran the last miles in 1978 on a route with just enough space for one runner to squeeze through. Every step had a fan, on each side, just inches from my ear, yelling encouragement."

Over the years Mile 24 has hosted a number of exciting lead changes, enthusiastic crowds, and even, occasionally, tragedy. Sadly, the Boston Marathon belongs to a world with free will, and sometimes that outside world works its way into the race. In 1957, a man trying to escape after murdering his ex-girlfriend was so frustrated by the traffic of the Marathon that he placed his gun on the passenger seat and turned himself in to a policeman responsible for crowd control. "I'm the guy you're looking for," he said. "I've just killed somebody, [and] I want to give myself up."

In the same block twenty-three years earlier, while the runners ran through Coolidge Corner, armed guards escorted a group of adults along the sidewalk, in pairs. Careful not to step out of line, the spectators came to the Boston Marathon to get away. This "remarkably average group of male Americans" was actually a group of jurors that had been sequestered for weeks while sitting on the case of the century—a machine-gun bank robbery, in which two policemen were killed in the town of Needham.

In the midst of the trial, the judge granted an approved furlough so the jurors could attend the Boston Marathon. The jury would watch Canadian Dave Komonen run to victory in 1934, and would leave the race only after Clarence DeMar had passed them. The jurors had become virtual celebrities; the *Globe* reported, "On every hand could be heard the cry, 'There's the Millens-Faber jury.' Pretty girls waved madly, but the jurymen, placid and sedate, conducted themselves with great propriety." Following the jury's verdict, the three defendants were sentenced to death.

On Patriots' Day, the world doesn't halt on its axis, but instead orbits around the Boston Marathon. The Marathon reflects the world around it, and the times. Sometimes the rest of the world intrudes and claims the Marathon as its podium. Over the course of the race's history, the Boston Marathon has never existed in a bubble. Moments of joy and community have been a constant, but there have also been stories of sadness and even death connected to the race.

In 1906, spectator James Carr left the race feeling sick, only to later die of heart failure.

In 1935 a Marathon fan was making his way home to Newton over the train tracks and was killed by a train.

Six years later a man named Noble from Boston was watching the race at the Harvard Club on Commonwealth Avenue when he fell into the street and perished, as did a man named McCue in 1968.

In 1984, longtime Boston Garden—and Boston Marathon—timekeeper Tony Nota died at the finish line.

In 2000, a pilot died when his plane crashed at Norfolk Airport. He was en route to Boston with the intention of towing an advertisement over the racecourse when his plane crashed and burned.

Three spectators died in the 2013 bombing, and hundreds more were injured.

Although the race isn't immune from sadness and tragedy, it has somehow found a way to coexist with the world. Since 1897, every April, headlines across the globe have brought news of America's Marathon. To many across the world, Boston is known not as the Athens of America, the City upon the Hill, or the Hub of the Universe, but simply as "Marathon City." The Boston Marathon and all its trappings, including the warm smiles of fans, the beautiful landscape, and the open front (and bathroom) doors of Hopkinton, make the race a wonderful ambassador of America and its people.

———

The mile moves past Coolidge Corner and works down the hill toward Boston. When Larry Brignolia ran down this hill in 1899 with the lead, he slipped on a rock and twisted his ankle. As he attempted to get up, medics held him down for five minutes to make sure he could continue the race, costing Brignolia the world record, and nearly, the championship. (He did go on to win, even after this mishap.) It was in this same mile in 2005 that Robert Kipkoech Cheruiyot ran an astonishing 4:36. (As a comparison, John McDermott's splits in 1897 were 6:41.)

For me, the very concept of splits was no longer part of the equation. I had slowed down to twelve-minute miles by this point. I wasn't running anymore; instead, I was sliding down the last part of the mile, like lava leaking into the ocean. By the time my brother and I made it through Coolidge Corner it was close to 4:30 p.m. I had been running for four hours, and only had two and half miles to go. For the first time since the six-mile mark, I started to think that maybe—just maybe—I had a chance of finishing.

Despite this slight moment of optimism, I still ran with a fragile psyche. Crowds had thinned at this point, but there were still some hearty fans cheering us on. As my mind kept moving from focusing to daydreaming, I wondered how bad I looked to the fans I passed. Suffering from an episode of paranoia, I listened intently for any disparaging comments from the crowd that might have confirmed my misery.

With my ears thus focused, all of the sudden I heard someone yell, "Hey, it's Michael Connelly—all right!" I shifted my gaze to the side and made out the images of Joe and Kevin Radley, the brothers of Michael and Jack.

It was great to hear their bighearted cheers and see their friendly faces, but nothing was going to help me at this point. I wondered if the other three had already passed by, and hoped they had. The thought provided me with some motivation to push on. I didn't want to be the only one of the four who didn't conquer the course.

So, I pushed on to Mile 25, where the famous Citgo sign sits on the horizon.

Mile 25

Adoption

Runner Craig Virgin called the last two miles of Boston "an eternity." After Coolidge Corner, the runners continue to be escorted by the C train, which runs along their left. The course is still descending, spilling runners into the city limits of Boston. Halfway through the mile, the train goes underground, and the runners are left to find the finish line without it. On the left side of the submerging train sits the local Irish pub, O'Leary's. The owner, Aengus O'Leary, is used to his steady customers throwing down a cold one and zipping out to see the leaders run by. He's also accustomed to having runners stop by the bar for some late carbo-loading. One year two Irish priests running the race pulled up a couple of stools and fueled up for the last mile, compliments of a properly poured Guinness. As to their condition, O'Leary had one thing to say: "They were thirsty."

⌁

Boston was founded in 1630 and named after St. Botolph, a town in Lincolnshire, England. It had previously been known by the name of *Shawmut*, the Native American word for "living waters." The city was originally dominated by three hills, with water on three sides. The hills were eventually scaled down and used as landfill to create the Back Bay and Copley Square out of the Charles River marsh.

Boston has played a central role in American history, through the events of the Boston Massacre, the Boston Tea Party, and the Battle of Bunker Hill, among others. In the first half of the nineteenth century, Boston was a center of the abolition movement, and many runaway slaves headed to Boston for refuge. The first all-black regiment, the 54th Massachusetts, came from Boston and fought valiantly during the Civil War.

Boston has always been known for its prominent citizens and affluent families, including the Franklins, Samuel Adamses, the Cabots, the Lodges, and the Saltonstalls, all of whom figured in the molding of this international city. (The Adamses, from nearby Quincy, and the Kennedys, from Brookline, also produced their fair share of statesmen.) Luckily for them, they didn't live long enough to have to commute through the construction of "The Big Dig"—the Central Artery/Tunnel Project—the most expensive road project in American history, costing over $20 billion and taking more than fifteen years to complete.

Today Boston is one of the world's greatest college towns and the largest city in New England, with a population of almost 600,000 people spread across an area of ninety acres. The professional sports teams have won twelve championships over the last twenty years, leading to some labeling Boston "Title-town." The late two-decade mayor of Boston, Thomas Menino, used to look forward each year to the running of the Boston Marathon: "It's incredible to me how, year after year, the Boston Marathon brings people together like that. The crowds aren't rooting for anyone in particular—they're rooting for everyone." He added, "No tradition quite captures the spirit of Boston like the Boston Marathon . . . as runners from all over the world run through the city's streets, spectators from all over rally together to welcome them and spur them on."

Running across the intersection of Park Street, the runners enter the Audubon Circle where, on the left, the Church of the Cross bears a sign that reads "God Is Our Refuge and Strength." Runners likely believe anything would help at this point. In days gone by, the circle used to be where Boston's affluent would race their horse-drawn sleighs over the winter snow for sport or leisure. The *Boston Globe* wrote in December of 1902, after the first storm of the year: "No matter where one happened to be, the jingle of silver-toned bells was to be heard."

Moving through the circle, runners look up and are confronted by the sometimes unexpected and never welcome obstacle called "Citgo Hill." This unpleasant bump in the course takes its name from the large neon sign advertising Citgo Fuel that shines high in Kenmore Square up ahead. The Citgo sign has dominated Kenmore Square since 1965. It was shut down during the energy crisis in the early 1970s, but it was soon relit and eventually listed as a historical landmark.

Two-time winner Geoff Smith covered this final hill in contrasting states during his consecutive championships. "In 1984, I didn't even know it was there. I felt great at the time, and just breezed over it. In 1985, when I struggled to make it to the finish line with cramps, I was shocked to find this hill in the middle of Mile 25. I wondered if it was always there, or if it was new." Three-time winner Sara Mae Berman echoed these thoughts. "Citgo Hill feels like Mount Washington," she said. "When you get to the base of the hill and look up, your body tells you that it doesn't want to go."

This one last incline rises for a grueling two hundred yards, giving the fresher runners an opportunity to gain ground and the worn-out runners an excuse to go limp. The rise over the Massachusetts Turnpike comes at a bad time on the course and has a surprisingly negative effect on the athletes. At this point, most runners are in the process of physically shutting down. Peripheral vision narrows to about two yards on either side, and the runners' hearing may be greatly impaired.

To me Citgo Hill, like Heartbreak Hill, wasn't any harder than any other step on the course. Every step was an effort. When I reached the hill's peak, I was still insecure, hedging the outcome of the race with negative thoughts. As I approached the end of the mile, I was closing in on the long-awaited sign that read "Just one mile to go!" Sadly, my excitement was diminished by the thought that one more mile equaled four trips around my high school football field—the same distance that I'd struggled to complete just six months earlier.

Despite the cloud of negativity that darkened my spirit, I moved forward. I ran with purpose and pain, knowing that every step brought me closer to Kenmore Square, which would in turn get me closer to the finish line.

In his book *The Alchemist*, Coelho talks about the final steps to one's destination being the most harrowing. "The closer he got to the realization of his dream, the more difficult things became."

Despite the fact that the finish line is drawing closer, the minds of anxious or exhausted runners will start to wander, as if to distance themselves from the body. This disorientation is almost like an out-of-body experience, not uncommon among marathoners in the last miles. Even elite runners sometimes find themselves running on automatic pilot while their minds vacate the premises.

While some have out-of-body experiences, it was here in 1996— during the 100th Boston Marathon—that one of the greatest of female runners had an out-of-this-world experience. Running through Mile 25, thirty-year-old Uta Pippig of Germany chose to stage one of the most courageous comeback victories in Boston Marathon history. Battling cramps and multiple internal ailments (including those common to women, and an impatient stomach that was desperate to purge), Pippig was chasing Tegla Loroupe from Kenya as they approached Citgo Hill. As she closed in on the front-runner, Pippig ran to the side of the road and grabbed a water bottle. She returned to the middle of the route, ripped the top of the container off with her teeth, slugged the water, spiked the bottle down on the ground, and then proceeded to pass Loroupe for good on her way to her third straight Boston Marathon victory.

After the race, Uta spoke retrospectively about her historic run. "Four different times during the race, the pain was so bad that I contemplated dropping out of the race altogether. Somehow, I kept going and pushed myself. As I approached Citgo Hill, I saw Tegla up ahead and I said to myself, 'Come on, Uta—this is your chance!' I just kept saying, 'Hey, you can do it—just go,'" said Pippig. " 'Push, push, and try to win the race.' I just started fighting and imagined I could fly. Somehow, I caught her. I don't know how I did it. I replay that part of the race in my mind, and I still can't explain how I did it. I guess I won't figure it out until I run the race again and pass that spot. In retrospect I would say [that] this was my greatest victory, with respect to overcoming mental and physical adversity."

This was Pippig's day. With her body shutting down, she ran past her competitors to break the tape. Although she had to be briefly hospitalized after the race, she would forever be the author of one of the greatest comeback stories in race history. Her resolve was even greater than her vast talent. She simply refused to quit. Those who choose to push through moments of adversity can actually build the muscle of "will." Uta Pippig said afterwards, "It's very special for me that I could come to this race in Boston with such an experience and such mental strength."

Uta Pippig's courageous run and beautiful smile endeared her to the people of Boston. Fans of the race and citizens of the city only ask for sincerity. The public saw her triumph as a great victory. It was impossible not to be enamored with her as a runner, and as a person. When she ran through the streets of Boston, the ten-deep crowd on the sidewalk chanted, "Uta, Uta, Uta!" In gratitude for the fans' support, she threw kisses to the crowd. Following her second win, Boston writer Dan Shaughnessy wondered kiddingly: "Could she be just a little more gracious, courageous, intelligent, and charming? Is that possible?"

Over the history of the race, Boston has grown fond of runners who have traveled to the city and shown courage and heart. Consequently, certain runners have been adopted as one of their own by the masses who line the eight towns along the racecourse. Despite the fact that Uta Pippig was born behind the Berlin Wall in East Germany, she is a New Englander to the millions who line the route to Boston.

Local runners such as DeMar, Kelley "The Elder," Kelley "The Younger," Rodgers, Bingay, Benoit Samuelson, and the Hoyts have been loved by Boston for their running, but also because they are one of them. When Arthur Roth won in 1916, he spoke of the pride of being from the city: "Victory in the race really belongs to the local boys . . . I am Boston-born, Boston-bred, and Boston-trained."

But in today's global world, for those who embrace the spirit of the city and give themselves to the race like Uta Pippig, the city is more than willing to open their arms and welcome them into the family.

In 1926, Boston was introduced to Johnny Miles of Nova Scotia. When he arrived at BAA headquarters to sign up for the first marathon of his life, he asked, "By the way, you won't be terribly disappointed if I win the race?" Race official Tom Kanaly would laugh, noting, "The kid has a sense of humor." The unknown runner wouldn't remain that way for long. Despite the fact that the twenty-year-old had never run in a race longer than ten miles before, he would shock the greatest field ever assembled in front of an estimated one million fans. The *Boston Globe* headline the following day read "Leaped from Obscurity into Ranks of Champions at a Bound." Miles's spunk and underdog spirit made him an immediate fan favorite.

Following his victory, the city fell in love with Johnny Miles, and wouldn't let him go home for a week. Finally, Nova Scotia needed their hero back home, compelling him to board a train at North Station, where fans mobbed him all the way to the steps of the train. Under his arm he held a newspaper from his hometown in Nova Scotia, with a front-page headline that read "Boston Goes Wild Over Johnny Miles." The champion returned home, where he was carried to the town hall on the shoulders of his people.

Former winner William Kennedy would finish eighth the year Miles won. Kennedy was also adopted by the people of Boston, engendering feelings of great warmth in those who watched him run. William Kennedy, known lovingly as the "Bricklayer," came from Chicago and New York, depending on where he could find work. He couldn't afford train fare, so he would hobo from train to train, sometimes taking days to arrive. Unable to afford a hotel room before or after the race, he would sleep wherever he could lay his head—sometimes on the floors of friends' homes, or on the pool table at BAA headquarters. But unlike Miles, Kennedy would often stay in Boston before and after the race, finding work as a bricklayer.

Before running in 1916, Kennedy worked on a home in the Back Bay during the day and then would train at night in the uniform of the common man: trousers, sweater, and cap. After winning Boston in 1917, he arrived at work the next morning at 5:30 a.m. and proceeded to lay over 1,500 bricks. The blue-collar hero further captured the hearts of Boston, inspiring America in the midst of the hardship and dourness of World War I. One of his fellow bricklayers was quoted as saying, about Kennedy, "[A]side from his running ability, he had already gained their friendship and esteem by his companionship qualities and ever-ready smile and words of encouragement."

While the host city welcomes runners and adopts them as honorary citizens, runners do the same by embracing Boston as a special place in their life. Three-time champion Ibrahim Hussein so loved the city that when he returned to Kenya, he affirmed his affection by naming his newborn son "Boston." Desi Linden followed suit after her 2018 victory, naming her beloved dog "Boston," as well.

Runners appreciate the love and affection that the city freely shares with them—so much so that many of them want to show their gratitude by giving back. In 2013, winner Lelisa Desisa of Ethiopia donated his medal back to the city of Boston, still suffering from the aftereffects of that year's bombing. "Sport holds the power to unify and connect people all over the world," Desisa said. In 2018, wheelchair champion Tatyana McFadden ran for Team Martin Richard, named for the smiling boy who perished in the 2013 bombing. After winning the race, she handed over her gold-dipped laurel wreath to 2013 hero Carlos Arredondo, in recognition for his bravery during the aftermath of evil.

With just over a mile to go, the runners scale Citgo Hill. At eleven o'clock on the runner's sight lines, the Citgo sign is smiling at the competitors. On the right is Boston's most storied landmark—Fenway Park, home of the beloved Boston Red Sox.

For eight decades, between 1918 and 2004, Fenway Park was the home of futility, where men like Bucky Dent, Tony Perez, and Mariano Rivera crushed the hopes and dreams of the Boston faithful. Being a fan of the Sox was like being a victim in an abusive relationship. Despite the pain we endured, we still blindly uttered at the end of each season, "Wait till next year." Since 2004, however, the Red Sox have not only brought joy to Boston, with four World Series championships, they've also been able to bring unity and healing to the city following the tragic Patriots' Day of 2013. In the days following the bombing, the Red Sox served as a galvanizing force. This position of leadership was personified by the team's captain, David Ortiz, who addressed a sold-out crowd at Fenway Park days after the bombing, saying in raw and honest language, "This is our fucking city. Nobody is going to dictate our freedom. Stay strong!" He then raised a fist, symbolizing the unity the city felt following those difficult days.

Later that season, the Red Sox won the World Series, and the city threw them a party to celebrate. The festivities called for the team to parade through the streets of Boston the way the Celtics had, back in 1962. But instead of convertibles like Bill Russell and Bob Cousy traveled in, the Red Sox rolled through the streets in World War II amphibious vehicles, known as Duck Boats. During the parade, the team made an impromptu stop at the finish line of the Marathon, where malevolence had visited earlier that year. This time, there was nothing but love. The team put the championship trophy down on the yellow paint of the finish line and the city sang "God Bless America" together.

Back in 1996, when I ran past Fenway Park, I was one of many frustrated fans in Red Sox Nation who didn't know that back in 1947, race officials contemplated moving the finish line of the race inside Fenway Park. The Fenway finish was considered a way to mimic the finishes in stadiums like those at the Olympics, and as runners did back in 1897 at the Irvington Oval, just down the road. Switching the race to Fenway wasn't the only radical change discussed by race officials; in 1964, they mulled the prospect of having the race start in Boston and end in Hopkinton.

At this point, I didn't care where the finish line was. I just wanted to finish. So, I ran over Citgo Hill, battling my love-hate relationship with the Sox. On my right, Fenway Park was sliding out of my vision as I ran toward the end of the mile, where Kenmore Square sits, below. This is where Red Sox fans have emptied out after their traditional morning game, held on Marathon Day since 1903. Passing Fenway may provide inspiration for runners; what seemed implausible now seems possible. Those 37,400 Red Sox fans now line the sidewalks of Kenmore Square, helping to propel the runners those final steps.

I would need every one of them to pull me through Mile 26.

MILE 26

Living in the Present

While on vacation with my wife in Scotland, we enjoyed a beautiful morning in the town of Pitlochry. We had breakfast looking out over the Highlands and took a stroll in town. The weather could not have been better. We poked in and out of shops before getting on the road to our next destination of St. Andrews.

Thirty minutes later we were driving south on the A9 when I turned to my wife and said, "At this very moment, everything is perfect. The weather, the company, the trip." It was the type of morning that invoked an overly affected existential assessment of life as it existed at that time. At that moment, not one minute before or one minute in the future, life could not have been better. I continued to drone on about soaking in the moment. "As far as the present is concerned—this is perfect."

Within a second of finishing my soliloquy, I saw something out of the corner of my eye. It was tough to identify because of the low autumn sun. It appeared to be some form of paper or trash that was suspended in the air. But then I became aware the object wasn't floating, but instead was tracking directly for our windshield. I had enough time to process that we were going to be hit by an object but could do nothing to affect the outcome. We were on a two-lane divided highway traveling with the flow of traffic at 65 miles per hour. If I'd swerved right, we would have crashed head-on with oncoming traffic. If I swerved left, we would have piled into the evergreen trees that lined the road.

The object turned out to be a twelve-by-twelve patio brick that had fallen off a truck going in the opposite direction. The brick hit the highway and bounced up and smashed into our windshield—a direct hit. It exploded, showering my wife and me with thousands of shards of glass. I was able to pull safely to the side of the road where we gathered ourselves. We lived to tell the story. For the next twenty-four hours we pulled glass out of our hair and skin and teeth (those fragments we hadn't swallowed).

You could say I was right when I'd made my assessment. You must enjoy the moment, because the future is subject to the random whims of a fickle world. Within a single second, life went from perfect to almost deadly. This is why living in the moment and enjoying one's blessings is so important.

In the twenty-sixth mile, it was imperative that I took in as much as I could. I was on the precipice of realizing a dream, in the midst of a life-changing moment. It was important that I cherish this experience. If it was my intention to change my life with this run, then it was incumbent on me to treasure, value, respect, and appreciate every step. It meant that "I had legs to take me where I wanted to go." I was blessed with good health, and I had a loving wife and son, parents, brothers and sisters, and friends. And here I was, in the last mile of the Boston Marathon, celebrating life as it existed at that very moment.

Henry David Thoreau said, "You must live in the present, launch yourself on every wave, find your eternity in each moment. Fools stand on the island of opportunities and look toward another land. There is no other land, there is no other life but this."

So, I ran each step, in thanks and in pain. Kevin served as my eyes and ears, updating me on the sights and sounds. We ran past the end of the bridge at Citgo Hill with the sun dropping and breezes picking up. Discarded cups from competitors were blowing across the course. Into Kenmore Square we ran. In my college days, my roommates and I had supported some of the local establishments. But not today—I only had the finish line and bed on my agenda.

In the old days, twenty-five miles would have been enough to finish the race, but King Edward VII of England ordered the race to be lengthened (from 24.5 miles to 26 miles, 385 yards), so that the 1908 Olympic Marathon would end in front of his royal box at Windsor Castle. Because of this edict, people have suffered for over a century in the closing steps of every marathon. The King could not have foreseen the ramifications of his decision. For decades, runners have struggled to finish the most demanding feat in sports because he was too lazy to take his carriage down the street.

Like a battered boxer forced to go extra rounds, the runners now have to traverse the last mile-plus with the burden of bankrupt legs and weakened resolve. The downhill into Kenmore Square is the last real chance for the sadistic course to wreak havoc on the field. Runners who wrote checks on the hills of Newton find them getting cashed in this last mile.

When the course finally leads the runners into Kenmore Square at the end of Beacon Street, the athletes arrive back on Commonwealth Avenue, the same street that houses the hills back in Newton. The route continues, on a level grade, through the square—just a mile from the finish line. Years ago, when beef stew was served to everyone at the finish line (to a far smaller field), the runners probably began to salivate here, as they could almost smell the finish. In truth, by this point in the race, most runners are more interested in finishing than eating.

Kenmore Square has long been compared to Times Square in New York City because of the intersecting streets (Beacon, Commonwealth, and Brookline) and the odd angles they make. Like Times Square, the location is ideal for billboard advertisements. The square is best known for its proximity to Fenway Park and the many bars and pubs that serve as a virtual "water stop" for thirsty Red Sox fans on game days. The square is also a bustling gathering spot for the thousands of downtown college students from Boston University and the colleges of Simmons, Emmanuel, and Wheelock. It was once known as Governor Square, and served as the center of Boston's hotel district. Hotels such as the Somerset, Braemore, Sheraton, Buckminster, and Kenmore all stood here, but they gave way to condominiums, nightclubs, and Boston University dormitories. In recent years, hotels have returned to the square, including the five-star Commonwealth Hotel, which is sold out every Marathon weekend.

The square takes its modern name from the Green Line train stop, set right in the middle. Thronged with students lugging schoolbooks, girls with purple hair, and commuters hustling to the T, Kenmore Square is a distinctive section of the Marathon, and the city.

World-class marathoner Craig Virgin found the fans and location at Kenmore Square taxing. "The crowd can suffocate you here and make you become claustrophobic." With thousands of Red Sox fans lining the sidewalks, the noise and mayhem of the square is palpable. This pandemonium was never more pronounced than in 1935, when John "The Elder" Kelley ran through Kenmore Square on the way to his first wreath. Kelley, who had gobbled chocolate glucose pills along the route, had been struggling with his stomach ever since Coolidge Corner. As he made his way over Citgo Hill, he was five hundred yards in the lead over Pat Dengis when his intestinal pains brought him to an abrupt halt, forcing the press car to slam on its brakes to avoid hitting the suddenly stationary runner.

The crowd—dismayed to see the hometown favorite bent over at the waist, clearly in pain—urged him on. Kelley unfolded himself and ran two steps before stopping again, sending the crowd into a frenzy. Behind him, Pat Dengis was closing the gap: Kelley had to move or lose. According to the following day's *Boston Globe*, a desperate Kelley applied the "Roman Cure," sticking his fingers down his throat to relieve himself. The trick worked, and Kelley ran on to the first of two championships. He had "overdosed on glucose pills," he later admitted.

Like Kelley, most runners plunge into Kenmore Square in some form of mental or physical free fall. By this stage the legs may no longer have the ability to brake; many runners let gravity throw their bodies down the hill, praying they will regain their balance without crashing. Glycogen is a distant memory, and the low fuel light is shining. When Greg Meyer was running through the square with the lead in 1983, a friend of his jumped out of the crowd and yelled, while pointing, "You've got to fucking go that-a-way." Halfway through the square, the runners pass by a sign with the most pleasant message known to a marathoner: "1 Mile to Go."

John "The Elder" Kelley had fond memories of this milestone from his wins in 1935 and 1945: "A mile from the finish, they have painted a wonderful sign, and when you know you have it won, you know if you can keep it up for another mile, it's all over, the chills go up and down your spine and tears are in your eyes and you know you've got the Boston victory, the one you wanted most of all."

On the left side of Commonwealth Avenue, in the square, is a bar called Cornwall's Pub that bears a sign reading "Rosie Ruiz Started Here," in reference to the woman who cheated her way to the laurel wreath (temporarily) in 1980 by jumping into the race in Kenmore Square. While Ruiz started in Kenmore Square, many runners struggle not to be finished here.

In 1936, an exhausted Tarzan Brown was trying to carry on and hold on to his lead. As he attempted to navigate the cars and fans, he swerved left and right, drunken-like, and was almost hit by a passing vehicle. Finally, Brown came to a complete halt, prompting his illegal attendant—who happened to be his coach—to douse the weary runner with water, reviving him and sending him off to victory. The coach was arrested for this, spending time in jail, while Brown enjoyed the fruits of his championship.

Ten years later, Mayor Maurice Tobin also violated the "no attendant" rule, but no one was going to arrest him. His runner of choice was Fred McGlone, a local harrier who had captured the attention of the city official. During the race, the mayor illegally jumped out of his car and provided water to McGlone. When Tobin got back into his car, he slammed the door on his hand, severing his fingers with a one-inch laceration. Approaching the finish line, McGlone would repeatedly collapse to the ground only to courageously rise each time. On his last fall a policeman couldn't take it anymore and helped McGlone to his feet. The runner would cross the finish line bleeding from both legs and with no recollection of the last three miles. In the clubhouse he would recover enough to be told that he'd been disqualified because he was aided by the policeman.

The race moves through Kenmore Square, past the Commonwealth Hotel on the right, up to the intersection of Charlesgate West. It was here in 1961 that John "The Younger" Kelley continued his stretch of frustrating runs when three-time winner Eino Oksanen passed him for the lead with less than a mile to go. (Over his career, Kelley finished second five times, and in the top ten no fewer than ten times. He won in 1957, becoming the only runner from the Boston Athletic Association ever to win the Boston Marathon.) Kelley was a favorite with the fans and the press, although his "close but no cigar" finishes frustrated the often-temperamental Boston media. After another one of Kelley's second-place finishes, the press ripped the Connecticut schoolteacher. Colin Heard of the *Boston Herald* wrote, "How stupid can a schoolteacher be?" John Gilhooley, also of the *Herald*, wrote, "If our schoolteachers are like that, it's no wonder our school system is in trouble."

After making it through Kenmore Square, the runners are greeted by the hysterical crowd in the Back Bay. Some line the streets, some hang out of apartment windows, and still others dangle from the rooftops of the highly priced brownstone condominiums. The athletes, who back at the starting line looked like kids on Christmas morning, now look like deserters from the Foreign Legion. The screams of "One more mile!" are finally—mercifully—accurate.

The runners move under the ramp to Storrow Drive, and then past Charlesgate East, where a statue of the Norse explorer Leif Erikson greets them. Like the doughboy statue at the starting line in Hopkinton, he also faces away from the finish line.

After the statue, the runners fork left down an underpass that travels under the Tom Leonard Bridge named after a local bartender/runner/supporter of the race. On the right at the Mass Avenue intersection sits the

Harvard Club, where members used to cheer from a temporary grandstand set up in front of the brick home of Harvard alumni and faculty. Now they watch the race from inside on a big-screen television, with the bar and grill open for the day.

Next door to the Harvard Club is where the Eliot Hotel, the old home of the legendary (and now extinct) Eliot Lounge was located. This watering hole, which served as a virtual clubhouse for runners, became famous in 1975 when a victorious Bill Rodgers told a national audience, while being interviewed, "I'm going to the Eliot Lounge." I'm sure Tom Leonard made Rodgers his favorite Blue Whale drink. In 1996, sadly, the lounge was closed. Crossing in front of the Eliot Hotel, the runners move over Massachusetts Avenue on their way toward the big right turn off Commonwealth Avenue, onto Hereford Street.

It was at Mass Avenue that 1897 winner John McDermott came to a halt when he ran into traffic. With less than a mile to go in the inaugural race, McDermott found himself running in front of a funeral procession and two trolleys, bringing all of them to a stop on his way to the finish line at the Irvington Oval. When McDermott entered the oval, the crowd was still wild with excitement from Boston College upsetting the favored Fordham in the hundred-yard dash at the annual BAA track-and-field handicap event. As McDermott circled the oval, he was said to have finished with the speed and strength of a half-miler.

Ever since 1965, the athletes have taken the 90-degree turn onto Hereford Street, eight-tenths into the mile. It's important for the leaders—as well as the runners who are trying to save every step—to cut the tangents on the five turns along the course. In 2008, Women's champion Dire Tune almost missed this turn altogether, running side by side with Russian Alevtina Biktimirova. Fortunately for her, she was able to double back onto the course and eventually win the race by two seconds.

Hereford Street moves up toward Boylston on a gradual incline as the course continues to punish the runner, even in the final steps. Over Newbury Street—where on the other 364 days of the year the sidewalks are filled with college kids who have trust funds and the Boston bourgeoisie, carrying their shopping bags—the runners need to grind out the final steps. Of course, they can't help but peek ahead at Boylston Street, which sits at the top.

The race now rises toward its crescendo. Throughout the day, the waiting fans have been updated on the race as they struggle to hold on to their viewing positions. These crowds are stacked sometimes fifteen deep in the last mile, and are known for their intensity and fervor.

A hazardous crowd inevitably becomes a problem for the runners. Especially in the early days, sidewalks lined with spectators can suddenly turn into streets crowded with mobs. In 1901, runners lost vital minutes off their times after they were forced to snake through the crowd. In 1905, Superintendent Pierce added patrolmen and mounted police to aid with crowd control. Their significant presence was welcomed by the *Globe*, who reported the following day that "they left the scene with every spectator feeling they were human and capable." The eventual winner that year, Fred Lorz, had to hopscotch over multiple discarded bikes to get to the finish line, where he caught his foot and crashed through the tape. Efforts to control the chaos over the years have sometimes only added to it. In the eleventh year of the race, 1907, police almost ran over the leader, Tom Longboat, in their zeal to control the crowd.

After crossing the intersection of Newbury Street, the road takes an unexpected and nasty little climb. Rising toward the last turn, I found myself getting giddy with excitement. Just around that corner—after one left turn at the top—my dream would become reality.

The thrill of rising to the top of Hereford Street was magical. It was the precursor to something special and memorable, like the smell of turkey on Thanksgiving morning. I was running toward the corner of Boylston Street—just 385 yards from my destiny.

385 Yards

Where Dreams Come True

Hopkinton seemed like it was years ago—a distant memory where excitement and the unknown coexisted. But now I was standing on the corner of Hereford and Boylston, where hard work, family sacrifice, and heavenly blessings had granted me the opportunity to run this race.

The day moves from sunrise to sunset, morning giving way to afternoon. At the top of Hereford Street, the runners arrive with their own story—their own dream. Working as one, their hearts and feet have brought them to the corner of Boylston Street.

As I slowly took the turn, I made sure I placed my feet carefully. There was no need for me to cut tangents. I just needed to get to that finish line. Now on Boylston Street, I allowed for a guilty pleasure and snuck a peek at the blue-and-yellow bridge for photographers that hovered over the finish line. After indulging my curiosity, it was back to one step at a time.

For months I had dreamt of this moment—running the last 385 yards of the Boston Marathon. For the first time since I'd stepped on the course in Hopkinton, I knew that I would conquer the route that had destroyed so many. For a century, hundreds of thousands of runners had lined up in Hopkinton with the dream of somehow defeating twenty-six-plus miles. Eight towns, four Newton Hills, a mile called Haunted, an overpass called Hell's Alley, and the madness of a vengeful course. Now I ran (albeit, slowly) with the blue-and-yellow banner of the BAA finish line in my sights. In minutes I would be realizing a lifetime aspiration to run Boston.

The needle in the knee, the catheters running through my body to my heart, the countless ice bags—all added to this moment. To be given this chance meant that God had deemed me worthy, for some reason, of His intercession.

In 1931, the *Boston Globe* reported after the race: "The old course could tell stories of shattered hopes, of triumphs lost when the goal seemed at hand, and of men who fought off seemingly insurmountable handicaps and managed to reach the finish line." This is the spirit that has enveloped the Boston Marathon for decade after decade, and the people who run it, watch it, work it, and love it.

Since that day at the end of the nineteenth century, when John Graham and Henry Holton had ridden their bikes out to Ashland in the back of the pack, marathoners have traveled east in search of glory and accomplishment.

To the pragmatic, the Boston Marathon is just a road race. It starts and finishes. It travels over pavement and, in the end, if the participants fulfill their goal of traversing these roads within the requirements, they are presented with a medal. But that's not why people run Boston. The medal is simply a symbol, the race, a metaphor.

People run Boston for reasons far beyond running. The race possesses the ability to literally change lives. People don't run it because it is there, but because of *what* is there. It's within those borders between start and finish that enlightenment can be found. It is here at the Boston Marathon that a person discovers who he or she is—and who he or she can be.

A mere 385 yards—1,155 feet—13,860 inches—that's all that's left. I ran down Boylston Street slowly but proudly, traveling the final steps over the greatest finishing stretch in the marathoning world. It is running down the stairs on Christmas morning; walking down the aisle on your wedding day; the sprint out the school door on the last day of classes. The runners move down Boylston Street like Caesar returning to Rome. Every athlete who runs these magical 385 yards is a winner on this day. The fans greet each and every one of them with the same fervor and sincerity, no matter their finishing time. As Dr. George Sheehan said about all Boston competitors: "Everyone who finishes the Boston Marathon has their own great moment in sports. Each one of us, on this day, has achieved greatness."

On Boylston Street, Boston's adopted daughter, three-time champion Uta Pippig—taken by the fans' compassion, enthusiasm, and sincerity—threw kisses and waved and flashed that smile in gratitude to the fans who had helped her get there. "Some people feel that I'm too emotional, but that's me," she said. "I feel a special connection with the people who line the streets to cheer, and I want to show these people who are sharing in the moment that I appreciate them, and the race."

Prior to being named Boylston Street, the thoroughfare was called Frog Lane, and then, Common Street. The street name was changed to honor philanthropist Ward Boylston back in the 1800s. Ward was previously known by the last name of Hallowell, but changed it to Boylston after his uncle, Dr. Zabdiel Boylston, pledged a share of his estate if he would take his name. Dr. Boylston, who was related to the famous Adams family of Quincy, Massachusetts, was a renowned doctor who became the first American physician to operate in this country. His radical methods of inoculating those afflicted by smallpox made him an outcast in the medical world, subjecting him and his family to violent rebuke, including a bomb attack.

The runners continue down Boylston Street, guided by the Old South Church steeple that stands behind the finish line, and its ringing bells. They glide past bars and restaurants that sit on the corners of the perpendicular streets of Gloucester and Fairfield. Up ahead on the right, just before the intersection of Exeter Street, the course moves past that Boston Marathon landmark, the Lenox Hotel. In 1948, Gerard Côté ran the final yards of Boston with his fourth victory in hand. As he passed the hotel, he looked up at the window of his room and signaled to friends and family that he was thirsty, so they would know to put his beers on ice.

The Lenox has long been associated with the Boston Marathon because of its proximity to the finish line. When the race used to finish outside of the BAA clubhouse, the hotel's side door on Exeter Street was often prominently displayed in newspaper photos of the winners breaking the tape. The hotel has 214 rooms and throws a party on the rooftop for their top clients on race day.

Just steps from breaking the tape, 1976 champion Jack Fultz experienced an out-of-body occurrence. With temperatures exceeding 90 degrees, he felt giddy as he soldiered on with the leaders. First, he started to giggle when he realized that he had a shot at achieving his greatest dream. Next, he found himself watching himself from above, like a sports commentator analyzing his run. Finally, Fultz caught himself rehearsing answers for the post-race press conference. He later explained, "If I was going to win it"—which he did—"I didn't want to be full of clichés and one-liners. I wanted to sound intelligent."

The 2005 champion, Hailu Negussie of Ethiopia, articulated the feelings of every runner: "Day and night, I was dreaming of winning the Boston Marathon. And I did what I was dreaming of."

Geoff Smith said after winning, "I'm going to be remembered."

During my training runs and physical therapy sessions, I used to envision myself running down Boylston Street in an exercise to justify the means for this most profound end. That it would be all worth it. I wondered and dreamed about how special the moment would be. The commitment and the agony were an investment in my life. Every step, every bead of sweat, every twinge of pain—all would have value.

As I worked my way down Boylston Street, I was bewildered to find that the finish line was still so far away. I decided to keep my head down and just work each step. My brother Kevin, fighting hard to slow his pace to stay with me, started to get excited. "Pick them up and put 'em back down. You're doing it! You're gonna do it! Listen to the crowd—they're all yelling for you. Keep it going!"

Champion Georgy Murray would say after one of his victories, "If you don't have a dream—then how can dreams come true?"

It's at the finish line of Boston where dreams are realized, and runners are rewarded with what eight-time champion Jean Driscoll describes as a goose bump–raising experience that causes all the stress of the journey to disappear. "It's a euphoric feeling whenever anyone achieves a goal," she says, "whether it's winning, beating a time, or just finishing the race."

With about a hundred yards to go and tears welling in my eyes, a burst of wind hit me in the face, almost knocking me over. As I continued toward the finish line, I realize that I was living the dream I had dreamed so often: I was running the last hundred yards of the Boston Marathon. It was one of those rare moments in life when dreams and reality become one.

As I crossed the finish line four and half hours after leaping over the starting line, I pumped my fist in the air twice with the last bit of strength I had left, and then leaned on my brother.

Kevin simply said, "You did it."

Rejoice, We Conquer

One weekend morning, I walked into church to see an elderly priest on the altar. I had never seen him before, and I was immediately concerned that the coming sermon could be a rambling diatribe about church dogma that would extend my stay unnecessarily. When it came time for his homily, I put my ears on autopilot and decided to get lost in my own personal prayers. That was until the slow-moving priest started preaching about legacy and our purpose in this world. The theme immediately caught my attention, so I slid up on the edge of the pew and suddenly found myself captivated by every word he said.

The priest was sharing a story about the great opera composer, Giacomo Puccini. He said that when the composer died, family members were going through his belongings when they came upon an opera that he had been composing up to the day that he passed, in 1924. The composition was named *Turandot*. Two years later, in Milan, the opera was to be performed for the first time at the Teatro alla Scala.

After the audience had taken their seats, conductor Arturo Toscanini was about to raise his baton when he turned to the crowd and said, "Tonight, Puccini lives. His soul and mind and heart are in the notes you will hear tonight. The same notes that will echo throughout this building. And the notes you will bring home with you tonight. The notes that will carry on for eternity. Puccini lives forever in this opera house and wherever his works are performed."

The priest then paused for effect, looked out at the congregation, and said, "I'm here to tell you that you can live forever. That you will never die if you leave something in this world. If you strive to make a difference. If you make your life matter and enhance the lives of others. So, I ask you—what are the notes of your life that will echo through time?"

I sat there with my mouth open, begging for more. In one five-minute sermon, the priest had challenged me to be better, to do more, to leave a legacy. That's why I went to Hopkinton that April Monday. Because when

I die, I want people to know that I lived. That I did something. I want my obituary to include a sense of purpose—that my time on this Earth meant something. By running Boston, I would have living, breathing evidence that all was possible.

There is a saying, "Anything said before the word 'but' is bullshit." I don't want my obituary to have that word in it. When my mother told me that I was a dreamer, she unknowingly put me on notice. She was telling me that it was time to act and achieve. No more excuses. So, I adopted the sentiment crystallized by Bill Olsen's grandfather—"Never mind the bullshit." You either do things—or you don't.

After his victory at Boston, John "The Elder" Kelley would say, "I've been looking forward to this moment since I was a kid." After winning, he would join former mayor John "Honey Fitz" Fitzgerald in a rousing rendition of the song "Sweet Adeline": "In all my dreams, your fair face beams; you're the flower of my heart."

Way back in 1897, when John McDermott entered the Irvington Oval for the final steps of the inaugural Boston Marathon, the crowd was said to have risen to their feet, cheering wildly for the runner on his last lap. As McDermott approached the tape, the crowd went strangely quiet. It was almost as if they were witnessing something so special, so extraordinary, that there was no precedent for how to respond. Then, in a collective release, they showered the runner with such a raw ovation of admiration that some were compelled to rush the track, place McDermott on their shoulders, and carry him around the oval for a spirited victory lap. "The race was a big success," a BAA official said the next day. "There is assurance that this event will be an annual fixture."

And it has been ever since.

Every April, for more than a century, runners have toed the line in Hopkinton in hopes that they too might enter through the gates of Boston to the cheers of the crowd, joining the ranks of John McDermott and all the others who have passed before them. In 1907, *Globe* writer Lawrence Sweeney wrote about those special few that have answered the call to run Boston: "The competitor possessed the sturdier legs, more lion-like heart, and [was] endowed with the spirit which carried Pheidippides into the marketplace at Athens."

No matter where in the pack a runner finishes, in those final steps, he or she realizes that if this is possible, then all is possible. Now they can clear any obstacle and accept any challenge in all the races of life. It's not even about running; it's about resilience, and a spirit that refuses to say no.

Nobody knows what motivates a runner to push past the limits that stop others. Is it the heart, or the mind, or the body? Is it the prize money or the pride of accomplishment? Is the glory for the runner, or for family, or country? Is it a rare spirit possessed by those in search of greatness? For those who want to, as marathon runner and heroic surgeon after the 2013 bombing Dr. David King said, "search for more within themselves"?

For the average marathoner, the medal is confirmation of his or her own personal victory. The ribbon with its attached pendant provides the runner with validation for the blood, sweat, and tears that have been shed in order to participate in this event. Each year after receiving his medal, Pat Williams ponders how a fifty-cent medal could be worth a million dollars. But it's clearly worth even more—it's about what it represents to each runner. For 1974 Women's winner Miki Gorman, "It was one of the most precious, memorable experiences in [my] life."

Like the competitors themselves, the race has persevered—through two world wars, a terrorist attack, bankruptcy, the transformation from an amateur contest into a professional one, rogue dogs, rambunctious police on motorcycles, spooked horses, manic media buses, chauvinistic officials, scorching heat, and slippery sleet. For more than a century, runners have worked their way through Hopkinton, Ashland, Framingham, Natick, Wellesley, Newton, Boston, Brookline, and back into Boston, in order to fulfill a dream held by runners the world over.

Pulitzer Prize–winning author John Cheever came to the race in 1979 to cheer on his son, and was moved by the effort and sincerity of the runners who passed in front of him. "The Marathon was one of the most impressive things I've ever seen. There are those thousands of men and women determined to find out something about themselves."

Runners step through a portal at the finish line—the line that separates those who do from those who don't—and go from challenger to conqueror. They know, like Women's champion Sara Mae Berman, that their run is eternal: "The wonderful thing about athletic achievement is that it is finite," Berman said. "There is no ambiguity. You did it, and no one can ever take that away from you."

For more than a hundred years, images from the Boston Marathon have been ingrained in the souls of those who came to challenge, conquer, or cheer.

The memories endure: Clarence DeMar's proud chest, breaking the tape; Uta Pippig's radiant Boylston Street smile; Bill Rodgers's gloved hands; John "The Elder" Kelley's immortal stride; the sight of a small boy on his father's shoulders. For competitors and spectators alike, being part of the Boston Marathon is a love affair. It is a link to our past. Like the New England seasons, it changes even as it remains constant. It represents tradition and—despite the horror of 2013—innocence. It is the one day of the year that people come from every corner of the world to share a bond.

After I crossed the finish line, I didn't feel like I'd walked through a portal. Instead, I was overcome by an overwhelming desire to fall asleep. Medical personnel recommended that I take a detour into the medical tent to regain my faculties. With a drained body, a stiff knee, blisters on my feet, and chills, I concurred with their diagnosis. I entered the tent and was led to an open cot. A nurse kindly attended to me while my brother Kevin went in search of some dry clothes. As the nurse completed her due diligence, she went through her litany of questions, including, "Any known medical problems?" That was when I realized that, for the first time in two decades, I didn't have to respond, "I have the heart disease WPW." My answer had changed thanks to my successful surgery months before.

What a win-win-win the entire event had been. Not only had I conquered the Boston Marathon, but I'd also strengthened my bond with Rad, Richie, and Jack—and, best of all, I had proven that I no longer struggled with the disease that had saddled me for so long. Lying on the cot, in disarray, I realized that the last six months had earned me invaluable long-term benefits. Running the marathon would pay me dividends for the rest of my life.

Still shivering, the volunteers bundled me up with blankets and moved a portable heater over to my side, allowing my system to slowly return to normal. Before being allowed to depart, I was required to drink twenty-four ounces of Gatorade, twelve ounces of water, and twelve ounces of cold chicken soup. After I had consumed sufficient fluids, two physical therapists made me take a lap around the tent to satisfy them that I was capable of walking. As I circled the tent, I noticed that there was a news camera, with its red light on, filming the scene. (Back at my parents' house, my mother called in to the kitchen to let my father know I was on TV. He ran into the den to watch his son being walked around the medical tent like a patient from the movie *One Flew Over the Cuckoo's Nest*.)

Eventually I completed my last lap of the day and was allowed to leave the tent and find my family at the Boston Common, a mile down Boylston

Street. As I walked down the street, with two Mylar blankets taped around me like capes, a well-meaning girl offered me a PowerBar. I felt like saying, "I don't need a PowerBar. I need to be read my last rites!"

It was almost six p.m., and the sun had gone down. The temperature had plummeted into the low forties, and the wind was howling. The thought of walking another mile was out of the question. Luckily a volunteer assessed my state and offered me a ride to the Boston Common in a wheelchair. Once there I found my wife, son, and brother—and the loneliness of the Marathon was over.

For me, the finish brought liberation. The long training runs, the hustle to find a babysitter, the ice bags—all would now fade into memory. Only the spirit of conquest would remain. I had satisfied the wild curiosity that had held me captive for years.

After arriving home from a muscle-stiffening thirty-minute cab ride, I was in no condition to party or dance into the night. As I unfolded from the taxi, I faced one more obstacle in my long day: the six steps of my front porch. For six months I had hopped down these steps en route to my training runs; now I was presented with the task of scaling up them. I clutched the banister, but my legs refused to cooperate. So, I turned around and mounted the steps backwards. Whatever it takes.

Shuffling across the porch where I always did my stretching, I eased myself over the threshold as my wife held the door open for me. I had arrived home, safe and sound. Twenty-four hours before, I had walked out that door a different man. Now I was the proud owner of a Boston Marathon "victory," and all the physical and mental benefits that come with it.

Later in the night, I sat at my kitchen table, barely in one piece, to have dinner with my family. My wife placed a delicious meal in front of me, which I struggled to keep down. When I had gathered enough strength, I made my way to the bathroom and sank into a nice hot tub, where I discovered that I had suffered a bad sunburn on the backs of my legs during my four-and-a-half-hour trek.

Around eight p.m., Richie called to see how I had done. We were both excited to hear that all four of us had been successful in reaching the finish line. If one of us had dropped out, the overall experience would have been tarnished. On this day the four of us had run in our own little private running club, and thankfully shared in the exhilaration of finishing.

Before Richie hung up, he reminded me of the pledge we had made to each other some eight months earlier. We had put our hands together like the Three Musketeers and vowed to each other to run the Boston Marathon. We had been true to our vow.

Five minutes later Michael and Jack Radley came by the house to make sure I still had a pulse. They were sore and tired but smiling. I was glad they had stopped by; I needed some closure to the event, and I wanted to see and hear from my three comrades. Later, as they headed out the door to settle in their own homes, Rad turned and said, "We did it." I echoed his sentiment with my own "We did it," as if I was saying it to myself in disbelief. Again, we shook hands and congratulated each other, parting with a special bond that would last a lifetime.

In all, twenty-six thousand runners ran a faster time than me that day, but as far as I was concerned, I was the winner of the Boston Marathon. Forever I would wear the figurative laurel wreath of victory. Half-century volunteer Tony Nota would say about those who complete the challenge of 26.2 miles, "The race itself is the real satisfaction. It makes no difference if you've beaten someone else, beaten your old time, or just beaten nature."

Fifteen minutes later I settled into bed with a sunburn, an injured knee, and a spent body. Staring at the ceiling, I couldn't help but revel in my day's accomplishment. Over and over, I replayed the race in my head and got goose bumps every time I crossed the finish line. Even two decades later, when I pass over the Marathon course, I find myself saying "I did it." The race was over, but the benefits would last forever.

For eight months, I'd ventured outside of myself in search of a sublime pot of gold at the end of an unknown rainbow. At age thirty-two, I knew that the world offered opportunities I had yet to explore. Little did I know that the intangible benefits of running twenty-six miles would serve me well in all aspects of my life. I had elected to take a trip back in October, choosing a destination and then running step by step down a path that would deliver me to my destiny. When I arrived, I was introduced to myself. I looked in the mirror and knew that my spirit possessed endless possibilities. I ran in order to answer the questions. After crossing the finish line, I unveiled layers of potential that would allow me to run any race.

Fulfillment comes in many shapes and colors. Running the Boston Marathon produced in me a profound sense of accomplishment. I ran from Hopkinton to Boston that day, unaware that my inner soul would be so seriously tested, and so richly rewarded.

In November of 1995, my heart had stopped. In April of 1996, my heart soared. I had run Boston.

Appendix

Men's Open Champions

1897	John J. McDermott, New York City, NY	2:55:10
1898	Ronald J. MacDonald, Cambridge, MA	2:42:00
1899	Lawrence J. Brignolia, Cambridge, MA	2:54:38
1900	James Caffery, Hamilton, Ontario	2:39:44
1901	James Caffery, Hamilton, Ontario	2:29:23
1902	Sammy Mellor, Yonkers, NY	2:43:12
1903	John C. Lorden, Cambridge, MA	2:41:29
1904	Michael Spring, New York City, NY	2:38:04
1905	Fred Lorz, New York City, NY	2:38:25
1906	Timothy Ford, Cambridge, MA	2:45:45
1907	Tom Longboat, Hamilton, Ontario	2:24:24
1908	Thomas Morrissey, New York City, NY	2:25:43
1909	Henri Renaud, Nashua, NH	2:53:36
1910	Fred Cameron, Amherst, Nova Scotia	2:28:52
1911	Clarence DeMar, Melrose, MA	2:24:39
1912	Mike Ryan, New York City, NY	2:21:18
1913	Fritz Carlson, Minneapolis, MN	2:25:14
1914	James Duffy, Hamilton, Ontario	2:25:01
1915	Edouard Fabre, Montreal, Quebec	2:31:41
1916	Arthur Roth, Roxbury, MA	2:27:16
1917	William Kennedy, Port Chester, NY	2:28:37
1918	Armed Services relay, Camp Devens, Ayer, MA	2:29:53
1919	Carl Linder, Quincy, MA	2:29:13
1920	Peter Trivoulidas, Greece	2:29:31
1921	Frank Zuna, Newark, NJ	2:18:57
1922	Clarence DeMar, Melrose, MA	2:18:10
1923	Clarence DeMar, Melrose, MA	2:23:37
1924	Clarence DeMar, Melrose, MA	2:29:40
1925	Charles Mellor, Chicago, IL	2:33:00
1926	John Miles, Sydney Mines, Nova Scotia	2:25:40

1927	Clarence DeMar, Melrose, MA	2:40:22
1928	Clarence DeMar, Melrose, MA	2:37:07
1929	John Miles, Sydney Mines, Nova Scotia	2:33:08
1930	Clarence DeMar, Melrose, MA	2:34:48
1931	James Henigan, Medford, MA	2:46:45
1932	Paul de Bruyn, Germany	2:33:36
1933	Leslie Pawson, Pawtucket, RI	2:31:01
1934	Dave Komonen, Ontario, Canada	2:32:53
1935	John "The Elder" Kelley, Arlington, MA	2:32:07
1936	Ellison Myers "Tarzan" Brown, Alton, RI	2:33:40
1937	Walter Young, Verdun, Quebec	2:33:20
1938	Leslie Pawson, Pawtucket, RI	2:35:34
1939	Ellison Myers "Tarzan" Brown, Alton, RI	2:28:51
1940	Gérard Côté, Sainte-Hyacinthe, Quebec	2:28:28
1941	Leslie Pawson, Pawtucket, RI	2:30:38
1942	Bernard Joseph Smith, Medford, MA	2:26:51
1943	Gérard Côté, Sainte-Hyacinthe, Quebec	2:28:25
1944	Gérard Côté, Sainte-Hyacinthe, Quebec	2:31:50
1945	John "The Elder" Kelley, Arlington, MA	2:30:40
1946	Stylianos Kyriakides, Greece	2:29:27
1947	Suh Yun-Bok, South Korea	2:25:39
1948	Gérard Côté, Sainte-Hyacinthe, Quebec	2:31:02
1949	Karl Gosta Leandersson, Sweden	2:31:50
1950	Ki-Yong Ham, South Korea	2:32:39
1951	Shigeki Tanaka, Hiroshima, Japan	2:24:45
1952	Doroteo Flores, Guatemala	2:31:53
1953	Keizo Yamada, Japan	2:18:51
1954	Veikko Karvonen, Finland	2:20:39
1955	Hideo Hamamura, Japan	2:18:22
1956	Antti Viskari, Finland	2:14:14
1957	John "The Younger" Kelley, Groton, CT	2:20:05
1958	Franjo Mihalic, Yugoslavia	2:25:54
1959	Eino Oksanen, Helsinki, Finland	2:22:42
1960	Paavo Kotila, Finland	2:20:54

1961	Eino Oksanen, Helsinki, Finland	2:23:39
1962	Eino Oksanen, Helsinki, Finland	2:23:48
1963	Aurele Vandendriessche, Belgium	2:18:58
1964	Aurele Vandendriessche, Belgium	2:19:59
1965	Morio Shigematsu, Japan	2:16:33
1966	Kenji Kimihara, Japan	2:17:11
1967	David McKenzie, New Zealand	2:15:45
1968	Ambrose (Amby) Burfoot, Groton, CT	2:22:17
1969	Yoshiaki Unetani, Japan	2:13:49
1970	Ron Hill, Cheshire, England	2:10:30
1971	Alvaro Mejia, Colombia	2:18:45
1972	Olavi Suomalainen, Otaniemi, Finland	2:15:39
1973	Jon Anderson, Eugene, OR	2:16:03
1974	Neil Cusack, Ireland	2:13:39
1975	Bill Rodgers, Melrose, MA	2:09:55
1976	Jack Fultz, Arlington, VA	2:20:19
1977	Jerome Drayton, Toronto, Canada	2:14:46
1978	Bill Rodgers, Melrose, MA	2:10:13
1979	Bill Rodgers, Melrose, MA	2:09:27
1980	Bill Rodgers, Melrose, MA	2:12:11
1981	Toshihiko Seko, Japan	2:09:26
1982	Alberto Salazar, Wayland, MA	2:08:52
1983	Gregory Meyer, Wellesley, MA	2:09:00
1984	Geoff Smith, Liverpool, England	2:10:34
1985	Geoff Smith, Liverpool, England	2:14:05
1986	Rob de Castella, Canberra, Australia	2:07:51
1987	Toshihiko Seko, Japan	2:11:50
1988	Ibrahim Hussein, Kenya	2:08:43
1989	Abebe Mekonnen, Ethlopla	2:09:00
1990	Gelindo Bordin, Milan, Italy	2:08:19
1991	Ibrahim Hussein, Kenya	2:11:06
1992	Ibrahim Hussein, Kenya	2:08:14
1993	Cosmas Ndeti, Kenya	2:09:33
1994	Cosmas Ndeti, Kenya	2:07:15

1995	Cosmas Ndeti, Kenya	2:09:22
1996	Moses Tanui, Kenya	2:09:26
1997	Lameck Aguta, Kenya	2:10:34
1998	Moses Tanui, Kenya	2:07:34
1999	Lameck Aguta, Kenya	2:09:47
2000	Elijah Lagat, Kenya	2:09:47
2001	Lee Bong-Ju, South Korea	2:09:43
2002	Rodgers Rop, Kenya	2:09:02
2003	Robert Kipkoech Cheruiyot, Kenya	2:10:11
2004	Timothy Cherigat, Kenya	2:10:37
2005	Hailu Negussie, Ethiopia	2:11:44
2006	Robert Kipkoech Cheruiyot, Kenya	2:07:14
2007	Robert Kipkoech Cheruiyot, Kenya	2:14:13
2008	Robert Kipkoech Cheruiyot, Kenya	2:07:45
2009	Deriba Merga, Ethiopia	2:08:42
2010	Robert Kiprono Cheruiyot, Kenya	2:05:52
2011	Geoffrey Mutai, Kenya	2:03:02
2012	Wesley Korir, Kenya	2:12:40
2013	Lelisa Desisa, Ethiopia	2:10:22
2014	Meb Keflezighi, United States	2:08:37
2015	Lelisa Desisa Benti, Ethiopia	2:09:17
2016	Lemi Berhanu Hayle, Ethiopia	2:12:45
2017	Geoffrey Kirui, Kenya	2:09:37
2018	Yuki Kawauchi, Japan	2:15:58
2019	Lawrence Cherono, Kenya	2:07:57

Women's Open Champions

1966	Roberta Gibb Bingay, Winchester, MA	3:21:40 *
1967	Roberta Gibb Bingay, San Diego, CA	3:27:17 *
1968	Roberta Gibb Bingay, San Diego, CA	3:30:00 *
1969	Sara Mae Berman, Cambridge, MA	3:22:46 *
1970	Sara Mae Berman, Cambridge, MA	3:05:07 *
1971	Sara Mae Berman, Cambridge, MA	3:08:30 *
1972	Nina Kuscsik, South Huntington, NY	3:10:26
1973	Jacqueline Hansen, Granada Hills, CA	3:05:59
1974	Michiko Gorman, Los Angeles, CA	2:47:11
1975	Liane Winter, Wolfsburg, West Germany	2:42:24
1976	Kim Merritt, Kenosha, WI	2:47:10
1977	Michiko Gorman, Los Angeles, CA	2:48:33
1978	Gayle Barron, Atlanta, GA	2:44:52
1979	Joan Benoit, Cape Elizabeth, ME	2:35:15
1980	Jacqueline Gareau, Montreal, Quebec	2:34:28
1981	Allison Roe, Takatuna, New Zealand	2:26:46
1982	Charlotte Teske, Darmstadt, West Germany	2:29:33
1983	Joan Benoit, Watertown, MA	2:22:43
1984	Lorraine Moller, Putaruru, New Zealand	2:29:28
1985	Lisa Larsen Weidenbach, Battle Creek, MI	2:34:06
1986	Ingrid Kristiansen, Oslo, Norway	2:24:55
1987	Rosa Mota, Porto, Portugal	2:25:21
1988	Rosa Mota, Porto, Portugal	2:24:30
1989	Ingrid Kristiansen, Oslo, Norway	2:24:33
1990	Rosa Mota, Porto, Portugal	2:25:24
1991	Wanda Panfil, Poland	2:24:18
1992	Olga Markova, Russia	2:23:43
1993	Olga Markova, Russia	2:25:27
1994	Uta Pippig, West Berlin, Germany	2:21:45
1995	Uta Pippig, West Berlin, Germany	2:25:11
1996	Uta Pippig, West Berlin, Germany	2:27:12

1997	Fatuma Roba, Ethiopia	2:26:23
1998	Fatuma Roba, Ethiopia	2:23:21
1999	Fatuma Roba, Ethiopia	2:23:25
2000	Catherine Ndereba, Kenya	2:26:11
2001	Catherine Ndereba, Kenya	2:23:53
2002	Margaret Okayo, Kenya	2:20:43
2003	Svetlana Zakharova, Russia	2:25:19
2004	Catherine Ndereba, Kenya	2:24:27
2005	Catherine Ndereba, Kenya	2:25:12
2006	Rita Jeptoo, Kenya	2:23:38
2007	Lidiya Grigoryeva, Russia	2:29:18
2008	Dire Tune, Ethiopia	2:26:11
2009	Salina Kosgei, Kenya	2:32:16
2010	Teyba Erkesso, Ethiopia	2:26:11
2011	Caroline Kilel, Kenya	2:22:36
2012	Sharon Cherop, Kenya	2:31:50
2013	Rita Jeptoo, Kenya	2:26:25
2014	Disqualified Winner	
2015	Buzunesh Deba, Ethiopia	2:19:59
2016	Atsede Baysa, Ethiopia	2:29:19
2017	Edna Kiplagat, Kenya	2:21:52
2018	Desi Linden, United States	2:39:54
2019	Worknesh Degefa, Ethiopia	2:23:31

* unofficial

Men's Wheelchair Champions

1975	Robert Hall, Belmont, MA	2:58:00
1976	No contestants	
1977	Robert Hall, Belmont, MA	2:40:10
1978	George Murray, Tampa, FL	2:26:57
1979	Kenneth Archer, Akron, OH	2:38:59
1980	Curt Brinkman, Orem, UT	1:55:00
1981	Jim Martinson, Puyallup, WA	2:00:41
1982	Jim Knaub, Long Beach, CA	1:51:31
1983	Jim Knaub, Long Beach, CA	1:47:10
1984	Andre Viger, Quebec, Canada	2:05:20
1985	George Murray, Tampa, FL	1:45:34
1986	Andre Viger, Quebec, Canada	1:43:25
1987	Andre Viger, Quebec, Canada	1:55:42
1988	Mustapha Badid, St. Denis, France	1:43:19
1989	Philippe Couprie, Pontoise, France	1:36:04
1990	Mustapha Badid, St. Denis, France	1:29:53
1991	Jim Knaub, Long Beach, CA	1:30:44
1992	Jim Knaub, Long Beach, CA	1:26:28
1993	Jim Knaub, Long Beach, CA	1:22:17
1994	Heinz Frei, Switzerland	1:21:23
1995	Franz Nietlispach, Switzerland	1:25:59
1996	Heinz Frei, Switzerland	1:30:14
1997	Franz Nietlispach, Switzerland	1:28:14
1998	Franz Nietlispach, Switzerland	1:21:52
1999	Franz Nietlispach, Switzerland	1:21:36
2000	Franz Nietlispach, Switzerland	1:33:32
2001	Ernst van Dyk, South Africa	1:25:12
2002	Ernst van Dyk, South Africa	1:23:19
2003	Ernst van Dyk, South Africa	1:28:32
2004	Ernst van Dyk, South Africa	1:18:27
2005	Ernst van Dyk, South Africa	1:24:11

2006	Ernst van Dyk, South Africa	1:25:29
2007	Masazumi Soejima, Japan	1:29:16
2008	Ernst van Dyk, South Africa	1:26:49
2009	Ernst van Dyk, South Africa	1:33:29
2010	Ernst van Dyk, South Africa	1:26:53
2011	Masazumi Soejima, Japan	1:18:50
2012	Joshua Cassidy, Canada	1:18:25
2013	Hiroyuki Yamamoto, Japan	1:25:33
2014	Ernst van Dyk, South Africa	1:20:36
2015	Marcel Hug, Switzerland	1:29:53
2016	Marcel Hug, Switzerland	1:24:01
2017	Marcel Hug, Switzerland	1:18:03
2018	Marcel Hug, Switzerland	1:46:26
2019	Daniel Romanchuk, United States	1:21:36

Women's Wheelchair Champions

1977	Sharon Rahn, Champaign, IL	3:48:51
1978	Susan Shapiro, Berkeley, CA	3:52:35
1979	Sheryl Blair, Sacramento, CA	3:27:56
1980	Sharon Limpert, Minneapolis, MN	2:49:04
1981	Candace Cable, Las Vegas, NV	2:38:41
1982	Candace Cable-Brookes, Las Vegas, NV	2:12:43
1983	Sherry Ramsey, Arvada, CO	2:27:07
1984	Sherry Ramsey, Arvada, CO	2:56:51
1985	Candace Cable-Brookes, Long Beach, CA	2:05:26
1986	Candace Cable-Brookes, Long Beach, CA	2:09:28
1987	Candace Cable-Brookes, Long Beach, CA	2:19:55
1988	Candace Cable-Brookes, Long Beach, CA	2:10:44
1989	Connie Hansen, Denmark	1:50:06
1990	Jean Driscoll, Champaign, IL	1:43:17
1991	Jean Driscoll, Champaign, IL	1:42:42
1992	Jean Driscoll, Champaign, IL	1:36:52
1993	Jean Driscoll, Champaign, IL	1:34:50
1994	Jean Driscoll, Champaign, IL	1:34:22
1995	Jean Driscoll, Champaign, IL	1:40:42
1996	Jean Driscoll, Champaign, IL	1:52:56
1997	Louise Sauvage, Australia	1:54:28
1998	Louise Sauvage, Australia	1:41:19
1999	Louise Sauvage, Australia	1:42:23
2000	Jean Driscoll, Champaign, IL	2:00:52
2001	Louise Sauvage, Australia	1:53:54
2002	Edith Hunkeler, Switzerland	1:45:57
2003	Christina Ripp, United States	1:54:47
2004	Cheri Blauwet, United States	1:39:53
2005	Cheri Blauwet, United States	1:47:45
2006	Edith Hunkeler, Switzerland	1:43:42
2007	Wakako Tsuchida, Japan	1:53:30

2008	Wakako Tsuchida, Japan	1:48:32
2009	Wakako Tsuchida, Japan	1:54:37
2010	Wakako Tsuchida, Japan	1:43:32
2011	Wakako Tsuchida, Japan	1:34:06
2012	Shirley Riley, United States	1:37:36
2013	Tatyana McFadden, United States	1:45:25
2014	Tatyana McFadden, United States	1:35:06
2015	Tatyana McFadden, United States	1:52:54
2016	Tatyana McFadden, United States	1:42:16
2017	Manuela Schar, Switzerland	1:28:17
2018	Tatyana McFadden, United States	2:04:39
2019	Manuela Schar, Switzerland	1:34:19

BIBLIOGRAPHY

BOOKS

Albom, Mitch. *Tuesdays with Morrie: An Old Man, a Young Man, and Life's Greatest Lesson*. New York: Doubleday, 1997.

Ballard, Elise. *Epiphany, True Stories of Sudden Insight to Inspire, Encourage and Transform*. New York: Harmony Books, 2011.

Benoit, Joan, and Sally Baker. *Running Tide*. New York: Alfred Knopf, 1987.

Benyo, Richard. *The Masters of the Marathon*. New York: Atheneum, 1983.

Coelho, Paulo. *The Alchemist*. New York: Harper, 1993.

Colvin, Geoff. *Talent Is Overrated, What Really Separates World-Class Performers from Everybody Else*. New York: Portfolio, 2008.

Curtis, John Gould. *History of Brookline*. Boston: Houghton Mifflin, 1933.

Daniels, John. *In Freedom's Birthplace: The History of Boston's Negroes*. Boston: Houghton Mifflin, 1914.

Derderian, Tom. *Boston Marathon*. Champaign, IL: Human Kinetics Publishers, 1995.

Falls, Joe. *The Boston Marathon*. New York: Collier Books, 1975.

Fixx, Jim. *The Complete Book of Running*. New York: Random House, 1977.

Frankl, Viktor. *Man's Search for Meaning*. Boston: Beacon Press, 2006.

Gaiman, Neil. *The Graveyard Book*. New York: HarperCollins, 2008.

Gladwell, Malcolm. *David and Goliath: Underdogs, Misfits, and the Art of Battling Giants*. New York: Little, Brown and Company, 2013.

———. *Outliers: The Story of Success*. New York: Back Bay Books, 2008.

Grzyb, Frank. *The Last Civil War Veterans*. Jefferson, NC: McFarland & Company, 2016.

Higdon, Hal. *A Century of Running Boston*. Emmaus, PA: Rodale Press, 1995.

Hinchcliffe, Elizabeth. *Five Pounds Currency, Three Pounds of Corn: The Wellesley Centennial Story*. Wellesley, MA: The Town of Wellesley, 1981.

Homer, Joel. *Marathons: The Ultimate Challenge*. Garden City, NY: Dolphin Books, 1979.

Hosler, Ray. *Boston: America's Oldest Marathon*. Mountain View, CA: Anderson World, Inc., 1979.

Johnson, Dick, and Frederick Lewis. *Young at Heart*. Waco, TX: WRS Publishing, 1992.

Kardong, Don. *Thirty Phone Booths to Boston*. New York: Macmillan, 1985.

Mandino, Og. *The Greatest Salesman in the World*. New York: Bantam Trade Edition, 1985.

McDougall, Christopher. *Born to Run: A Hidden Tribe, Superathletes, and the Greatest Race the World Has Never Seen*. New York: Vintage Books, 2009.

Natick Federal Savings & Loans Associates. *The Story of Natick*. Natick, MA: Suburban Press, 1948.

Rodgers, Bill, and Joe Concannon. *Marathoning*. New York: Simon & Schuster, 1980.

Stafford, Francis A. *Brief History of Hopkinton*. 1915.

Temple, Josiah H. *History of Framingham, Massachusetts, 1640–1885*. Framingham, MA: Framingham Historical & Natural History Society, 1988.

PERIODICALS

Accomplishments of Henry Wilson, 1993
Boston American, 1904–1961
Boston Athletic Association Program, 1996
Boston College Magazine, 1996
Boston Daily Advertiser, 1813–1929
Boston Daily Record, 1951–1961 (available archives)
Boston Globe, 1872–2013
Boston Herald (Traveler), 1950–2013
Boston Journal, 1833–1917
Cincinnati Enquirer, 1909
Dallas Morning News, 1885–present
History of the Boston Public Library, 1987
Lexington Leader, 1919–present
Magazine of History, Vol. XII, February 1911
Massachusetts Municipal Profiles, 1994–1995
Middlesex News, 1980–1997
Natick Bulletin & Sun, March 17, 1983
Newton Registry, 1896
Patriot Ledger, 1837–present
The Paper, April 18, 1973
Providence Journal, 1829–present
Runner's World, 1969–2013
A Social & Architectural History of 19th Century Natick, Massachusetts, 1988
Sports Illustrated, September 16, 1996
Springfield Republican, 1824–present
The Week, July 26, 2019
Winnipeg Tribune, 1910–1912

INTERNET

Adair, Aly. "Astronaut Sunita Williams Runs Boston Marathon from Space," April 17, 2007 (http://voices.yahoo.com/astronaut-sunita-williams-runs-boston-marathon -from-305845.html).

"Andrew Sockalexis," SR/Olympic Sports (www.sports-reference.com/olympics/ athletes/so/andrew-sockalexis-1.html).

"The Axis Conquers the Philippines: January 1942–July 1942," HowStuffWorks.com (https://history.howstuffworks.com/world-war-ii/axis-conquers-philippines9.htm).

"Baseball's Greatest Sacrifice" (http://www.baseballsgreatestsacrifice.com/ world_war_ii.html).

"Bataan Death March," ISM, World War II (https://sites.google.com/a/ismanila.org/ wwii/home/war-crimes/axis-war-crimes/bataan-death-march).

"Boston Marathon: Girls of Wellesley," *Runner's World*, April 21, 2008 (www.runners world.com/photos/boston-marathon-girls-wellesley).

Cronin, Brian. "Sports Legend Revealed: A Marathon Runner Nearly Died Because of Drugs He Took to Help Him Win," *Los Angeles Times,* August 10, 2010 (http://latimesblogs.latimes.com/sports_blog/2010/08/sports-legend-revealed-a-marathon-runner-nearly-died-because-of-drugs-he-took-to-help-him-win.html).

Douglas, Scott. "Marathon Sports at Epicenter of First Boston Bomb," *Runner's World,* April 17, 2013 (http://www.runnersworld.com/races/marathon-sports-at-epicenter-of-first-boston-bomb).

Ducharme, Jamie. "Q&A: Marathon Legend Bill Rodgers," *Boston Magazine,* June 10, 2013 (www.bostonmagazine.com/health/blog/2013/06/10/bill-rodgers-boston-marathon).

"Fenway Park Timeline," mlb.com (https://www.mlb.com/redsox/ballpark/museum/timeline).

FindaGrave.com.

Gambaccini, Peter. "Denise Dillon," *Runner's World,* March 20, 2006 (http://www.runnersworld.com/runners-stories/denise-dillon).

Golen, Jimmy. "Soldier Honored for 'Shadow Marathon' in Iraq," *The Big Story,* April 12, 2013 (http://bigstory.ap.org/article/soldier-honored-shadow-marathon-iraq).

Goodreads. Disability Quotes (https://www.goodreads.com/quotes/tag/disability).

———. Quotes (http://www.goodreads.com/quotes).

Helliker, Kevin. "One Running Shoe in the Grave," *Wall Street Journal,* November 27, 2012 (http://online.wsj.com/news/articles/SB10001424127887323330604578145462264024472).

Herbaugh, Tracee. "Boston Marathon Winner Returns His Medal to City," Associated Press (http://usnews.nbcnews.com/_news/2013/06/23/19102305-boston-marathon-winner-returns-his-medal-to-city).

Hinchliffe, Beth. "About the Town of Wellesley," Town of Wellesley, Massachusetts (http://www.wellesleyma.gov/pages/wellesleyma_webdocs/about).

"Jerome Drayton," Time-to-Run, December 31, 2006 (www.time-to-run.com/marathon/athletes/men/jerome-drayton).

Kotz, Deborah. "Injury Toll from Marathon Bombs Reduced to 264," *Boston Globe,* April 24, 2013 (www.bostonglobe.com/lifestyle/health-wellness/2013/04/23/number-injured-marathon-bombing-revised-downward/NRpaz5mmvGquP7KMA6XsIK/story.html).

Long, Tom. "Boston Marathon Man Johnny Kelley Dies at 97," Boston.com, October 8, 2004 (www.boston.com/news/globe/obituaries/articles/2004/10/08/boston_marathon_man_johnny_kelley_dies_at_97).

Marathon Running Statistics, Statistic Brain (www.statisticbrain.com/marathon-running-statistics).

Martindale, Martin. "Figs, a Little Port Wine and Some Blue Cheese," *Foodsite Magazine,* August 8, 2012 (http://www.foodsitemagazine.com/2012/08/08/15698).

McCabe, Neil, Sgt. "Boston Marathon Comes to Iraq," www.Army.Mil, April 27, 2010 (http://www.army.mil/article/38116).

NKOTB@Boston Strong Concert, May 30, 2013 (https://www.youtube.com/watch?v=54M0PWOzsFw).

"Peerless Runner," Boston.com, April 20, 1901 (www.boston.com/zope_homepage/ sports/marathon_archive/history/1901_globe.htm).

"The Poorest Countries in the World," *Global Finance*, 2013 (http://www.gfmag.com/ component/content/article/119-economic-data/12537-the-poorest-countries-in -the-world.html#axzz2kYatg7Vu).

Rainsberger, Lisa, interview with Gary Cohen, GaryCohenRunning.com, September 2010 (www.garycohenrunning.com/Interviews/Rainsberger.aspx).

Reese, Robert. "Women in Marathons," *Runner's World*, April 8, 2013 (www.runners world.com/womens-running/women-in-marathons).

Rita Hayworth Pin-Up, Iconic Photos (https://iconicphotos.wordpress.com/ 2009/05/10/rita-hayworth-pin-up).

Robbins, Liz. "Air Traffic Controller Tells Gripping Tale of Hudson Landing," *New York Times*, February 24, 2009 (http://www.nytimes.com/2009/02/25/nyregion/25 crash.html).

"Robert Murray Hanson," www.findagrave.com/cgi-bin/ fg.cgi?page=gr&GRid=8121665.

"Running Legend Frank Shorter on Boston," *Outside* (https://www.outsideonline .com/1922336/running-legend-frank-shorter-boston).

Ryan, Bob. "Their Absence Didn't Last Long," *Boston Globe*, April 16, 2002 (http:// www.highbeam.com/doc/1P2-7719859.html).

Sandrolini, Mike. "Well Rounded Corner," Sports Spectrum, Fansite.com.

Schoenberg, Shira. "Carlos Arredondo, Who Helped Boston Marathon Bombing Vic- tims, Is Honored in Sept. 11 Ceremony," September 11, 2013 (www.masslive.com/ politics/index.ssf/2013/09/carlos_arredondo_who_helped_bo.html).

Shaw, Jene. "Perfect Your Downhill Running Form," *Competitor: Your Online Source for Running*, August 6, 2013 (http://running.competitor.com/2013/08/training/ perfect-your-downhill-running-form_52804).

"Split-Toe Running Shoe Won the 1951 Boston Marathon," *Zero Drop*, April 10, 2011 (http://zero-drop.com/?p=1474).

"Through the Years," Boston Red Sox (http://boston.redsox.mlb.com/bos/fenway park100/timeline.jsp?year=1949).

"Transcript: Obama's Remarks at Boston Marathon Memorial," *Los Ange- les Times*, April 18, 2013 (http://articles.latimes.com/2013/apr/18/news/ la-pn-transcript-obama-boston-marathon-memorial-20130418/2).

Wikipedia. Framingham Station (https://en.wikipedia.org/wiki/Framingham_station).

Williams, Mel, PhD. "Sports Science Research—Can it Improve Your Marathon Time?," Marathon and Beyond, 2003 (www.marathonandbeyond.com/choices/ williams.htm).

TELEVISION

Courage in Sports, CBS Sports Spectacular, November 17, 2013.

INTERVIEWS

Abele, Susan
Arredondo, Carlos
Barron, Gayle
Berman, Sara Mae
Driscoll, Jean
Duffy, Martin
Fannon, Dick
Flynn, Raymond, Mayor of Boston, Ambassador to the Vatican
Foran, Tom
Fortier, David
Fultz, Jack
Gaffney, Charlie
Hall, Robert
Hussein, Ibrahim
Kelley, John "The Elder"
Kelley, John "The Younger"
Ketterle, Wolfgang
King, Dr. David
Knaub, Jim
McGillivray, David
McGuire, Carolyn
McIntyre, Joey
Meagher, Thomas
Menino, Thomas, Mayor of Boston
Meyer, Greg
Nelson, Laura
Pippig, Uta
Ralston, Thomas
Rodgers, Bill
Sanders, Summer
Smith, Geoff
Staines, Henry
Sullivan, Bob
Switzer, Kathy
Yanni, Lee Ann